GHOST
WRITING

GHOST
WRITING

Haunted Tales by Contemporary Writers

Edited by

ROGER WEINGARTEN

INVISIBLE CITIES PRESS
MONTPELIER, VERMONT

Invisible Cities Press
50 State Street
Montpelier, VT 05602
www.invisiblecitiespress.com

LIBRARY OF CONGRESS CATALOGING-IN-PUBLICATION DATA

Ghost writing : haunted tales by contemporary
writers / edited by Roger Weingarten.
p.   cm.
ISBN 0-9679683-0-5 (alk. paper)
1. Ghost stories, American. 2. Ghost stories, English.
I. Weingarten, Roger.

PS648.G48 G5 2000
813'.0873308—dc21   00-057242

Manufactured in the United States of America

Book Design by
Peter Holm
Sterling Hill Productions

FIRST EDITION

For Michael Grimaldi, Joel Bernstein, Ann Brandon,
Kate Fetherston, and Ra pha el Ben Myer

CONTENTS

ACKNOWLEDGMENTS

Thanks to Pamela Painter, Douglas Glover, Ellen Lesser, Ann Brandon, Michael Grimaldi, Joel Bernstein, Judith Jones, Jeffrey Weingarten, Carl Taylor, Carl Brandon, Adam Sherman, Ralph & Libby, Bruce, and above all, Kate Fetherston.

INTRODUCTION

I wanted to know if contemporary writers whose storytelling gift I admire had a ghost story up their sleeves or would scare one up for a collection that gives them the latitude to write anything from a traditional haunted tale to something that skates the perimeter of the genre frame.

You will be pleased to know the answer was yes.

If you have a yen for fabulist or realist stories that possess at least one supernatural element that drives the narrative into the twilight zone of your reading pleasure, or,

If you can't get enough black comedy, phantom sex, phantom sex with a serial killer and caterer, calendar murders, or characters much more frightening than ghosts, or,

If you're ready to be haunted by: clothes, a plaster virgin, a sanitorium turned private home, a wig, doors, a troll, a mirror, insomnia, a circus giantess in a museum, a wallet, a lake, and a couch, or,

If you just want to indulge in wonderfully crafted stories, then *Ghost Writing* is the book you've been waiting for.

ROGER WEINGARTEN

THE PARTY OVER THERE

Gordon knew she was dead the moment he entered the house. It wasn't any kind of evidence, nothing untoward or obvious. It was more her special kind of resonance that was missing, gone as if he'd imagined it had ever been here, and now the house hung silent around him, carefully decorated with a sure professional touch, delicately set with crystals and luxuries.

But empty.

"Sylvie?" His voice was uncanny in the stillness, too loud. He expected the curtains to move with the force of it, the crystal to shatter from the volume. Gordon's fingers curled around the hardwood banister. He started up the stairs to the second floor. She was up there, of course; whatever she'd done, she'd done it up there.

He'd known something was up for the past few weeks. Something had changed in her. Her eyes were brighter and her step quicker and the depression had settled away from her. He'd thought she was on her way to finding religion or some such nonsense and he'd tolerate it, as long as she had the sense to keep it out of his way.

Briefly he'd considered that she might have taken a lover, but got away from that thought fairly quickly. She wasn't the sort. And she knew the consequences. Too well. Which was why he'd been glad the depression had lifted, that Sylvie's sad eyes were smiling again, although her quick, nervous movements seemed geared toward hiding something from him. Once he grabbed at her, thinking she was hiding something from him, right there, in her hands, and he left her wrists bruised but there was nothing in her hands, just a curious little smile around her mouth. She hadn't cried out or protested.

His feet were on the stairs of their own volition. He wasn't sure he wanted to go up. Sylvie changed the house by her presence or absence. Now the Victorian seemed old and decayed, as though he walked a crumbling mansion, alone in the moonlight and haunted. Gordon shrugged off the thought. "Sylvie?"

The upper hall was empty. As it would be. Unlikely she'd be in the hall. Her room was empty, clean and lacy in an ordered, neat way. She always knew where everything was.

He always knew where she was. She couldn't hide from him. "I'm coming," he said, hearing his voice drop. He tried to keep it light. Hide and go seek. Just a game. She wasn't running.

She knew better.

Except perhaps this time she had run, and beyond his reach.

The bedroom was empty, the room he'd shared with her until a few months ago, after one bad night, when she'd moved down the hall and all the demands, promises and gifts in the world weren't enough to draw her back.

He passed from her bedroom to the master bathroom. The door stood closed, a beacon, letting him know where she hid. He never allowed her to close the door, always insisted she leave it open. She was taunting him. Gordon forgot what he knew and stepped to the bathroom. The door flew open so hard it bounced back, caught him against the forearm he had raised.

He was hardly aware of it.

The bath water was red. Sylvie's red curls dropped into it, the ends floating limp upon the surface, and one of her arms had slipped outside the tub, perhaps thrown there in a moment of fear. Blood had dripped from the jagged line along her wrist; drops of it marred the white bath mats where more than once he had taken her.

"Sylvie."

Her face was slack, eyes closed, mouth a little open. He could just see her tongue between her teeth. The bathroom was full of candles, their light flickering weirdly over her face, causing little movements that weren't hers.

"Sylvie."

He moved her arm, returned it to the edge of the tub, as if she'd laid it out of the water to cool down a little. The water was very warm. She hadn't been here long. Gordon reached over and pressed two fingers hard against her neck, unafraid of hurting her. The pressure sent her head rolling back against the porcelain. There was no fluttering beat under his fingers, no rapid quick breaths, no pulsing ebb and flow of life. He looked at her still face.

"Sylvie."

She'd gone where he couldn't' follow, left him here, alone.

"Sylvie."

She'd left him. Gone away. Gotten away.

"Sylvie!"

The mirror shimmered as he slammed the door back open, threatened to crack as the door rebounded and he slugged it again. His footsteps were thunder through the house, pounding to her room, throwing back open the door there. Inside he grabbed the first thing he came to, an ornate, crystal clock he'd given her after the first time. It shattered against the wall satisfactorily, the wall gouged behind it as it fell, a nasty place of darker paint, chipped and scolded. With one hand, he swept the shining collection of cut glass and crystal from the top of her dresser, left a scatter of sharp-edged light on the floor. The pillows shredded under his hands.

She'd left him, run. Where he couldn't bring her back. She'd gotten away. She'd defied him. He heaved the mattress from the bed,

3

upended it, threw it against the wall, knocking books from the case, cracking the window. He reached down again and then stopped.

Under the mattress, against the box springs, lay a book, wine-dark leather bound with gold, something fancy but inexpensive. His motion stopped and he dropped to the bed.

The leather was coarse under his fingers, a nubby texture. A gold fountain pen lay beside it so he wasn't surprised to open the thing and find her spidery, elegant writing.

"Sylvia Chase Newton," she'd written, her full name, including maiden, banished from her usually. "Sylvia Chase Newton. My life." It was dated several weeks back, about the time the change in her began. About the time she'd started planning her escape, he'd bet on it. "Sylvia Chase Newton. My life." And the date. He took a shuddering breath. Not your life any longer. You messed up there. You haven't won, haven't won.

The first page tore under his fingers. Gordon struggled to control his breathing, turned the page to the first page of script.

"Gordon's tantrums continue, growing worse. I've stopped trying to do anything about them. I don't know what to do. My days would be so long, waiting for him to come home, except they're all spent on the house. Cleaning, fixing, bringing it to life. I don't know if he loves the house or hates it but if it's at all messed up—"

She didn't finish the sentence. Gordon tore the page, crumbled it in his hand. Bitch. Slut. It was all for you. Too lazy to understand. Had to be forced to keep up the house.

Another entry.

"Can't go out. Usually not my face, but lately—he's awful. The least little thing sets him off. I was trying to put aside some money, but he must have caught on and he took the checkbook. I don't know what to do. Ever since he killed Fluffy, I think I'd do anything to get away."

He couldn't see for an instant, couldn't see even when the room returned around him, couldn't see past the pain in his hand. Plaster lay on the floor, lacy chips of paint beside her dainty pillows. The book had resisted him; he could still read the words.

"Found a box in the basement today. Some previous owner's? Books on magic. Ready to scoff but one of them is so old and it looks real. It has all these crazy things in it, love spells and how to make a poppet, the appearance of the sleeping death and the hand of glory. And one of the newer books tells about scrying, looking for people or things through a mirror. Doesn't have to be a fancy mirror or magic or anything of the sort. Just a mirror. Like the one on the back of the bathroom door. Which actually is fancy, with that ornate frame, and I wonder if the person who owned the books ever tried it."

Bitch. Bitch. How often had she closed the door? How often to be so familiar with the mirror that shimmered there?

The book smashed against the wall, just to the right of the place the clock had made. The pages riffled as it fell, wounded birds found out on the creamy carpet. Gordon paced. One hand smashed the dresser and a few last crystal apologies fell, a bright sound as they hit the shattered mass on the floor. He stared toward the bathroom but he couldn't go in there yet. This, all this in her room, he could explain. Moments of grief. Overcome, officer. And the book would be long gone before the police came. But if he touched her—

The next entry was written five days earlier. Her writing was all over the place, excited curlicues dancing along the margins.

"It works. The scrying. I can really see things in the mirror. A fog comes up and then—I found Tom. Tom, from college, who asked me to marry him, but I'd already met Gordon and he was so handsome and attentive, already taking the bar, driving a Porsche. And Tom, he wasn't ready to marry, wasn't even ready to have a career."

The pages bent and ripped and smeared under his sweating fingers. Found him how? Because she'd barely left the house at all, he'd seen to it.

And never would again, now. Remember. It's okay. She hasn't won. She ran, but she hasn't won.

"It works. The scrying. And Gordon is so into work, he hasn't noticed. It's almost okay right now, because he's not home. I was about ready to run, but he says he'll kill my parents and I believe him. But he's going to kill me if I don't—yesterday I was waiting for him to leave and thinking about coming up here to the mirror and he started demanding to know what I had and why I was smiling. I didn't have anything, just a book of matches to light the candles when he left, but he grabbed me and almost broke my fingers. After he left I came up and Tom was there. He's often with a group of people, Cindie and Jason, Kelli and Georgio, Kay and Dave. I feel like I know them. But Tom's always alone. And he looks the same. And I thought he saw me. Just for an instant. Shit! He's home—"

The writing stopped. Gordon left the book on the tumbled dresser, went down the hall into the bathroom. Among the candles were other things she'd taken there, incense, a short knife, some kind of herbs, a hammer, crystals. The mirrors were still steamy, the room humid from the heat of the bath water. Sylvie's head lay tipped to one side, as it had when he'd felt for her pulse.

Her arm had fallen into the water again but the bleeding had stopped. Gordon stared, thinking she'd moved. "Bitch."

He expected her to flinch, but she didn't move. Was she truly dead, then? Truly run, actually escaped? Gordon slapped the door open. He couldn't remember closing it. For an instant the mirror shimmered, about to reveal something other than the bathroom, misty with heat, and then the door hit the wall. He thought about slamming it shut again, pummeling the mirror, breaking her door, stopping her escape. But that was crazy. Crazy as she had become. There was no escape, not from him. He kept track of his property. She hadn't run, she'd died. Packed it all in chasing a dream and was gone not won, not won.

"Dead. You're dead, Sylvie," he said but he was already back in her room, down the hall, and he needed to call the police soon, the bereaved widower, and there was the rest of her carefully transcribed insanity to get through. He perched on the end of the box springs, and turned the next page. It was dated the day before.

"Tom was talking about me to Kay and Dave. I know he still misses me. He said he thought he'd seen me, can't stop thinking. I know how to get to him. I can go through the mirror. It's dangerous, but I can do it. If I mess up, I'm dead. But if I stay, I'm dead. Gordon is going to kill me, sooner or later. I'm going thorough the mirror tomorrow."

He took a deep breath, trying to control the rage that crawled and coiled in his chest. He lashed out at the room, tore the curtains from the rods and left them shredded on the bedroom floor.

"Sylvie!"

The bathroom was no cooler, as if hotter water had been run. He thought she'd moved. He headed for the tub but movement behind stopped him. He spun as the door clicked shut, leaving him in the bathroom with her, and a mist was stealing across the mirror, a fog coming up and then burning off and there she was, Sylvie, laughing within the mirror, taunting him. She pointed, laughed, and when he turned fully to stare, she ran. Ran. Away from him. He couldn't see where it was she ran, only her feet hitting the ground over and over, only her form pulling away from him. He moved without thinking, grasped the frame of the mirror, and pulled himself through, thought he heard something in the bathroom behind him and then he was running, away from the mirror, after the bright flame of Sylvie's hair and even that was becoming dimmer, as if she faded.

"Sylvie!"

Her laugh came back. He ran harder, into nothing, into a nowhere world that surrounded him, a dim gray world, a flip side of their house, empty, gray and cold. A world where forever he would be walking up the stairs to find Sylvie dead.

"Sylvie."

"Here." The voice was behind him. Impossible. He spun, found himself facing the bathroom. She stood in front of him, wan and beautiful, framed in the mirror. He couldn't think for an instant, spun again, still looking. Impossible. "Sylvie, you bitch, let me—"

"Gordon," she said, clearly her voice. He stared out at her, at the bathroom behind her, the blood on her wrists, her hair, damp from the bath water. The cleverly colored bath water. The scratches on her wrists. He started forward. Bitch. He saw the fear rise up in her eyes. As well it should. He was only a couple steps from the edge of the mirror and this time she wouldn't be able to run from him. This time he was going to teach her a lesson she'd never forget. Good thing he hadn't phoned the police yet. He'd hate to report a suicide before it happened.

"Gordon," she said again. Something in her voice stopped him. He looked at her again and she was smiling. "Gordon. I won." She stood in front of the mirror, blocking the exit from the gray world. Gordon ran, but he was still three steps from the mirror. She brought down the hammer and shattered the world.

THE MIRACLE AT BALLINSPITTLE

T here they are, the holybugs, widows in their weeds and fat-ankled mothers with palsied children, all lined up before the snotgreen likeness of the Virgin, and McGahee and McCarey among them. This statue, alone among all the myriad three-foot-high snotgreen likenesses of the Virgin cast in plaster by Finnbar Finnegan & Sons, Cork City, was seen one grim March afternoon some years back to move its limbs ever so slightly, as if seized suddenly by the need of a good sinew-cracking stretch. Nuala Nolan, a young girl in the throes of Lenten abnegation, was the only one to witness the movement—a gentle beckoning of the statue's outthrust hand—after a fifteen-day vigil during which she took nothing into her body but Marmite and soda water. Ever since, the place has been packed with tourists.

Even now, in the crowd of humble countrymen in shit-smeared boots and knit skullcaps, McGahee can detect a certain number of Teutonic or Manhattanite faces above cableknit sweaters and pendant cameras. Drunk and in debt, on the run from a bad marriage, two DWI convictions, and the wheezy expiring gasps of his moribund mother, McGahee pays them no heed. His powers of concentration run deep. He is forty years old, as lithe as a boxer though he's done no hard physical labor since he took a construction job between semesters at college twenty years back, and he has the watery eyes and doleful, doglike expression of the saint. Twelve hours ago he was in New York, at Paddy Flynn's, pouring out his heart and enumerating his woes for McCarey, when McCarey said, "Fuck it, let's go to Ireland." And now here he is at Ballinspittle, wearing the rumpled Levi's and Taiwanese sportcoat he'd pulled on in his apartment yesterday morning, three hours off the plane from Kennedy and flush with warmth from the venerable Irish distillates washing through his veins.

McCarey—plump, stately McCarey—stands beside him, bleary-eyed and impatient, disdainfully scanning the crowd. Heads are bowed. Infants snuffle. From somewhere in the distance come the bleat of a lamb and the mechanical call of the cuckoo. McGahee checks his watch: they've been here seven minutes already and nothing's happened. His mind begins to wander. He's thinking about orthodontia—thinking an orthodontist could make a fortune in this country—when he looks up and spots her, Nuala Nolan, a scarecrow of a girl, an anorectic, bones-in-a-sack sort of girl, kneeling in front of the queue and reciting the Mysteries in a voice parched for food and drink. Since the statue moved she has stuck to her diet of Marmite and soda water until the very synapses of her brain have become encrusted with salt and she raves like a mariner lost at sea. McGahee regards her with awe. A light rain has begun to fall.

And then suddenly, before he knows what's come over him, McGahee goes limp. He feels lightheaded, transported, feels himself sinking into another realm, as helpless and cut adrift as when Dr. Beibelman put him under for his gallbladder operation. He breaks out in a sweat. His vision goes dim. The murmur of the crowd, the call of the cuckoo, and the bleat of the lamb all meld into a single sound—a voice—and that voice, ubiquitous, timeless, all-embracing, permeates his every cell and fiber. It seems to speak through him, through the broad-beamed old hag beside him, through McCarey,

Nuala Nolan, the stones and birds and fishes of the sea. "Davey," the voice calls in the sweetest tones he has ever heard. "Davey McGahee, come to me, come to my embrace."

As one, the crowd parts, a hundred stupefied faces turned toward him, and there she is, the Virgin, snotgreen no longer but radiant with the aquamarine of actuality, her eyes glowing, arms beckoning. McGahee casts a quick glance around him. McCarey looks as if he's been punched in the gut, Nuala Nolan's skeletal face is clenched with hate and jealousy, the humble countrymen and farmwives stare numbly from him to the statue and back again . . . and then, as if in response to a subconscious signal, they drop to their knees in a human wave so that only he, Davey McGahee, remains standing. "Come to me," the figure implores, and slowly, as if his feet were encased in cement, his head reeling and his stomach sour, he begins to move forward, his own arms outstretched in ecstasy.

The words of his catechism, forgotten these thirty years, echo in his head: "Mother Mary, Mother of God, pray for us sinners now and at the hour of our—"

"Yesssss!" the statue suddenly shrieks, the upturned palm curled into a fist, a fist like a weapon. "And you think it's as easy as that, do you?"

McGahee stops cold, hovering over the tiny effigy like a giant, a troglodyte, a naked barbarian. Three feet high, grotesque, shaking its fists up at him, the thing changes before his eyes. Gone is the beatific smile, gone the grace of the eyes and the faintly mad and indulgent look of the transported saint. The face is a gargoyle's, a shrew's, and the voice, sharpening, probing like a dental tool, suddenly bears an uncanny resemblance to his ex-wife's. "Sinner!" the gargoyle hisses. "Fall on your knees!"

The crowd gasps. McGahee, his bowels turned to ice, pitches forward into the turf. "No, no, no!" he cries, clutching at the grass and squeezing his eyes shut. "Hush," a new voice whispers in his ear, "look. You must look." There's a hand on his neck, bony and cold. He winks open an eye. The statue is gone and Nuala Nolan leans over him, her hair gone in patches, the death's-head of her face and suffering eyes, her breath like the loam of the grave. "Look, up there," she whispers.

High above them, receding into the heavens like a kite loosed from a string, is the statue. Its voice comes to him faint and distant— "Behold . . . now . . . your sins . . . and excesses . . ."—and then it dwindles away like a fading echo.

Suddenly, behind the naked pedestal, a bright sunlit vista appears, grapevines marshaled in rows, fields of barley, corn, and hops, and then, falling from the sky with thunderous crashes, a succession of vats, kegs, hogsheads, and buckets mounting up in the foreground as if on some phantom pier piled high with freight. *Boom, boom, ka-boom, boom,* down they come till the vista is obscured and the kegs mount to the tops of the trees. McGahee pushes himself up to his knees and looks around him. The crowd is regarding him steadily, jaws set, the inclemency of the hanging judge sunk into their eyes. McCarey, kneeling too now and looking as if he's just lurched up out of a drunken snooze to find himself on a subway car on another planet, has gone steely-eyed with the rest of them. And Nuala Nolan, poised over him, grins till the long naked roots of her teeth gleam beneath the skirts of her rotten gums.

"Your drinking!" shrieks a voice from the back of the throng, his wife's voice, and there she is, Fredda, barefoot and in a snotgreen robe and hood, wafting her way through the crowd and pointing her long accusatory finger at his poor miserable shrinking self. "Every drop," she booms, and the vast array of vats and kegs and tumblers swivels to reveal the signs hung from their sweating slats—GIN, BOURBON, BEER, WHISKEY, SCHNAPPS, PERNOD—the crowd lets out a long exhalation of shock and lament.

The keg of gin. Tall it is and huge, its contents vaguely sloshing.

You could throw cars into it, buses, tractor trailers. But no, never, he couldn't have drunk that much gin, no man could. And beside it the beer, frothy and bubbling, a cauldron the size of a rest home. "No!" he cries in protest. "I don't even like the taste of the stuff."

"Yes, yes, yes," chants a voice beside him. The statue is back, Fredda gone. It speaks in a voice he recognizes, though the wheezy, rheumy deathbed rasp of it has been wiped clean. "Ma?" he says, turning to the thing.

Three feet tall, slick as a seal, the robes flowing like the sea, the effigy looks up at him out of his mother's face in miniature. "I warned you," the voice leaps out at him, high and querulous, "out behind the 7-Eleven with Ricky Reitbauer and that criminal Tommy Capistrano, cheap wine and all the rest."

"But Mom, *Pernod?*" He peers into the little pot of it, a pot so small you couldn't boil a good Safeway chicken in it. There it is. Pernod. Milky and unclean. It turns his stomach even to look at it. "Your liver, son," the statue murmurs with a resignation that brings tears to his eyes, "just look at it."

He feels a prick in his side and there it is, his liver—a poor piece of cheesy meat, stippled and striped and purple—dangling from the plaster fingers. "God," he moans. "God Almighty."

"Rotten as your soul," the statue says.

McGahee, still on his knees, begins to blubber. Meaningless slips of apology issue from his lips—"I didn't mean . . . it wasn't . . . how could I know?"—when all of a sudden the statue shouts "Drugs!" with a voice of iron.

Immediately the scene changes. The vats are gone, replaced with bales of marijuana, jars of pills in every color imaginable, big, overbrimming tureens of white powder, a drugstore display of airplane glue. In the background, grinning Laotians, Peruvian peasants with hundreds of scrawny children propped like puppets on their shoulders.

"But, but—" McGahee stutters, rising to his feet to protest, but the statue doesn't give him a chance, won't, can't, and the stentorian voice—his wife's, his mother's, no one's and everyone's, he even detects a trace of his high-school principal's in there—the stentorian voice booms: "Sins of the Flesh!"

He blinks his eyes and the Turks and their bales are gone. The backdrop now is foggy and obscure, dim as the mists of memory. The statue is silent. Gradually the poor sinner becomes aware of a salacious murmur, an undercurrent of moaning and panting, and the lubricious thwack and whap of the act itself. "Davey," a girl's voice calls, tender, pubescent, "I'm scared." And then his own voice, bland and reassuring: "I won't stick it in, Cindy, I won't, I swear . . . or maybe, maybe just . . . just an inch. . . ."

The mist lifts and there they are, in teddies and negligees, in garter belts and sweat socks, naked and wet and kneading their breasts like dough. "Davey," they moan, "oh, Davey, fuck me, fuck me, fuck me," and he knows them all, from Cindy Lou Harris and Betsy Butler in the twelfth grade to Fredda in her youth and the sad and ugly faces of his one-night stands and chance encounters, right on up to the bug-eyed woman with the doleful breasts he'd diddled in the rest room on the way out from Kennedy. And worse. Behind them, milling around in a mob that stretches to the horizon, are all the women and girls he'd ever lusted after, even for a second, the twitching behinds and airy bosoms he'd stopped to admire on the street, the legs he'd wanted to stroke and lips to press to his own. McCarey's wife, Beatrice, is there and Fred Dolby's thirteen-year-old daughter, the woman with the freckled bosom who used to sunbathe in the tiger-skin bikini next door when they lived in Irvington, the girl from the typing pool, and the outrageous little shaven-headed vixen from Domino's Pizza. And as if that weren't enough, there's the crowd from books and films too. Linda Lovelace, Sophia Loren, Emma Bovary, the Sabine women and Lot's wife, even Virginia Woolf with her puckered foxy face and the eyes that seem to beg for a good slap on the bottom. It's too much—all of them murmuring his name like a crazed chorus of Molly Blooms, and yes, she's there too—and the mob behind him hissing, hissing.

He glances at the statue. The plaster lip curls in disgust, the adamantine hand rises and falls, and the women vanish. "Gluttony!" howls the Virgin and all at once he's surrounded by forlornly mooing herds of cattle, sad-eyed pigs and sheep, funereal geese and clucking ducks, a spill of scuttling crabs and claw-waving lobsters, even the odd dog or two he'd inadvertently wolfed down in Tijuana burritos and Cantonese stir-fry. And the scales—scales the size of the Washington Monument—sunk under pyramids of ketchup, peanut butter, tor tilla chips, truckloads of potatoes, onions, avocados, peppermint candies and after-dinner mints, half-eaten burgers and fork-scattered peas, the whole slithering wasteful cornucopia of his secret and public devouring. "Moooooo," accuse the cows. "Stinker!" "Pig!" "Glutton!" cry voices from the crowd.

Prostrate now, the cattle hanging over him, letting loose with their streams of urine and clots of dung, McGahee shoves his fists into his eyes and cries out for mercy. But there is no mercy. The statue, wicked and glittering, its tiny twisted features clenching and unclenching like the balls of its fists, announces one after another the unremitting parade of his sins: "Insults to Humanity, False Idols, Sloth, Unclean Thoughts, The Kicking of Dogs and Cheating at Cards!"

His head reels. He won't look. The voices cry out in hurt and laceration and he feels the very ground give way beneath him. The rest, mercifully, is a blank.

When he comes to, muttering in protest—"False idols, I mean like an autographed picture of Mickey Mantle, for christsake?"—he finds himself in a cramped mud-and-wattle hut that reeks of goat dung and incense. By the flickering glow of a bank of votary candles, he can make out the bowed and patchy head of Nuala Nolan. Outside it is dark and the rain drives down with a hiss. For a long moment, McGahee lies there, studying the fleshless form of the girl, her bones sharp and sepulchral in the quavering light. He feels used up, burned out, feels as if he's been cored like an apple. His head screams. His throat is dry. His bladder is bursting.

He pushes himself up and the bony demi-saint levels her tranced gaze on him, "Hush," she says, and the memory of all that's happened washes over him like a typhoon.

"How long have I—?"

"Two days." Her voice is a reverent whisper, the murmur of the acolyte, the apostle. "They say the Pope himself is on the way."

"The Pope?" McGahee feels a long shiver run through him.

Nods the balding death's-head. The voice is dry as husks, wheezy, but a girl's voice all the same, and an enthusiast's. "They say it's the greatest vision vouchsafed to man since the time of Christ. Two hundred and fifteen people witnessed it, every glorious moment, from the cask of gin to the furtive masturbation to the ace up the sleeve." She's leaning over him now, inching forward on all fours, her breath like chopped meat gone bad in the refrigerator; he can see, through the tattered shirt, where her breasts used to be. "Look," she whispers, gesturing toward the hunched low entranceway.

He looks and the sudden light dazzles him. Blinking in wonder, he creeps to the crude doorway and peers out. Immediately a murmur goes up from the crowd—hundreds upon hundreds of them gathered in the rain on their knees—and an explosion of flash cameras blinds him. Beyond the crowd he can make out a police cordon, vans and video cameras, CBS, BBC, KDOG, and NPR, a face above a trenchcoat that could once belong to Dan Rather himself. "Holy of holies!" cries a voice from the front of the mob—he knows that voice—and the crowd takes it up in a chant that breaks off into the

THE MIRACLE AT BALLINSPITTLE

Lord's Prayer. Stupefied, he wriggles out of the hut and stands, bathed in light. It's McCarey there before him, reaching out with a hundred others to embrace his ankles, kiss his feet, tear with trembling devoted fingers at his Levi's and Taiwanese tweed—Michael McCarey, adulterer, gambler, drunk and atheist, cheater of the IRS and bane of the Major Deegan—hunkered down in the rain like a holy supplicant. And there, not thirty feet away, is the statue, lit like Betelgeuse and as inanimate and snotgreen as a stone of the sea.

Rain pelts McGahee's bare head and the chill seizes him like a claw jerking hard and sudden at the ruined ancient priest-ridden superstitious root of him. The flashbulbs pop in his face, a murmur of Latin assaults his ears, Sister Mary Magdalen's unyielding face rises before him out of the dim mists of eighth-grade math . . . and then the sudden imperious call of nature blinds him to all wonder and he's staggering round back of the hut to relieve himself of his two days' accumulation of salts and uric acid and dregs of whiskey. Stumbling, fumbling for his zipper, the twin pains in his groin like arrows driven through him, he jerks out his poor pud and lets fly.

"Piss!" roars a voice behind him, and he swivels his head in fright, helpless before the stream that issues from him like a torrent. The crowd falls prostrate in the mud, cameras whir, voices cry out. It is the statue, of course, livid, jerking its limbs and racking its body like the image of the Führer in his maddest denunciation. "Piss on sacred ground, will you," rage the plaster lips in the voice of his own father, that mild and pacifistic man, "you unholy insect, you whited sepulcher, you speck of dust in the eye of your Lord and maker!"

What can he do? He clutches himself, flooding the ground, dissolving the hut, befouling the bony scrag of the anchorite herself.

"Unregenerate!" shrieks the Virgin. "Unrepentant! Sinner to the core!"

And then it comes.

The skies part, the rain turns to popcorn, marshmallows, English muffins, the light of seven suns scorches down on that humble crowd gathered on the sward, and all the visions of that first terrible day crash over them in hellish simulcast. The great vats of beer and gin and whiskey fall to pieces and the sea of booze floats them, the cattle bellowing and kicking, sheep bleating and dogs barking, despoiled girls and hardened women clutching for the shoulders of the panicked communicants as for sticks of wood awash in the sea, Sophia Loren herself and Virginia Woolf, Fredda, Cindy Lou Harris and McCarey's wife swept by in a blur, the TV vans overturned, the trenchcoat torn from Dan Rather's back, and the gardai sent sprawling—"Thank God he didn't eat rattlesnake," someone cries—and then it's over. Night returns. Rain falls. The booze sinks softly into the earth, food lies rotting in clumps. A drumbeat of hoofs thunders off into the dark while fish wriggle and escargots creep, and Fredda, McCarey, the shaven-headed pizza vixen, and all the gap-toothed countrymen and farm wives and palsied children pick themselves up from the ground amid the curses of the men cheated at cards, the lament of the fallen women, and the mad frenzied chorus of prayer that speaks over it all in the tongue of terror and astonishment.

But oh, sad wonder, McGahee is gone.

Today the site remains as it was that night, fenced off from the merely curious, combed over inch by inch by priests and parapsychologists, blessed by the Pope, a shrine as reverenced as Lourdes and the Holy See itself. The cattle were sold off at auction after intensive study proved them ordinary enough, though brands were traced to Montana, Texas, and the Swiss Alps, and the food—burgers and snowcones, rib roasts, Fig Newtons, extra dill pickles, and all the rest—was left where it fell, to feed the birds and fertilize the soil. The odd rib or T-bone, picked clean and bleached by the elements, still lies there on the ground in mute testimony to those three days of tumult. Fredda McGahee Meyerowitz, Herb Bucknell and others cheated at cards, the girl from the pizza parlor and the rest were sent home via Aer Lingus, compliments of the Irish government. What became of Virginia Woolf, dead forty years prior to these events, is not known, nor the fate of Emma Bovary either, though one need only refer to Flaubert for the best clue to this mystery. And of course, there are the tourism figures—up a whopping 672 percent since the miracle.

McCarey has joined an order of Franciscan monks, and Nuala Nolan, piqued no doubt by her supporting role in the unfolding of the miracle, has taken a job in a pastry shop, where she eats by day and prays for forgiveness by night. As for Davey McGahee himself, the prime mover and motivator of all these enduring mysteries, here the lenses of history and of myth and miracology grow obscure. Some say he descended into a black hole of the earth, others that he evaporated, while still others insist that he ascended to heaven in a blaze of light, Saint of the Common Sinner.

For who hasn't lusted after woman or man or drunk his booze and laid to rest whole herds to feed his greedy gullet? Who hasn't watched them starve by the roadside in the hollows and waste places of the world and who among us hasn't scoffed at the credulous and ignored the miracle we see outside the window every day of our lives? Ask not for whom the bell tolls—unless perhaps you take the flight to Cork City, and the bus or rented Nissan out to Ballinspittle by the Sea, and gaze on the halfsize snotgreen statue of the Virgin, mute and unmoving all these many years.

VISITATION

S he was visited one night by the ghost of her old lover. He was wearing the blue shirt she loved, the one he gave her which she threw away when he left her, and was carrying his penis in his hand like a little bird. He squeezed it and it raised its head and then he let it go limp again. He showed her how to make it go up and down and let her play with it. It was weightless and felt like a cylinder of light in her hand, though it pulsed faintly when she squeezed and released it, making it rise and fall, rise and fall, remembering how fond of it she once had been. When she pressed it into that place between her legs so familiar to it, it felt no more substantial than in her hand: something that was felt, yet not felt, teasingly present, yet not quite there, like an image in a movie. She took the phantom penis out and tried to give it back to him, but he had withdrawn into a corner and was fading away, so she put it back in, for when she'd removed it, it had left a strange chill behind like an airy echo of itself, and she understood then the nature of his haunting.

He was visited one night by the ghost of his former lover, who arrived wearing an old shirt he'd once given her because she looked so beautiful in it. When her hand wrapped his penis it was as if it were gripped by a warm damp breath, though she remained withdrawn in a far corner, watching him with a look of infinite sorrow, an expression of the distance between them. When she gave him her vagina to taste, it reminded him of a hillside in Italy where they'd gone to gather herbs that last summer, though it did not taste of herbs but more like what the sky might taste like if one could taste it, or at least like something blue, a flavor not quite a flavor, in the way that infinity is not quite a measurement, and one that would haunt him, he knew, for the rest of his days. He thought that her vagina whispered to him as it withdrew, but whether of love or the betrayal of it, he could not tell. Her hand slowly lifted from his penis then and, even as it and she faded from sight, remained hovering in the air just above its anguished stretch, grazing its tip with a phantom finger.

RUN RAGGED

I t isn't new for me, this being perplexed by clothes. They burdened me when I was a kid and swithering between the Snoopy tee-shirt and the Linus one. Worse than ever they burden me now. Mornings I have often lain in bed quite unable to decide. If it's a cold day I can wear a sweater and not worry about what kind of shirt underneath, but then, if I go into the warm, I might have to take that sweater off, and then the shirt would count. Which shirts are clean and mostly button up? Will anybody, any lady, any guy in the locker room see my underpants today? Do I need to look for holes? And the shirt, what color? Not a blue one again. I wear so much blue I'll be taken for a cop on his way to work, or I would be taken if everyone in Tulley's Gore didn't know my face. Pants. Is it splashy out? Should I wear something dark? What pair of pants doesn't have a crotch like the inside of a piano? If I don't sit down in public, maybe it doesn't matter, not if it isn't very cold and I find the underpants without the holes. The variety gets me down. It would be quicker if we all wore uniforms.

Yet you couldn't have said before that I was scared of clothes. Worried, yes; embarrassed, certainly; betrayed, perhaps; and bullied, probably. But, before the first Monday in January, never scared.

Get me right. The anxious type I may be; easily intimidated I am, even to the point that I'd rather spend an extra hour in bed than come to grips with my wardrobe. Every free weekend I have a stomach like a witch's cauldron—all the way from Friday night to Monday morning. I can only sing in public when I've had three beers, and I never drink that many for my bladder's sake because you never know when you might not have the chance. Rather than face my Aunt Eunice from Boston, her with the opinions about Sunday School and dobermans, I've been known to spend all day in my car, and I don't enjoy driving. I get nervous, sweat-nervous, but I don't get scared. I didn't, that is to say.

Don't get me wrong. I am a cautious, logical man; I don't scare at what can't be explained, not always. The cigarette smoke, for example. Many times when I'm lying in bed, around nine in the morning, always that time, I smell a cigarette. Now *that* I gave up years ago—eleven years ago, if you want the facts—excepting the occasional one when I've had too much to eat or I want my breath to smell of cigarettes instead of bad gums. I have smelled that smell of cigarettes—filters, I would say—when I have not had even that occasional one in weeks, when I've been alone, with no one besides myself in the building. Who comes to sit by me, smoking patiently? Am I peeking under the curtain at what's in store? It's bad, I know, or I wouldn't smell those smells, bad enough to come seeping back from the future. Some days I think it's a last hour with some lady before she dies of cardiac arrest or suicide; some days it's an interrogation, with the interrogator dragging away while I squirm, chained to my seat. But I'm not scared about it. Leastways not yet, and if it doesn't scare me now, it never will.

Of course, clothes may have weird habits. We all know the shirt that goes AWOL for entire months. One day it's there begging to wear me, please, and the next, however many times you push the hangers up and down the rack, it isn't. Not hiding between two big, assertive chamois shirts; not there at all. And the next day it is again, complaining hey, you didn't wear me in months. I have one just like that, a blue check with short sleeves. I couldn't find it since square-dance classes—there was this woman, you see, who thought the classes would be a blast—and that was seven years ago, going on nine, but on Monday back it had come, telling me I'm just wasted on you. Oh yes, I know all about invisible borrowing. I know about shirts—underpants and socks as well, let's not forget—spirited away to be worn someplace else.

But worn right where I am?

So I don't get scared, and I've gotten accustomed to shirts and underpants and socks and (I forgot before) belts and shoes with weird habits. Fair enough. I mean, who doesn't like surprises?

But enough is enough. Mornings are hard enough as it is. There were too many choices. Maybe I was chosen.

That Monday, or really Tuesday morning—yes, the clock-radio shone 2:45 when I turned to look at it, so it was the morning—I lay there thinking about or, truthfully, trying not to think about infinity . . . eternity. Me snug in bed in a structurally sound apartment building in Tulley's Gore, Maine—a job of sorts and an actuarial chance at forty more years of life unless in case of nuclear war or accident when all premiums null and void—thinking about eternity and infinity. Couldn't think about them, couldn't not think of them. What came before, what comes after, how would you not get bored in heaven, what's *outside*, that sort of thing.

Ridiculous, sure, but I was lying there, sweat pouring off me like spring break-up, thinking of time without end, amen, when suddenly, from over by the deacon's bench where I generally drop my clothes (I sleep naked except in hospital, and there they don't let you) comes a stirring. Damn, a mouse. Tomorrow, today, this afternoon, I'll have to go down to the hardware store to get me a trap. How I hate to see their little eyes popped-out and glassy, but it's them or me. Anyways, no more infinity. I start to think about the day and the letter I have to write to the credit-card company about being over-charged fifty-nine dollars and thirty cents by that rental car company when I went to see my aunt, and while I'm composing the letter, which should have been written two weeks ago, it all gets too complicated and I cosy up to my deep pillow and go back to sleep.

Except for buying the trap and trying to decide between farm-house cheddar for the home-loving rodent or Monterey Jack for the adventurous kind, I wouldn't have thought any more about the stirring round the deacon's bench if it hadn't have been for the warmth. My bedroom's quite cold, you know, not cold like part of a big house shut off for the winter where the squirrels and the coons move in, but pretty damn cool. Every fall I try to catch my landlord before he tacks those foggy plastic sheets to all the window frames, because I want to be able to open a few windows on a mildish day. He complains of the expense, and I remind him it's good to have a longtime tenant and I'm saving him the price of an ad in the *Shopper*. Mostly that shuts him up. Rather too cool than too warm, then, but that means chilly mornings. No wonder I don't get up at once. And, with a job that starts at noon, who cares? It's chilly and so are my clothes. Usually, when I've decided what to wear, I grab everything and head for the bathroom. There aren't any windows there.

That Tuesday morning, my clothes were still warm. I picked up my last night's shirt, sniffed it in the obvious places, and decided it would last another day. That shirt was warm. I picked up my under-pants and socks to toss them in the laundry basket—I am not a dirty person—and they were warm. My sweater—white, Aran—was warm too.

To warm up that much clothing would take a lot of mice. I like the idea of preheated clothes, sort of like Napoleon having a man just to break in his boots, but so many mice—no thank you.

Yet there was no mousy smell, and not a single mouse turd rolled out of my things when I shook them.

26

My shirt and sweater were warm, my pants too, but the room was cold enough to freeze the balls off a polar bear. I ran for the bathroom.

During lunch break, which I get at four o'clock in the afternoon, I went down to Duboeuf's and bought three traps. Then I stopped in at the IGA, where I chose Monterey Jack and farmhouse cheddar. Turds or no turds, I would get those mice.

Helped by two hot rums and a copy of *Statutes of the State of Maine, Revised* that came with the apartment, I fell asleep and stayed that way. When I woke the next morning, well rested, I found a chilly shirt and, in the traps, three lumps of cheese untouched and drying out.

Nevertheless, I baited those traps again and set them out Wednesday evening. Liquor wasn't needful, and I never could abide the law. The very sight of my pillow had me nodding and yawning. The mice had likely been a one-night stand and, if they hadn't been, well, I was ready.

I wasn't ready for what happened next. At first it was like a dream. A lovely woman's scent, like the perfume counter in a ritzy Boston store, was making me smile in the dark. Something would happen to me, something good. It felt like she had floated up the stairs to my apartment, glided on in and straight to my bedroom. I could imagine her, hear her almost, dropping her clothes, shoes, skirt, sweater, blouse and the rest, ready to slip between the sheets and cuddle. I did hear her too—could distinctly hear garments fall, one after another, just so.

I stretch out a bit and wriggle, not wondering how she came to be here, just relaxing and enjoying as though it's all settled.

The phone rings. It's an instinct—right?—that when the phone rings, even when you're in bed and starting in on the erotic experience of a lifetime, you stretch out a hand and answer. So I do.

It's my pal Max in California, where it's ten o'clock. Drunk again, just like in Mainz, Germany, in the army. "Not now, buddy, not now.

Everybody loves you. Go to bed. That's where I am. Busy, know what I mean? Take care now." Down with the phone. Silence. Did I spoil the mood? Where did the perfume go? She can't have left. "Honey, are you there? Don't be catching cold. Warm in here. Come on, I know you're there. Hey, don't be a tease."

I switch on the bedside lamp. No one there. Not a sound, not a sight of anyone.

Nothing but yesterday's clothes in a heap.

Hopeful mostly, I sleep in a king-size bed. On the floor, not on my side, away from the phone and the lamp, my clothes have been dropped in a heap. I didn't leave them there. A faint perfume, a honeysuckle scent, still lingering.

I certainly wasn't going to buy more cheese. The rest of the night inched by in the light of my bedside lamp equipped with a 100-watt bulb, soft white. I dozed—neither asleep, nor awake.

During my day at the lab I broke two flasks, spilling gold and orange reagents across the floor. All my energy went in getting ready for the coming night. Driving home, on the curve above the gorge where spray from the falls slicks the road even on the coldest day, I all but hit a light pole. I made a big pot of coffee to go with my ham-and-cheese sandwiches. Usually too much coffee will get me up in the night, but that wouldn't matter now. This night I wasn't going to sleep at all. My clothes were folded just like for kit inspection in the service. I was the mousetrap.

Of course I had to turn off the lights. Because, maybe, of the excitement, I wasn't afraid of doing that. Sex fools us all, and I didn't mind being fooled—didn't think of it even. I just thought of that honeysuckle perfume, and I lay there in the darkness smelling pictures, seeing pictures of necks and breasts, the crossing place between the breasts, that tender place beneath the ears. It was all I could do to keep my hands off of myself. I tried to think of something else . . . Thanksgiving as a kid, going over every dish from celery and

California olives with a hole in them to that real creamy pumpkin pie my mother learned from her mother. Next it was Christmas, then a picnic for Memorial Day. . . .

And I woke up with the sun streaking through the gaps between the curtains. Darkness and exhaustion had beat the coffee. It was quarter after eight.

My visitor had come all right. This time my clothes lay all around the room: socks on the center light, pants on the deacon's bench, sweater wadded in a corner, shirt dangling over the edge of the bureau like a climber hiking himself onto a ledge. The perfume lingered softly, but the clothes scared me. No one that mad about being rejected was going to share my bedroom in the dark.

Some clothes do have a history, no doubt about it. My blue silk dressing gown, which always hangs first in the walk-in closet so as I have something to wear while I make up my mind, came from my missionary Uncle Tad who got himself knifed in Burma. Girlfriends have borrowed sweaters when men's sweaters were the fashion, neckties when it was neckties. Once, after an evening of fooling around under the pines at Rushbee's Pond, I put on Arlette Honan's denim shirt while she put on mine, and we didn't even notice until I breathed too hard and all the buttons popped. Then there are jackets. I don't mind admitting that I buy my jackets at the hospital rummage sale. You find a good class of tweeds there, some of them shot in the pocket, but some of them hardly worn, like that brown herringbone I picked out, with the label of a store in an Ivy League town, for only two-fifty that has lasted me so far three-and-one-half winters. It's not as though I lived on Park Avenue in New York City.

Like an old house, then, or one of those Indian swamis, you might say some of my wardrobe had lived previous lives. And like an old house, my wardrobe might be haunted.

There, I've admitted the word. I didn't then. The most I would say was that some of my pants and shirts and jackets were experienced.

They had seen too much, heard too much, felt too much, and done too much. You might even say they knew too much. It was time to invest in a little innocence.

On my day off, which is Friday because even in these bad times the mill works around the clock, I drove very carefully into Bangor. That made the choosing harder than in Tulley's Gore, but it sure saved money. I wandered up and down for a couple of hours and then decided on two completely new sets of everything except a jacket. I didn't intend to be that extreme—only to have two completely new and inexperienced outfits. The jacket I did without because often I don't wear one, but new shoes I bought, gray Bangor moccasins. Yes, the choosing was a worry, but I did my bit for the local economy.

Although my company had not returned, I had a hunch it might be coming—and I had no wish to meet it. After a clam-strip dinner in Orono I drove on up through a night of sharp stars and hard cold. I sat up till around midnight playing Linda Ronstadt and Emmylou Harris, feeling sad along with the music. Then I went to bed, but before undressing I set out one of the new outfits all ready to go in the morning, and I tossed my old stuff away in the bathroom. As an industrial chemist, I believe in experiments.

This one, you could say, had negative results, but that didn't make me sorry. Friday night was as quiet as a snowbound Sunday.

I spent a peaceable Saturday, work and all. Before going to bed, though, I put on my blue silk dressing gown and stood in the closet just to see what I could see. All those shirts, all those pants, and, courtesy of the hospital auxiliary, a whole bunch of jackets. Everything a little frayed, a mite tattered—dressing came a little hard. Maybe I should do some casting off, but how I hated even the idea. No matter how leaky or how squeaky, even with nails sticking out, when a pair of boots goes west, I feel an urge to play taps for it. Does anybody else apologize to neglected belts and vests?

In a display of neatness that might have squeezed a smile out of my old sergeant, I stripped the second new outfit of its wrappings, all those pins and plastic clips, and laid it out. Then I hung up my blue silk dressing gown in the closet and climbed into bed. Peace came in gentle waves.

Cradled in the waves, oh yes, up and down like a babe in arms, lapped by the waves, the waves lapping around me, lapping at my face. I woke up. Something was stroking my cheeks, lapping at my face. I tried to call out. The moment I opened my mouth it was filled, stuffed with fabric. As I gasped for air, the fabric jammed itself against my nose; my head buzzed and rang. A massive weight slumped across my chest.

I fought back. A salmon on a line couldn't fight harder. My body arched from the bed. I twisted around. With a heave I wrenched my right arm free of the bedsheets. I tugged at what was stifling me and pulled it clear of my face. I gave another great heave which flung me out of bed. The carpet needed a shampoo. The sour smell and the clotted pile were real comforting.

Well, for a few seconds they comforted me, until I thought about what was in the dark with me. Like a kid waking from an ugly dream, scared of the dark, scareder still of what the light would show, that is how I felt. I am not a child, however, but a logical man, trained to be inquisitive. First I got to my knees; then, with my eyes shut against the glare, I turned on the light.

Though fearing much worse, I expected at least a shambles of blankets and sheets. All was tidy. After flailing about like a patient on the electroshock machine, you would expect a certain amount of disturbance. Yet the bed looked orderly, almost untouched, in much better shape than after a normal, quiet night's sleep. Only one thing was out of place. I had set my new clothes on the deacon's bench. There they still sat. But my dressing gown, my blue silk dressing gown from Burma lay spread-eagled on the pillow, for all the world as if it had been making love.

I am a logical man, a cautious man, some say a tight-fisted man. Nevertheless, not even halfway through the month I was ready to throw my deposit away. It was a sick apartment, of that much I was sure. Something I had done, something I hadn't done, maybe neither, maybe the start of a new year had started it—had provoked it, if you like. I wasn't going to stick around and let it provoke me back.

Fortunately for me, the Penobscot County rental market in mid-January doesn't offer a whole lot of options. Between the creaky top floor of a triple-decker with exposed wiring and a snug little house right on the edge of town, even I had no trouble deciding. "If you're the handy sort," said the realtor, "you could fix that floor yourself."

Even with the expense, it was good to be out of the apartment. Ruthless for once, I managed to give quite a lot of clothes, the really unwearable ones that needed tailor work, back to the hospital auxiliary. The dressing gown went in a parcel, third class, to the Sailor's Home in Portland. Anything newer or without a history would move with me. And yes, I kept the two new outfits. Seeing that I was on my way to fresh, healthy quarters, there was no point in giving them up.

Jeff Pancheon helped me with my stuff. He thought I was crazy moving on an impulse, but I lied and said the heating pipes kept banging, stopping me from sleeping. That's what I told the landlord too.

We loaded everything into Jeff's truck on a snowy day. I left nothing but the *Statutes of the State of Maine, Revised*, abandoned in the middle of the bedroom floor. I felt a little sad now that the place was empty. It may have given me a bad time, but I had no hard feelings. I looked around one last time, the way you do when you're leaving.

At the new place, Jeff helped me erect the bed and position the couch and stereo. Then he sat around awhile, drinking beer, talking pro football, which doesn't particularly interest me because I only care about the college kind. I wanted him to go so I could putter around, but I did owe him the beers. Before, I had always moved around Labor Day. Doing it mid-winter felt like breaking all the rules. Even if the change had been forced on me, I was going to enjoy it.

At last, at last Jeff drove away, taking his Dolphins and Patriots along with him. Now that the snow had stopped, the sky was clear violet. When I came out one last time to find an outlet and plug in my car, the air felt like pincers around my skull. Another bitter night was on its way.

I could worry later about windows that didn't open. For now I was glad of the warmth of the basement furnace and the solid pile of logs beside it.

When you walk into someone else's new apartment, you see the bareness; you notice how makeshift everything seems. But when it's your own apartment, better still a little house, every nail in the wall's a work of art and every new-hung calendar a Michelangelo. I wasn't going to make any rushed decisions about what pictures would go where, but, taking care for the newly-spackled plaster, I did tap in half a dozen nails. Quite enough excitement for one evening. I opened some albacore tuna in spring water, spiked it with green Tabasco, ate it from the can, chasing it down with the last of Jeff's beer, and considered bed. It was ten o'clock. Prospects looked good.

And now, six hours later, they have never looked worse. Only to find out what sense it made, I have gone over everything that has happened, but the going-over has not helped at all. Nothing is left. I am a logical man, and nothing is left. All around my new bedroom, my clothes, familiar ones and new additions, lie shredded and tattered just as I found them when I woke. My bureau drawers slew off their runners. My shirts have been unstitched and torn— streamers flapping in every breath of air. The severed legs of my slacks sprawl in mismatched pairs, gray with green and brown with black. Returned to their original threads and fibers are things I cannot even name.

I went tranquilly to sleep in my warm, rented house. At most an hour later, I woke. I heard no noise, saw no movement, but I felt the whole room still and exhausted. This time I did not hesitate to switch on the light, yet even before I put my hand out to the lamp, I knew I had brought the wrongness with me.

There should be smoke though, the smoke of cigarettes. Where has my smoker gone? I smell nothing but spackling and fresh paint.

One day in the lab a tiny bug started to crawl down the inside of a funnel. The funnel hung in the neck of a bottle of glycerine and was thinly coated with the stuff. I tried to rescue it, but the surface was too slick. Round and round, down and down. My fingers tasted sweet.

What now? I have no clothes to wear, no house can shelter me. Everything or nothing; nothing and everything. Because I am a cautious man, although I am a cautious man, I have to squeeze my options from the darkness.

I might gather up the fragments, all the spurned tatters, bundle them all together, wriggle beneath and wait, wait for the smoker, the one last cigarette, the final match.

I might walk outside, into the open, before the dawn exposes me, naked, feeling the indrawn breath cake in my nostrils, the snow closing around my feet, the ice draping my shoulders. Naked I came into the world, naked I can end.

I rock upon a fulcrum sharp as an icicle, hot as a reddened poker. To and fro. Which will clothe me, fire or ice? The hair on my chest bristles, sweat chills my groin. My heart is going one and zero, one and zero, one and zero, one and zero, as I wait to be decided.

FLOGGINGS

And just what do you think you're doing?" the voice asked, making the young man, Lucien, drop the hem of the petticoat from his soft freckled fingers, whereupon it spread out against the wall in a white fan, like a wave spreading across the beach, the eyelet shirred and smelling of fish. The petticoat was tacked to the wall at its enormous waistband; beside it was displayed an equally enormous pair of bloomers, hand-sewn of flannel, the seams finished off in the French manner with stitches so tiny they appeared to be the work of mice. "Qu'est-ce que tu fais?" the voice asked, coyly this time. "Or are you a mute?" It was late afternoon and through the room's single window the light issued in a single yellow block, as if the glass Lucien had polished just that morning wasn't there, and the light was a corporeal substance of which there was too much. He looked around. The museum had been closed for an hour, but that didn't always stop the tourists—people who, no doubt, in their normal lives respected the message of locked doors—from lifting the peevish faces of their offspring up against the windows, hinting by gesture at the need for a bathroom. But the room was empty. "Like tree trunks," the voice said. "Or so the Captain claimed. *He* was my equal, and he adored my legs. Mes jambes. He had a tongue in him the size of a hand and, let me tell you, the manual dexterity to go with it."

Lucien beat each of his ears, in turn, against the flat of his palm. Although his skin was of that inordinate paleness and sheen which so often characterizes people with red hair, making it a bad idea for them to spend too much time in the sun, Lucien bathed in the sea every morning, and he knew the trick for releasing from his earholes the trapped voices of the drowned—that oddly dry and brittle buzzing—as if it were a fact of nature that the souls of sailors emerged, after watery death, in the form of insects. In this case the trick didn't work. Anyone might have told him it wouldn't: the wide, seething body of the North Atlantic is undoubtedly sentient, but inarticulate. Still, with his final whack, Lucien managed to dislodge a little trickle of water, and it amazed him how warm it was, like soup.

"Hello?" he said. "Hello?" But there was no answer. A moth flew out from under the remarkable three-tiered wedding gown on the opposite wall, its infinitesimal innards working hard to digest a hundred-year-old fiber. "Shoo," Lucien said. And then Thomas walked into the room, the trowel of his face digging into the book he carried—Proust, Proust, these days always Proust!—and Lucien noticed how he had combed his brown hair so that it looked exactly like the cap on an acorn.

"Were you calling me?" Thomas asked.

From its vantage point on the ceiling of the room the ghost of Wanda Broom—famous Wanda Broom, the giantess of Margaree, without whom there would never have been a museum—relaxed in certain knowledge. Since her death she had swelled to the size of a dirigible, making such containment uncomfortable, but preferable to contention outdoors with the unpleasant winds as they swooped down from Labrador: masculine winds, every one of them, filled with boastful tales of waterspouts and submerged kayaks. The white and spotted one, the ghost realized, was the *youngest* brother. Traditionally a dunderhead: faithful and true, but a dunderhead nonetheless. As for the older one, she probed him briefly, but the sensation was too painful; he felt like a wet sock, wrung in knots, releasing a single gray drop of moisture.

Certainly they didn't look like brothers. In fact, many of the tourists who wandered through the front door, their curiosity stirred by the sign Thomas had painted—MARGAREE MUSEUM AND TEA SHOPPE—assigned to their relationship an explicitly sexual interpretation. It is possible Lucien never noticed; Thomas, on the other hand, registered every raised eyebrow or smirk and, while the affection between the two of them occasionally grew wings and tried to turn itself into love, he found himself overcome with the desire to explain to anyone who would listen how that love had never assumed an incestuous nature. Still, every person on earth manages to entertain every conceivable idea at least once in their lives. Thomas could not forget how, when he and Lucien were younger, their mother made them take baths together. The bathtub was shaped like a boat with stunted legs and nervous paws. The soap was Ivory, which meant that it floated. Lucien suggested a game called Milking the Cows.

"Well?" Thomas asked.

Lucien stood grinning, embarrassed. "I thought I heard someone talking to me," he said.

Thomas set his book down on a table just below Wanda Broom's large white chemise. A dangerous juxtaposition: the ectoplasmic torso of Wanda Broom swarmed in all of its mothy parts towards that lacy white receptacle, seduced by the inevitable rising cloud of language; the ghost torso recalled with Proustian thoroughness just what it had been like to be alive. How sweetly her heart had beat— average-sized, as she'd been informed by the family physician— within her capacious breast. The Captain had lifted from his plate a prawn and inserted it lovingly between her partly opened lips. It had been her eighteenth birthday. The calliope juggled its pluvial notes in the blue air outside. Wanda Broom was aroused. Ghosts are, in any event, composed of pure desire. The first time the Captain slid his wide hand up under that chemise was nothing compared with this! Into the room escaped the faintest odor of cinnamon.

Hers had been a short life, as the mimeographed biography that Lucien and Thomas sold to the tourists for one dollar explained. She had been born to parents of normal dimension, and had lived with them in a farmhouse on the outskirts of what was now the town of Margaree: her father had made a special large bed for her, and a special large chair, so that she could eat with the rest of the family. Like a normal child, she was sent off to school. But then the schoolmaster began complaining that she took up too much room; whether he was referring to the size of her body, or to the size of her brain—for Wanda was very intelligent—is unclear. Whatever the nature of his complaint, one day when Wanda showed up for school he sent her home, and for the next two years she languished, spending most of her time walking along the beach, thinking of how even the largest creatures of the sea were small in proportion to all that water. It was not until she was older that she realized how human happiness is a matter of discovering context.

Margaree, for example, was situated along the Gulf of Saint Lawrence, at the tip of the Gaspé Peninsula. The whole universe could be perceived as radiating outwards from that spot or, conversely, it could contain more than one focus, like a wildly improbable geometric figure, and each of these foci would be the city or town in which the circus put up its tents. For, when Wanda was eleven years old, her father sold her to P. T. Barnum. And so it came to pass that it was Sarabelle, the Queen of Fatland, rather than her own mother, who ended up guiding her through the mysteries of the ménarche, in exchange for which Wanda learned how to fasten Sarabelle's stays without catching in their teeth clamlike morsels of flesh.

Then, one day, the Captain joined the circus. He was a handsome man, eight feet tall—taller than Wanda by one inch. Their courtship was brief, and received considerable attention in the press. "World's Tallest Man to Wed World's Tallest Woman!" the headlines announced. No doubt people took the story so much to heart because it reinforced their belief in love's inevitability: that for every person on earth there was one perfect lover; that all one had to do was be patient, and that lover would come along.

At least this was the interpretation May Swicegood gave to the phenomenon, the first afternoon she'd appeared in the museum. "It was a simpler time," she had said ruefully, as she sat on one of the chaste Sheraton chairs in the tearoom, a muffin crumb enchantingly lodged on her upper lip. Her voice was a little husky and breathless, as if she'd just run in out of the rain, even though she'd been sitting at the table for almost an hour waiting for the rain to let up. "Husbands and wives had separate bedrooms," she'd said. "Every time they came together it was like a tryst. I can just picture the way it must've been for Wanda and the Captain. They must've been happy in a way we can't even begin to imagine."

"Happy?" Thomas, in a familiar gesture, had removed his eye-glasses and blown on the large, thick lenses, wiping them off on the sleeve of his shirt, so that Lucien found himself wondering once again if, for his brother, all incomprehensible human behavior appeared to be nothing more than a result of dirt. "How could they have been happy?" Thomas had asked. "They were freaks."

"And I suppose," May Swicegood had said, tapping with the long, square nail of her index finger at Thomas's book, "that you think this guy was perfectly normal? Let's face it, Proust was a freak."

"You've read Proust?" Thomas had asked.

"Sure. I suffered through him in college. Didn't everyone?" Then May had turned her slightly wall-eyed yet beautiful gaze on Lucien: her eyes were long and shaped like minnows, the gray irises apparently tugged at, ever so delicately, by those apparitions we all catch glimpses of from the corners of our eyes. "The muffins were delicious," she'd said. "Maybe sometime I could paint your portrait, with you holding one of them in the palm of your hand?"

For May Swicegood, it turned out, was an artist; she lived in a large house in New Hampshire with, as she said, "a group of like-minded women." She was thirty-one years old—four years older than Thomas—and ever since her twenty-fifth birthday she had specialized in portraits. "I woke up and looked at myself in the mirror," she'd said, "and I *knew* that everything anyone needed to know about me was right there." Her talent was for the revelation of character through an obsessive and intricately crafted accumulation of detail. Already she'd had several one-woman shows in New York, despite the fact that the prevailing aesthetic was for anything but the representational.

Every year, at the giddy and pivotal moment when the faces of her friends began assuming, as did the greenish-black faces of the trees, that internal shine which precedes the dropping off of excess matter—as if by choice, rather than in thrall to the coming storms—May undertook a bicycle trip through the Gaspé. She wanted to avoid the frenzy of canning and pickling that beset the household; she wanted to escape the prevailing sense that things could be gotten under control. She knew they couldn't: her own parents had been pig farmers in upstate Pennsylvania. The one thing May remembered with chilling clarity was the day her father, a man dedicated to the idea that there was no part of a pig he would let go to waste, came running into the kitchen screaming that the antichrist had taken up residence in their barn. Three piglets had stood together with their hind ends facing him and their tails read 666—the devil's own number. May remembered helping her mother put up beets as, outside, the sun heated up the lawn, melting white sheaths of frost from the grass blades. She thought she could see each blade; coming from the barn she could hear reedy squeals and panicking, tiny hoofbeats.

"Holding a *muffin*?" Lucien had been skeptical.

But May had explained how in the greatest portraits the inclusion of symbolic objects intensified the viewer's relationship to the subject. She produced from out of her rucksack a print of a painting by Hans Holbein, the Younger, her idol. In it a man in long robes stood slightly to the left of a table on which there sat a globe of the world. Hanging in the air between the table and the man there was a strange, white, cigar-shaped object. "That's a human skull," May had said. "Rendered in anamorphic projection. If you hold your head at just the right angle, you can see it perfectly clearly. The point is, the guy in the picture was a cartographer, and Holbein wanted us to understand the connection between the charting of unfamiliar places and the skeleton that is always right there, really, waiting inside of our bodies."

That had been three years ago. May's portrait of Lucien now hung in the entrance hallway to the museum. Visitors exclaimed over the likeness, marveling at the exactitude with which the artist had managed to record even the smallest freckles on Lucien's face. The more visually astute noticed how each freckle asserted an individual shape — shapes echoed in the crumb of the muffin, invitingly split open and extended on the palm of Lucien's hand. For, although Lucien had hoped that May would paint the muffin anamorphically — a golden-brown blur just above his head was what he'd imagined — she had refused. According to May such an interpretation would be a lie: Lucien lived in the here and now, she insisted; a person looking at the painting should feel their powers of taste and smell and touch awakening. "It's the way you are," May had said. "It's your gift."

Now, as the ghost of Wanda Broom — made drowsy by so much skirmishing at the boundaries — rested within its frothy sack of dimity, Lucien and Thomas continued preparations for May's annual arrival. They swept the floors. Thomas dusted the top of the dresser in the guest bedroom, while Lucien put fresh sheets on the little maple bed. For May's first visit to Margaree had assumed the contours of ritual: every fall she would arrive just after Labor Day to spend a month with the two brothers. She even kept an easel and a roll of Utrecht linen in the closet, as well as a bundle of wooden stretchers, and the jars of pigment she would mix with egg yolks or oil to make paint.

Lucien and Thomas were both in love with her, although they'd never discussed the fact with each other. Thomas believed that May preferred his company; certainly she appeared to revel in those late-night conversations when they would sit side by side in two wicker rockers on the porch, drinking the peculiar wine Lucien concocted out of rosehips and bearberries. As Lucien slept they would talk about everything—about life and art and the great mystery of the human spirit. Then the moisture would condense on their skin, so that Thomas found himself convinced that May's lips had covered every exposed part of his body, even though neither one of them ever got up out of their chairs.

Lucien, for his part, merely knew that he adored her. If his brother, as an intellectual, made sense out of the world through comparison and judgment, Lucien was content to observe. In this way, despite May's assertion that he existed in the here and now, Lucien was more like the ghost of Wanda Broom: an invisible, watchful presence occasionally ballooning outwards in all directions, subsuming—but never willfully, like a ghost—the objects of his observation.

Before May, Lucien had fallen in love three times in his life. When he was very little, no more than four years old, he had fallen in love with a russet potato. This potato, among other less wonderful potatoes on the kitchen counter, had been slated by his mother for roasting alongside a leg of lamb; because he had wept, his mother had given it to him, and he kept it for almost a year in the pocket of whatever he was wearing, removing it only at bedtime so that it could sleep on his pillow next to his right ear. Later, when he was twelve, he had been walking home from the village one afternoon and had noticed how the Tatros' barn was set into the side of a steep hill, with two heavy leglike posts holding up the part of the barn that extended out into space—it almost broke his heart the way all that gray wood, spilling out light through its cracks like a thing filled with hope, looked like it was about to start walking, staggering first and then picking up speed, down through the thick grass to the winking seam of Phinney's Brook, below. August Tatro, steering his tractor around and around the field, making his second cutting of hay, found himself wondering what the boy was up to, standing there beside the barn for hours in the sun. It looked like he was patting the barn wall, the way some people pat the flanks of nervous horses.

The third time Lucien fell in love—which until the arrival of May Swicegood, he had taken to be the third and final of the Tall Loves allotted him in his lifetime—it was with Jesus Christ. Or, more specifically, it was with the stories Jesus Christ told, which Lucien absorbed in an energetic and personal fashion.

"They aren't just stories," Thomas had repeatedly insisted. "They're parables. If you take them at face value, you're missing the point." In those days, before he had given up on philosophy and embraced literature, Thomas was reading Kierkegaard, whose own parables he spent hours trying to unravel, until his brain was as tangled up as the ancient hosiery of Wanda Broom—that most recent and unexplained gift which had appeared one day in a pink hatbox on the front stoop of the museum. By way of example, Thomas had read Lucien a passage describing a custom whereby a prince, from the day of his birth, was provided with a companion of simpler extraction whose sole purpose was to receive the floggings. "Most people," Thomas had said, "would sympathize with the poor companion. But Kierkegaard says that it was much more horrible for the prince, who knew that he'd done wrong, and never had a chance to experience physical pain. The prince had to watch his companion being flogged, without being able to do anything about it."

"But he was a prince," Lucien had said.

43

"Forget it," Thomas had mumbled. "I don't know why I ever try explaining these things to you."

"He could have smote upon his own breast. He could have humbled himself. In the story of the Pharisee and the publican, the Pharisee is abased because he exalts himself, but the publican humbles himself and is exalted." Lucien had waited, but it became clear, as Thomas turned in his chair and adjusted the angle of the reading lamp, that the conversation was over.

It was beginning to get dark by the time May pedalled her bike up the last steep rise out of Bayhead; the wind was picking up, unrolling tubular swells so that she could see, off to her left and down a sharp cliffside, the ocean's white froth, as if to remind her of her own secret and persistent excitement. The froth shone, as did the widening and narrowing band of beach; along the side of the road vetch grew, which she remembered Lucien explaining was the thing called *tares* in the Bible. A weed. May was thinking about her next painting, which she understood only insofar as it was to be her personal version of Van Eyck's famous portrait of Giovanni Arnolfini and his bride. *May Swicegood fui hic* over the mirror. People would look at the painting and think that it was a self-portrait, since the only person in it would be May, herself. But during the last year she had made a choice. Her idea was to provide evidence of the identity of her prospective bridegroom through the inclusion of objects. A domestic setting, breathtakingly realistic, replete with disguised symbolism of the most subtle kind: May began making lists up in her head; she began seeing the finished painting so clearly that when the lights of Margaree appeared in front of her she mistook them for opaque dots of white paint, applied with the tiniest of her sable brushes, highlighting the thousands of seed pearls sewn into the bodice of Wanda Broom's gown. The natural world, May thought, will be made to contain the world of the spirit in such a way that the two actually become one. I love you! she thought. Please, oh please don't disappoint me! She was a modern woman, and conceived of the painting as a thinly veiled proposal of marriage.

By the time she arrived at the Margaree Museum and Tea Shoppe it was pitch dark: clouds had flown in from the north, mimicking in their configuration the by-now violent scalloppings of foam in the sea. May rested her bicycle against the porch railing and then, before going inside, looked through the window into the little dining room. Thomas was sitting at one of the tables, a book open in front of him. But he wasn't reading. In fact, his glasses were lying on the damask tablecloth in the middle of the three place settings of Haviland china—they were lying there folded up, as if no longer necessary. May could see the rosebuds and gilt vine on the china. Include? she wondered. As she watched him, Thomas looked around anxiously, and for a moment May felt something like a cat's tongue licking at her heart. Guilt, she told herself. Oh, God, this is going to be harder than I thought. Then Lucien walked in, carrying a blue vase filled with wild asters. The wind was blowing wildly; as May finally opened the front door and closed it behind her she felt as if she was leaving a party of deities to their furious pleasure.

In the days that followed, May tried not to let her anticipation of what would happen once her painting was finished get the better of her. At least, it was to such anticipation that she ascribed her general feeling of uneasiness. The truth is, May felt as if she were being watched. She had set up her easel in the Wanda Broom Room; she explained that this was because of the fact that its single window was northward-facing, but in actuality it was because she knew that the wall upon which the immense bridal gown was displayed would form the backdrop for her portrait. The first time she set the canvas in place and then stood back to survey her preliminary arrangement of objects, she thought she could see, in the mirror she'd propped up against the wall to catch her own reflection, the reflection of another face: a big, chalky head, like a plaster casting of an antique funeral bust, its proportions epic and expressionless.

"Of course you feel like you're being watched," Lucien said, as they walked together the next morning to the beach. "It's the tourists. Maybe you should work somewhere else. It'd be okay with me if we moved the dress. There's that room at the end of the hall. No one ever goes there."

"The one with the two-headed calves?" May asked. "No thank you. I hate those things. I don't know why you don't get rid of them."

"They came with the place," Lucien said.

It was an unseasonably warm day: the mist that was everywhere was just beginning to lift up so that, as Lucien pointed out, the only parts of their bodies that were really visible were their ankles and feet. Through the crisp and stinging bodies of flies, rising particulate within the singular body of mist, Lucien and May plunged, tidal muck oozing up between their sharply focused toes, towards the sea. They had left their clothing behind in two neat piles on the dunes and, as they swam, Herve LeGare and Tootie McPheeny—playing hooky from school—amused themselves by tying the arms and legs together in knots.

"Le Chien! Le Chien! " Herve and Tootie were doubled over with laughter, rolling around like horrible puppies in the sand. They watched as May and Lucien emerged from the water; by now the mist was like the floor of an enormous elevator car, ascending with greater and greater rapidity above their heads, carrying the noisy gulls inside it upwards.

"Why do you let them call you that?" May asked. She was in-furiated: the boys' three eyes—for Herve wore a pirate's patch over his left eye—fixed on her naked body. They were staring at her pubic hair, their curiosity fastening moistly to her arms and legs and breasts, like seaweed.

"Come on, May," Lucien said. He held out a towel to her, and then picked up her jeans and flannel shirt.

For the first time, as she watched his fingers tenderly working out the knots, May understood the sexual implications of her decision: a channel extending throughout her body filled in with a silvery and molten seam of metal which, as Lucien set the shirt down across her shoulders, solidified. Could the two little boys see how her nipples had become erect? May held the towel tightly against her chest. "I mean it, Lucien," May said.

But Lucien just stood there, jumping on one leg, pulling up his chinos, pausing, as May had noticed men had to, to take into account the soft pouch of sexual organs, before yanking the zipper closed. The two boys—disappointed, no doubt, by the lack of response—began wandering off towards the water. They walked like drunks, aimlessly bumping up against each other; occasionally Tootie stooped down to pick up a shell, which he would heave with a neat flick of the wrist into the sky, aiming at gulls.

"You'll get yours!" May screamed. "Just wait! Little bastards!" She shook out the towel violently, so that it made a noise like a gun going off.

"Hey," Lucien said. "Hey." He put his arm around May's shoulders and patted her upper arm. Of course she didn't realize it, but it was precisely the way he had patted the side of the barn, almost fifteen years earlier. "They're just kids," he said.

"They're monsters." May realized, suddenly, that she was crying. "You don't understand," she said. "I've missed you so much."

"We've missed you, too," Lucien said. He smiled. He was the younger brother, and he really didn't understand. He really didn't. Now May began work on her painting in earnest. Whatever sense she'd had of being watched had been replaced by a general feeling of good will and companionship. Never before had her hand moved with such certainty across the canvas. Nor did she remember ever before experiencing such a pliant attitude in relationship to her composition. The blue vase filled with wild asters all but spoke out loud. *Wrong! Wrong! All wrong!* it decreed. *Lilies in the Meissen pitcher!* it insisted. It was difficult to obtain lilies in Margaree, but May worked out an arrangement with a florist in Fontanelle. The mirror provided her with a version of her face she had never seen before: a little shy, her eyelids lowered. She unbound her thick blond braid and wore her hair loose to her shoulders. One day she sent Lucien out in search of mousetraps. Why? May wasn't sure, all she knew was that the painting called for two mousetraps, one to be placed on the window ledge, the other on the floor near her feet. It would appear that there was an unconscious pattern of symbolism, insistent on asserting itself.

The truth is, of course, that the ghost of Wanda Broom was profoundly involved in all of May's actions. It had taken almost a century, but finally the ghost saw a way out of the dim and blurry waystation of its grieving. Indeed, as May completed her under-painting, and began laying on translucent glazes, bringing the room into sharper and sharper focus with each consecutive layer of madder, or cerulean, or Naples green, the ghost saw in the process the first hints of its own transformation into pure spirit.

It had been so unfair that, to begin with, she had been born a giantess. Or, more precisely, that the world could not love anything so threatening to its system of aesthetics, so contrary to its unfair rules of proportion. After all, whatever rules held true for people, certainly didn't hold true for trees. Think of the thumb-sized birch trees of the tundra! Think of the redwoods! Still, if she had been born a normal size, she would never have married the Captain. Hadn't her own father, climbing up on a sideboard to kiss he cheeks just minutes before her wedding, pointed out to her how lucky she was? And even though he was a fool—even though Wanda had never really forgiven him for giving her upin exchange for a sum of money only large

48

enough to buy a single milk cow—the fact of the matter was that he was right. Wanda and the Captain had loved each other fiercely, sweetly. The notches and the spurs of their great bodies slipped together perfectly. And, in the boatlike canopied bed of their nuptial chamber—for May Swicegood was wrong; they did not sleep in separate rooms—they created, twice, the possibility of a child. Twice.

The ghost's sorrow, beyond containment, surged out through the open window where, in the pervasive chill of the first killing frost, it compressed itself into the form of a bird something like a sparrow, except for the fact that it had four wings. The sparrow came to rest on the window ledge, just beside the mousetrap, the significance of which was not lost on Wanda Broom. According to Saint Augustine, God had to appear on earth in human form so as to fool Satan— "The cross of the Lord," Saint Augustine said, "is the Devil's mousetrap." Two babies. Both carried full term and both born without even the tiniest puff of breath in their bodies. Little babies, both of them. Why couldn't they have lived? The ghost wrapped May Swicegood in a dense, filamental cocoon. She would recall this, later, as a sensation of having been whittled down into a single-celled creature, all eyestalk, pump, and nerve. That was the same morning she painted, as if in a daze, a peculiar four-winged bird, perched on the window sill. Its eyes were the palest blue, like drops of water.

"What's that supposed to be?" Lucien had asked.

"I'm not sure," May had answered. "But I think one of these days we'll find out."

Lucien had sighed. "I never saw a bird before that looked *sad*," he'd said.

The elder brother, Wanda Broom noticed, kept his fascination with the painting to himself. In the middle of the night she would feel the jumpy beam of a flashlight sliding like a finger along her pellicular surface, and then she would see him, shuffling across the floor in bedroom slippers and a plaid robe. At these moments he reminded her of her father, setting forth on moonless nights with his coon hounds, furtive and excited. Thomas studied the painting; he stuck his head as close to its surface as he possibly could, so that all he could see were the brush strokes—as if in the individual strokes he might be able to discover the identity of May's future bridegroom.

Wanda felt sorry for him. She'd been listening the morning May revealed to the two brothers the painting's secret meaning, and she'd watched the way Thomas stood with his head turned towards the window—the way Thomas tried to appear disinterested, even as the wick of his face took fire, casting its bright reflection across all four quadrants of the glass. It was drizzling outside, and the room was filled with a strangely pleasant mixture of smells: muffins baking, tea steeping, the damp exhalations of the walls, as if the sea itself lapped up against the clapboard. Lucien didn't even try to hide his amazement. He looked back and forth, again and again, from the painting to May.

"I don't understand," he said. "It's just you. I don't see anyone in the picture but you."

Thomas laughed, as if he were trying to jar loose a fish bone no larger than a hair, lodged dangerously in his throat. "May likes surprises. Even *you* should know that by now. Why else do you think she waits until the last minute to tell us when she's coming?"

"I thought it was because she didn't like making plans," Lucien said.

Wanda Broom, then, had concentrated all of her attention on the young woman's brain, on the sudden synaptic flickerings which made her think of the stars that time she had watched them from underneath a sweetgum tree, its leaves moving in a hot wind. The Captain's tongue had lapped and lapped at the minute central point of disturbance in her body, that fleck, layering it with moisture until it hardened into a pearl.

"But you're both wrong," May Swicegood was thinking.

And Wanda Broom understood that the young woman was worried because, as she stood there looking at the painting, she knew that it was almost finished. The lace panels of the bridal gown still needed work: the finest tracery of white paint, unmediated by any distillate, would indicate the play of light across the gown's bodice. Likewise May was thinking about how she would have to intensify the juxtaposition of light and shadow in the area immediately above the Haviland saucer—that masterpiece of chiaroscuro by which she hoped to imply the presence on the apparently empty saucer of an object otherwise invisible to the human eye. The light opaque, the shadow translucent: that is how one creates the illusion of reality in classical painting. Whereas Wanda Broom saw the object with perfect clarity; it had been, after all, her idea. The child was seated cross-legged within the saucer's faint indentation, a miniature girl, her skin bluish-white and thin like whey, through which Wanda Broom could see stalks and buds quickening—by which Wanda Broom understood that the child was alive.

A buzzer sounded in the kitchen, and Lucien left the room to return, a few minutes later, carrying a basket full of freshly baked muffins. "Here," he said to May, who took one and bit into it absently. It could have been anything she was putting into her mouth.

"How much longer do you think it'll be?" Thomas asked. "How much longer before you're finished?"

"Two days?" May shook her head so that her braid came to rest over one shoulder like a stranger's arm. "Three days? I don't know," she said, a little irritably. "Soon."

From the basket a thick cloud of steam poured forth, an aromatic molecular disturbance that ascended towards the ceiling. If redemption of memory is the ghost's curse, then it has as its accessories those devices without which memory cannot exist: in a ghost the senses are manifold and acute, unhoused and, consequently, impossible to act upon. Imagine the desire to taste, in the absence of a mouth or a tongue! *My darling, how I hunger for your touch*. And who is he fooling, the romantic who says such a thing, knowing in his heart of hearts that, ultimately, the consummation of his desire is possible? But to be without a body! Damply farinaceous, the skins of hundreds of blueberries darkly bursting with juice—such an odor as the muffins exuded was torture to Wanda Broom. She remembered her mother's kitchen. The broad back of her mother stooping towards the oven. Snow falling outside and the sound of her father's axe, chopping wood. She'd been maybe six years old; a whiskeyjack had landed on the tree outside the window, so tame it would later eat the leftover crumbs right out of her hand.

"Yum, yum," the ghost said. "Muffins."

Its feeling of melancholy was pervasive. Tears welled up, suddenly, in May Swicegood's eyes. "Don't mind me," she explained. "I just burnt my tongue."

In any coastal area the winds, as they blow in off the sea, are filled with ghosts: the ghost of the young matron who perished in her stateroom, her hand poised above the sheet of paper on which she was writing a letter to her best friend; the ghost of the fisherman yanked from his boat and then swept dizzyingly downwards by a huge fish, his breath slowly rising towards the light like a necklace; even the ghost of the brigand, a knife clenched between his teeth. This is why in coastal areas the winds clutch at you with the manifold hands and fingers of a mob: I was beautiful, once; I was married with three children; I was strong like Hercules—if you listen you can hear those plaintive voices. They think you are their last hope. And, if you pause long enough so that out of all that clamoring you begin to feel the isolate heat of just one voice within your ear, then perhaps they are right. A ghost cannot take possession of a living body. It cannot move in. But a ghost can speak to the soul.

The day on which May Swicegood finished her painting the winds hurled themselves up against the walls of the Margaree Museum and Tea Shoppe. All morning and afternoon the place had been filled with tourists, their faces hammered flat and burnished by a fear they assumed was unreasonable; their desire for the familiar had drawn them inside and then—my God!—all they encountered was the grotesque. The two-headed calves! The photographs depicting the seventy-some-odd whales beached and putrescent on the dark sand of the harbor! The undergarments of a giant! How could they explain such deviations from the familiar to themselves, let alone to their children, who ran giddily from one end of the building to the other, screaming with monstrous delight? Even their tea was served to them by a young man with the obsessed and stunted features of a monk. Stunted, that is, except for his eyes, which swelled to the size of golfballs behind the lenses of his glasses. And Earl Grey tea, with its lacing of bergamot, always manages to conjure up thoughts of vegetation gone queer, of ergot poisoning and subsequent madness.

In the kitchen Lucien swooned and stumbled around, the whole top of his head latched onto by the voracious teeth of a moray eel— he had been, as a child, prone to migraines, but he had thought they were a thing of the past. Everything he put in the oven came out burned. Wind blew in through the round exhaust fan over the stove. The kettle whistled and Lucien was infuriated. "Shut up!" he yelled, and a tiny girl with corn-colored hair peeked through the door and laughed.

It wasn't until very late—until the last of the tourists had scribbled their comments in the guest book on the hallway table—that May carried her canvas into the tearoom and propped it up on one of the Sheraton chairs. She was, to borrow a term from Wanda Broom, in her best bib and tucker: for the first time since Lucien and Thomas had known her she was wearing a dress, an antique dress of a pale green color with a high collar and muttonchop sleeves. Her waist appeared to be impossibly small, and the soft gathers of the skirt ran across her hips like water from the mouth of a faucet. Somehow she had managed to contain all of her hair in a knot at the top of her head; her face was pale, her expression both tentative and tyrannical.

"Well," she said, "here it is."

For all of its lapidary and somnolent details, the painting suggested events springing into motion. If the four-winged bird had just lit on the windowsill, it was about to take to flight; if the woman who was May Swicegood sat smiling wistfully down at the empty saucer, she was about to rise up and turn to the wall the face of the convex mirror, in which the artist's own face, tiny and distorted, peered as if through a peephole into the room. The folds of the bridal gown implied, in their subtle disarrangement, the first insufflation of spirit; on her saucer the invisible child's chest began to rise and fall.

The two brothers stood side by side in the darkening tearoom, staring at the painting. May had twisted the shade of the floorlamp so that all of its light was directed on the canvas; it was, consequently, hard for her to make out the expression on Lucien's face. Was he frowning? Was he angry? Thoughtful? *Let us in! Let us in!* the windy ghosts yelled, hurling themselves against the sides of the building. They might have been frightening, but they served a purpose, standing between the three people in the tearoom and the steady seepage into the landscape of the infinite.

"The book?" Thomas asked, hopefully. "Is the book a clue?" It lay open on the table, next to the saucer, the pages ruffling as if in a spring breeze.

"Everything's a clue," May said.

"But there's no way of telling what book it's supposed to be," Thomas said.

Lucien sat down then, suddenly. "Yes there is," he said. He began rubbing at his eyes with his knuckles. "The edges of the pages are red and so are some of the words. It's a Bible, isn't it? And that black knobby thing that wasn't there before is my potato. Next to the mousetrap." He sounded agitated, his voice scandent, twining and

54

putting forth tight little clusters of words, many of which cracked open releasing the high music of adolescence. "But it isn't *me*," he insisted. "You didn't mean it to be *me*, did you?"

"I thought it was so obvious." May's arm flicked out to encircle the thin escaping body of Thomas, to draw it back away from the door. "Thomas," she said, "please. Listen."

"Listen?" Thomas yanked himself free. "What do you think I was doing, all those nights? Did you think I was just an insomniac? And when you gave me that copy of *Swann in Love*, the one you found at the yard sale? 'I can't imagine a more appropriate gift'—those were your exact words, in case you've forgotten."

"I'm sorry," May said. "I never wanted to hurt you."

"You told me I was the only man you'd ever met who could understand the female sensibility. You said I reminded you of that poet, that friend of El Greco's. You made me take off my glasses. Jesus! "

"Fray Felix Hortensio Paravicino," May said. "And you do. You look just like him, without the beard."

"No," Lucien said softly. His voice came as a surprise, the single word emerging out of a deep, riparian groove, filling up the shadowy corner of the room in which he was sitting.

"Since when have you become an expert on mannerist painting?" Thomas muttered.

"That's not what I mean." Lucien got up and walked over to where May was sitting, her spine unnaturally straight, her beautiful minnowy eyes darting from side to side. "I mean, no, I can't marry you. All along I've thought it must be Thomas in the painting, because I couldn't see myself in it anywhere. I kept checking. I wanted to be sure. I wanted to warn you, if it was me, that you were making a mistake."

"I don't understand," May said. She reached over and turned off the lamp, so that the room was suddenly filled with that agitated blackness through which one is able to catch sight of those viral loops and chains called floaters; of those elusive negative images of whatever one was staring at, before the lights went out. "Are you saying you don't *want* to marry me? Is that what you're telling me?" In the darkness May saw Lucien's face bobbing around, sprinkled with unfamiliar and glittering constellations. Freckles, she reminded herself. However many times she had imagined this scene, she had never once entertained the possibility that Lucien would refuse her. She was a proud woman; ever since she'd been a child she'd believed that refusal was not a matter of choice—the gray pork chop on her plate, for instance, had to be eaten, just as the adulation of her peers was inevitable.

"What I'm *telling* you," Lucien said, "is the saddest of all the stories. It's the one about the fig tree. As soon as its branches become tender and put forth leaves, you know that summer is coming. The signs are everywhere, exactly as Jesus said. And then two women will be grinding at the hand mill; one will be taken away and the other left. Two men will be in the field; one will be taken away and the other left."

"This is so humiliating," May said as, in the darkness, Thomas approached; she could feel the heat and shape of his body, even when he was still inches from her; she could anticipate the future: the space between them growing smaller and smaller, Thomas's hand reaching out to touch her breast and then, because the hand and the breast, themselves, had reduced to spinning particles, there would be nothing left to prevent the particulate hand of Thomas from dipping into her heart.

On the beach, in full daylight, the ghost of Wanda Broom threaded itself through the emerald green casing of a falling wave. The ghost could move faster than the wave could finish falling: in one end and out the other, attenuated and fluent, it then flew straight up into the air, a spectacular mile-high pillar, before circling back down to repeat the process. The ghost was practicing. In one end and out the other! it hummed. A length of embroidery silk without a knot! it hummed. O, and when I was a living woman with a mouth and lips, I remember sucking the snail out of the shell. Such pleasure, that tiny moist spook, like swallowing up all the millions of babies from out of the tip of the Captain's penis. Here today, gone tomorrow! the ghost hummed. Gone today, here tomorrow! At the precise moment after the human man and woman had latched together—at the precise moment when the cock prepared to explode within the cunt— the ghost would loop itself like a glimmering, hermaphroditic bracelet through both bodies. The timing would have to be perfect! And then, with the tiniest and most heart-stopping of *clicks*, the two ends of the bracelet would clasp together; the ghost sperm would enter the ghost egg, and the baby would begin forming within the human woman's womb. Through the great noose of the ghost's passage gulls flew, squawking. Such arrogance! The ghost flew in increasingly smaller circles until its noose tightened around the neck of a single gull, tightened and squeezed until the gull plummeted, lifeless, into the sea.

"Holy shit," said Tootie McPheeny, "did you see that?"

But he needn't have asked. Herve LeGare was standing with his mouth hanging open, staring out to where, only moments earlier, a green hand of water had reached up to close its sparkling fingers down around the unaccountably strangled body of a bird.

"I don't know about you," Tootie said, "but I'm getting the hell out of here." He began running, but Herve called him back.

"Look!" Herve said.

Just a little ways beyond the breakers the water erupted in a thin fountain, from the frothy apex of which the two boys could see white feathers shooting forth, hundreds of white feathers shooting upwards and coalescing, high above the sea, into something gigantic and protean. Now they were really frightened. The thing of white feathers interposed itself between the two boys and the sun, so that the beach fell under its shadow.

"What is it?" Herve asked. He lifted his eyepatch, as if whatever the apparition was, it might reveal itself fully only to an eye of stone, an eye unmuddied by images from the world of the familiar.

"It looks like the Holy Ghost," Tootie whispered.

They were, after all, young boys—no more than ten years old. They were still young enough to believe that every event in their lives was separate from all the others: that if there was such a thing as fear it slid, at random intervals, onto the lengthening string of beads that was their experience. They were immune to the concept of motive; the only thing that really interested them was how long the string was becoming, how various and brightly colored were its many parts. Perhaps, by the time they were as old as May Swicegood, they might come to share her suspicion that fear, itself, was the constant; for now, as they ran together—Tootie in the lead, Herve flat-footed several paces behind—all they felt was the exhilaration of escape, combined with a relentless desire to make something happen. In other words, they wanted to prove to themselves that they were still alive. In this way they were not so different from the ghost of Wanda Broom, except for the fact that they had hands and feet; except for the fact that they could actually squash their faces up against the windows of the church where the freckled man they called Le Chien was standing off to one side, waiting for the moment when he would be called upon to hand a wedding ring over to his brother.

The ghost of Wanda Broom had reduced itself to the size of a mote, indistinguishable from the millions of motes of dust with which the yellow light in the church was swarming, stirred into violent motion by even the most restrained of gestures: May Swicegood, for example, turning her head discreetly away from the minister's serious face to see what the sound was at the window. If she saw Tootie and Herve she gave no sign. Instead, she swiveled her head back until she was, apparently, looking at her husband-to-be. Thomas had removed his glasses for the occasion; he couldn't see a thing.

"What's going on?" Herve asked.

"A hockey match," Tootie said, rolling his eyes. "What d'you mean what's going on? It's a wedding, asshole. The blond chick is marrying the skinny dude."

"I know that," Herve said. "But isn't that the wrong guy?"

Their noses, pressed flat, had looked like mushrooms—Tootie's, with its flaring nostrils, like a cultivated mushroom sliced in two; Herve's was more like a truffle. At least this was what May Swicegood had thought when she glanced over towards the windows. It was cold in the church and her dress was thin and gauzy; goosebumps sprang up on her arms and thighs. She could hear Lucien trying to stifle a sneeze. So what, she was thinking. So what if I never paint again. She believed that the painting had exerted a will of its own. As, of course, it had, although May had misunderstood the nature of its communication. The doors of the church flew open, admitting winds and ghosts, admitting two boys in blue jackets, their faces lively, anticipating the consequences of their daring.

"Stop the wedding!" yelled the one with the eye patch.

"You're making a big mistake!" yelled the other one, the one named Tootie.

May looked back over her shoulder and realized that they were both leering at her.

"We've seen you," Tootie said. "Remember?"

But, to her great relief, May never got a chance to answer them; before anyone could say another word, Lucien dragged both of the boys with him out of the church.

"'Is a lamp brought and put under a basket or under a bed?'" he said. "'Is it not put on a lamp stand?'"

"What's wrong with you, man?" Tootie asked. "How could you just stand there and let her get away with that?"

"'For there is nothing hidden,'" Lucien said, "'which will not be uncovered; and nothing done in secret which will not be revealed.'"

. . .

For her seventh birthday Rosa asked for the following presents: a doll with golden hair, a pair of silver shoes, a red bicycle, a set of binoculars that really worked. Her father had explained to her that this was a tall order; he had sat her down and made her listen while he talked solemnly about money and reasonable expectations. Rosa knew that he was doing the best he could. She knew, because she had heard the story many times, how difficult it had been for him; how he'd had to struggle to take care of her, after her mother left. According to her father, exactly one year after Rosa's birth, her mother had walked out the door, climbed up onto her bicycle, and ridden away. She had pedaled quickly; it had been a brilliant day and, as she pedaled over the crest of the hill, it had looked to Rosa's father as if the sun had reached down its flat, shining hand and scooped her up. Still, during that year, the first year of Rosa's life, she had been a perfect mother. "She nursed you, and bathed you, and changed your diapers," Rosa's father would say, the expression on his face pinched and surprised, as if he'd just gotten his fingers caught in a door. "She sang to you." For a while he had tried to find out where she'd gone; eventually he gave up.

Rosa would never have known what her mother looked like, for her father had kept no photographs, if it hadn't been for her Uncle Lucien. One day, not too long before her seventh birthday, he led her upstairs and into his room; his finger was pressed right up against his lips to let her know that she shouldn't make a sound. Then he opened his closet door and took out a large painting of a beautiful woman with long yellow hair, sitting on a chair in the room where the giant's dresses hung. Even though the woman was very beautiful, the painting scared Rosa. It made her feel the way she did sometimes when she knew she was all alone in her bed at night, but could sense vague and independent stirrings of the sheets and blankets. Her Uncle Lucien told her that her father was wrong; that her mother hadn't ridden away on a bicycle. "She would never have done that," he said. "She loved you too much."

Instead, according to her Uncle Lucien, her mother had been walking along the beach one day when, from over the horizon, a small wooden boat had sailed towards them. As they watched, the little boat came in closer and closer to shore; even though it was a cloudy day the boat's wake sparkled, as if the sun were shining right under the surface of the sea, so that the keel had sliced through it, letting out the light. The sailor was a tall, bearded man. His accent led the two of them to think, at first, that he was from the north, probably from Newfoundland—that he had sailed all the way from L'Anse aux Meadows, where the dead Vikings slept under their green quilts of grass.

Uncle Lucien told Rosa how her mother had removed the little sack in which she carried Rosa on her back, like a papoose, and handed her to him. Then she had waded out into the water to meet the man, who stood smiling and waiting. They talked briefly, earnestly—Lucien hadn't been able to hear what they were saying; it wasn't until Rosa's mother waded back, her cheeks flushed and her eyes, for the first time, perfectly focused, that he found out the cause of her excitement. The man in the boat was the promised bridegroom. There could be no question about it. "In this painting," Uncle Lucien explained, running his finger along the edge of the canvas, where Rosa could see tiny silver nails tacking the linen to the wooden stretcher. "The hidden bridegroom." He told her that if she wanted proof she could look in the back of the woodshed, where she would find her mother's bicycle hidden behind a pile of cardboard boxes. "She was very happy because she knew, finally, that her painting had told the truth."

"Is that when she left?" Rosa asked.

"No," Uncle Lucien said. "She didn't leave for about a month. She came back here and painted another picture—her masterpiece, she called it. She worked on it day and night; during that time she made me promise to keep the painting and the sailor a secret from your father. She painted it for you, Rosa, and she told me that I was supposed to give it to you on your seventh birthday."

"Can I see it?" Rosa asked.

"On your birthday," Uncle Lucien said. "And not a moment sooner. It would be very wrong for me to go against her wishes. Besides, it wasn't just anybody on that boat—it was Jesus Christ of Galilee."

"Jesus Christ?" Rosa asked. "But how could you tell?" She was accustomed to her uncle making these kind of remarks; still, his conviction, this time, frightened her a little.

"Because it was summer," Uncle Lucien said, mysteriously. He said how even though they were too far north to see it, in the hot countries to the south of them the fig tree was beginning to send out its tender shoots of new growth; how from the palms of the sailor's hands, when he reached out to help her mother up onto the boat, it was possible to make out the yellow-green unfurling of new leaves. "He didn't come to make peace on earth, Rosa," Uncle Lucien continued, "He came to make divisions. That's what He told His disciples; it's written down, word for word, in the Bible."

Rosa loved her Uncle Lucien, but she had come to suspect, along with many of the other residents of the town of Margaree, that he was, as her father put it, "unhinged." So it was with a degree of skepticism that she looked for her mother's bicycle in the woodshed—but, sure enough, there it was, leaning up against the far wall, its contours fuzzy within a dense pod of spider webs. With a rag Rosa wiped the bicycle clean. The bell was rusty and Rosa had to yank hard at the lever before it gave out a small, musical *ding*. But the presence of the bicycle, alone, didn't prove the accuracy of her Uncle Lucien's story.

On the day before her birthday Rosa went for a walk along the high road out of town and noticed, for the first time, a row of spruce trees growing out of the top of a small hill. There were five trees, evenly spaced—as Rosa looked at them she began to feel strange, as if the bodies of the trees were empty like the fingers of a glove into which, as she watched, an invisible substance was extending upwards, filling every nook and cranny. Briefly, all five fingers waggled, adjusting the fit. "Mother?" Rosa said, experimentally, But the trees stood motionless—there was not even the smallest breeze to stir their branches. A blue car drove past her, stopped, and backed up. In it sat a man with a patch over one eye. "Need a lift?" he asked, but Rosa refused, having been well schooled by her father regarding the dangers of accepting rides from strangers. "You never know when one of them's going to turn out to be a freak. And there're more of them around than you'd think. Not all of them are as easy to spot as *she* was," her father'd said, pointing across the hallway to Wanda Broom's room.

Now the man stared at her out of his one shiny eye. "You live around here?" he asked. Then, when Rosa began walking away from him, he tooted his horn. "I know you," he yelled. "You're the kid who lives at the museum. Your father still hang out on the beach all day long?"

"You must be thinking of my uncle," Rosa said, walking faster. "My uncle's the one who likes to spend time on the beach."

"Sure," the man yelled. "If that's what you want to believe." He gunned his engine, so that the car flew off and over the hill, all at once, like a spooked horse.

On the morning of her birthday, Rosa got dressed early and came downstairs. Her Uncle Lucien was in the kitchen making a special breakfast just for her: popovers and bacon, clouds and airplanes, he called it—it was her favorite breakfast. He laid the bacon strips in crosses among the high, puffed bodies of the popovers, arranging them all on a sky-blue plate. She could smell cocoa; it was the special kind which came out of a box with a picture of a little Dutch child on its front.

"Sit down," Uncle Lucien said, pulling back her chair. Then he bent over and kissed her on the forehead. "Happy birthday, Rosa," he said. Sunlight was all over everything in the room, lively and unpredictable, like cats. It was early October, the most beautiful time of the year; it was the time of year when you could see right through walls and faces, or all the way up into the sky to the place where the angels' wings flashed their many colors down onto the sparkling waves of the sea.

As Rosa sipped her cocoa, her father walked through the door, holding a doll stiffly out in front of him, as if he were afraid that if he carried it too close to his body he might inflict damage on its long satin dress, or muss its long yellow hair. "I looked all over," he said. "I hope this is what you wanted." Why did he always act that way around her, Rosa wondered; why was he always so formal and embarrassed, never looking her straight in the eye?

"Thank you, Daddy," she said.

He lifted the hem of the dress and pointed to the doll's shoes. "I couldn't find any that would fit you," he said. "But at least *these* are silver."

"She looks just like my mother," Rosa said, taking the doll into her arms, smoothing the shining hair with her fingers.

"What makes you say that?" her father asked. He was staring angrily at Uncle Lucien, who just stood there staring back at him.

"I don't know," Rosa said. She realized she'd made a mistake. "I was just guessing," she explained.

But Uncle Lucien shook his head and smiled at her, sadly. "It's all right, Rosa. We can't keep the light hidden under the bushel forever. That would be a sin." He reached behind the sideboard and slid out a large, flat rectangle wrapped in brown paper. "I'm sorry, Thomas," he said. "I tried to get her to tell you about this, but you remember what she was like. She made me swear. She even made me sign a pact in blood."

"I don't remember anything," Thomas said. He sat down cautiously, reminding Rosa of the way the old women tourists settled themselves into beach chairs, as if they were afraid they'd never be able to get up again. "Go ahead," he said. "Open it. Don't let me stop you."

For the rest of her life Rosa would never forget the way she felt as she peeled the brown paper off of her mother's painting. Sometimes, in fact, she thought that she'd never actually taken a full breath before that moment: taken into her body all the air of this world, so that everything in the world hovered around her in a perfect vacuum, the implements of a juggling act of cosmic proportions, in radiant suspense everywhere. And then she breathed out; the mundane luck of gravity reentered the room.

The painting was a landscape, seen from high up, as if through the eyes of a bird. And yet, even from such an elevated vantage point, the elements of the landscape were all rendered with supernatural clarity: the houses of Margaree, for instance, were complete as to every architectural detail, the thousands of shingles on every rooftop not merely alluded to but painted to show a crack here, a glaucous smudge of bird excrement there; it was even possible to make out the decomposing shapes of leaves, lodged within individual gutters. Due to a trick of perspective, not only were the rooftops visible, but also the sides of the houses: Rosa could look through the windows and see, alternately, the face of Mrs. Roland Badeau, scowling down at the fly she was trying to swat; the tuberous begonia with a dead bloom just about to fall onto Josie MacFarland's windowsill. And there was her father! Standing on the porch, in the act of raising one arm, his mouth open as if he were screaming. His teeth glittered and she could see grackles reflected in the lenses of his glasses. So many things to look at! The sea formed the faintly curving line of the horizon, its surface dimpled with the shadows of innumerable tiny swells; where the sunlight touched the water it raised into prominence a pattern of shining ridges like the print of an enormous finger.

"May was right," Uncle Lucien said, "this is her masterpiece."

"It's an instrument of torture," Rosa's father corrected. "I feel like my eyes are being shoved back into my head. It's the work of a mad-woman. And what's *that* supposed to be?" He pointed to a narrow, grayish stretch of beach, where Herve LeGare was shown—still a young boy—hunched over, holding a bloodstained handkerchief to his nose. Tootie McPheeny stood knee-deep among the swordlike grass of the dunes, a frightened expression on his face, his right hand clenched in a fist.

"I don't know," Uncle Lucien said. Suddenly he reached out and grabbed Rosa's arm, drawing her closer. "'And the servant who knows the wishes of his master, and does not make ready according to his wishes, will receive a severe beating,'" he said to her. "'But he who does not know, and does what is worthy of punishment will receive less beating.'"

"Is that from the Bible?" Rosa asked. "It's hard to understand; is it from the Bible?"

She had just discovered, their bodies almost hidden behind a scrubby clustering of beach plum, her mother and her Uncle Lucien, lying side by side in the sand. They wore no clothes; they were facing each other and, due to the angle of perspective, she could only see her mother's face, although she knew the other body belonged to her Uncle Lucien, because the skin was so very white and marked with freckles.

"'For to whomever more is given,'" Uncle Lucien said, "'of him more will be required; and to whom much is entrusted, more will be required of his hand.'"

Her mother's face was smiling, tilted back a little, looking upwards as if into the far-off face of her observer: high above, attentive and hungry—voracious, even!—for evidence. A small white banner, such as one might find on a church altar panel, scrolled outwards from her mother's mouth. *Amor fuit hic,* it said.

"Cover it up," Rosa's father mumbled. "I don't want to look at it anymore."

"But it's Rosa's painting," Uncle Lucien said. "And it would be blasphemy to cover it up."

"Blasphemy? Since when is it blasphemy to abhor such a twisted vision? It's evil. It's the work of a freak."

Rosa pulled away from her uncle's arm and went over to where her father sat. Gently she peeled her father's hands back from where they covered his eyes like bandages. "But it's just the world," she said. "It's just the world seen from very high up."

Uncle Lucien nodded his head. "She's right, Thomas. Evil has nothing to do with it. Evil has been vanquished into its pit and Our Lord Jesus Christ is ascending into heaven. We can't see it, but Heaven is spreading open to take Him in; even so, He has to take one last look—after all, He was the child of a mortal woman. It won't be very long before He will sit in judgment on us all, but for one final moment He pauses to watch: the trees, the houses, the birds—everything."

"Leave me alone," said her father, but Rosa frowned and moved in closer, so that she could see the way her breath made her father's hair shudder, like the grass of a meadow when the wind passes over it.

"It isn't Jesus Christ," she said. "It isn't Him at all. It's only me. Someday," Rosa said, "I am going to be that tall. Maybe I won't ever stop growing."

LE MOOZ

Margaret had exhausted three husbands, and Nanapush outlived his six wives. They were old by the time they shacked up out in the deep bush. Besides, as Ojibweg in the last century's first decades, having starved and grieved, having seen prodigious loss and endured theft by agents of the government and *chimookomaanag* farmers, they were tired. You would think, at last, they'd just want simple comfort. Quiet. Companionship and sleep. But times did not go smoothly. Peace eluded them. For Nanapush and Margaret found a surprising heat in their hearts. Fierce and sudden, it sometimes eclipsed both age and anger with tenderness. Then, they made love with an amazed greed and purity that astounded them. At the same time, it was apt to burn out of control.

When this happened, they fought. Stinging flames of words blistered their tongues. Silence was worse. Beneath its slow-burning weight, their black looks singed. After a few days their minds shriveled into dead coals. Some speechless nights, they lay together like logs turned completely to ash. They were almost afraid to move, lest they sift into flakes and disintegrate. It was a young love set blazing in bodies aged and overused, and sometimes it cracked them like too much fire in an old tin stove.

To survive in their marriage, they developed many strategies. For instance, they rarely collaborated on any task. Each hunted, trapped, and fished alone. They could not agree on so little a thing as how and where to set a net. The gun, which belonged to Nanapush, was never clean when it was needed. Traps rusted. It was up to Margaret to scour the rifle barrel, smoke the steel jaws. Setting snares together was impossible, for in truth they snared themselves time and again in rude opinions and mockery over where a rabbit might jump or how to set the loop. Their avoidance only hardened them in their individual ways, and so when Margaret beached their leaky old boat one morning and jumped ashore desperate for help, there was no chance of agreement.

Margaret sometimes added little Frenchisms to her Ojibwemowin, just the way the fancy-sounding wives of the French voyageurs added, like a dash of spice, random *"le"*'s and *"la"*'s. So when she banged into the cabin screaming of "le Mooz," Nanapush woke, irritated, with reproof on his lips, as he was always pleased to find some tiny fault with his beloved.

"Le Mooz! Le Mooz!" she shouted into his face. She grabbed him by the shirt so violently that he could hear the flimsy threads part.

"Booni'ishin!" He tried to struggle from her grip, but Margaret rapidly explained to him that she had seen a moose swimming across the lake and here were their winter's provisions, easy! With this moose meat dried and stored, they would survive. "Get up, old man!" She grabbed the gun and dragged him to the boat before he'd even mentally prepared himself to hunt moose.

Nanapush pushed off with his paddle, sulking. Besides their natural inclination to disagree, it was always the case that, if one of them was particularly intrigued by some idea, the other was sure to feel the opposite way just to polarize the situation. If Nanapush asked for maple syrup with his meat, Margaret gave him wild onion. If Margaret relished a certain color of cloth, Nanapush declared that he could not look upon that blue or red—it made him mean and dizzy. When it came to sleeping on the fancy spring bed that Margaret had bought with this year's bark money, Nanapush adored the bounce while she was stingy with it, so as not to use it up. Sometimes he sat on the bed and joggled up and down when she was gone, just to spite her. For her part, once he began craftily to ask for wild onion, she figured he'd developed a taste for it and so bargained for a small jar of maple syrup, thus beginning the obvious next stage of their contradictoriness, which was that they each asked for the opposite of what they really wanted and so got what they wanted in the end. It was confusing to their friend Father Damien, but to the two of them it brought serene harmony. So, when Margaret displayed such extreme determination in the matter of the moose that morning, not only was Nanapush feeling especially lazy but he also decided that she really meant the opposite of what she cried out, and so he dawdled with his paddle and tried to tell her a joke or two. She, however, was in dead earnest.

"Paddle! Paddle for all you're worth!" she yelled.

"Break your backs, boys, or break wind!" Nanapush mocked her.

Over the summer, as it hadn't been the proper time for telling the sacred Ojibwe *adisookaanag*, Father Damien had tried to convert Nanapush by telling as many big-fish tales as he could remember, including the ones about the fish that multiplied, the fish that swallowed Jonah. Soon, Father Damien had had to reach beyond the Bible. Nanapush's favorite was the tale of the vast infernal white fish and the maddened chief who gave chase through the upper and lower regions of the earth.

"*Gitimishk!*" Margaret nearly choked in frustration, for the moose had changed direction and they were not closing in quickly enough for her liking.

"Aye, aye, *Ahabikwe!*" shouted Nanapush, lighting his pipe as she vented her fury in deep strokes. If the truth be told, he was delighted with her anger, for when she lost control like this during the day she often lost control once the sun went down also, and he was already anticipating their pleasure.

"Use that paddle or my legs are shut to you, lazy fool!" she growled.

At that, he went to work and they quickly drew alongside the moose. Margaret steadied herself, threw a loop of strong rope around its wide, spreading antlers, and then secured the rope tightly to the front of the boat, which was something of an odd canoe, having a flat, tough bottom, a good ricing boat but not all that easy to steer.

"Now," she ordered Nanapush, "now, take up the gun and shoot! Shoot!"

But Nanapush did not. He had killed a moose this way once before in his life, and he had nothing to prove. This time, he wasn't so anxious. What was happening to them was a very old story, one handed down through generations, one that had happened to his namesake, the trickster Nanabozho. He would not kill the moose quite yet. He hefted the gun and made certain that it was loaded, and then enjoyed the free ride they were receiving.

"Let's turn him around, my adorable pigeon," he cried to his lady. "Let him tow us back home. I'll shoot him once he reaches the shallow water just before our cabin."

Margaret could not help but agree that this particular plan arrived at by her lazy husband was a good one, and so, by using more rope and hauling on first one antler and then the other with all their strength, they proceeded to turn the beast and head him in the right direction. Nanapush sat back, smoking his pipe, and relaxed once they were pointed homeward. The sun was out and the air was cool, fresh. All seemed right between the two of them now. Margaret admonished him about the tangle of fishing tackle all around his seat, and there was even affection in her voice.

"You'll poke yourself," she said, "you fool." At that moment, with the meat pulling them right up to their doorstep, she did not really even care. "I'll fry the rump steaks tonight with a little maple syrup over them," she said, her mouth watering. "Old man, you're gonna eat good! Oooh," she almost cried with appreciation, "our moose is so fat!"

"He's a fine moose," Nanapush agreed passionately. "You've got an eye, *Mindimooyenh*. He's a juicy one, our moose!"

"I'll roast his ribs, cook the fat with our beans, and keep his brains in a bucket to tan that big hide! Oooh, *ishte*, my husband, the old men are going to envy the *makizinan* that I will sew for you."

"Beautiful wife!" Nanapush was overcome. "Precious sweetheart!"

As they gazed upon each other with great love, holding the rare moment of mutual agreeableness, the hooves of the moose struck the first sandbar near shore, and Margaret cried out for her husband to lift the gun and shoot.

"Not quite yet, my beloved," Nanapush said confidently, "he can drag us nearer yet!"

"Watch out! Shoot now!"

The moose was indeed approaching the shallows, but Nanapush planned in his pride to shoot the animal just as he began to pull them from the water, thereby making their task of dressing and hauling mere child's play. He got the moose in his sights and then waited as it gained purchase. The old man's feet, annoyingly, tangled in the fishing tackle he had been too lazy to put away, and he jigged, attempting to kick it aside.

"Margaret, duck!" he cried. Just as the moose lunged onto land he let blast, completely missing and totally terrifying the animal, which gave a hopping skip that seemed impossible for a thing so huge, and veered straight up the bank. Margaret, reaching back to tear the gun from her husband's hands, was bucked completely out of the boat and said later that if only her no-good man hadn't insisted on holding on to the gun she could have landed, aimed, and killed them both, as she then wished to do most intensely. Instead, as the moose tore off with the boat still securely tied by three ropes to his antlers, she was left behind screaming for the fool to jump. But he did not, and within moments the rampaging moose, with the boat bounding behind, had disappeared into the woods.

"My man is stubborn," she said, dusting off her skirt, checking to make sure that she was still in one piece, nothing broken or cut. "He will surely kill that moose!" She spoke hopefully, but inside she felt stuffed with a combination of such anxiety and rage that she did not know what to do—to try to rescue Nanapush or to chop him into pieces with the hatchet that she found herself sharpening as she listened for the second report of his gun.

Bloof!

Yes. There it was. Good thing he didn't jump out, she muttered. She began to tramp, with her carrying straps and an extra sharp knife, in the direction of the noise.

In fact, that Nanapush did not jump out of the boat had little to do with his great stubbornness or his bravery. When the moose jolted the boat up the shore, the tackle that had already wound around him flew beneath his rear as he bounced upward and three of his finest fishing hooks stuck deep into his buttocks as he landed, fastening him tight. He screeched in pain, further horrifying the animal, and struggled, driving the hooks in still deeper, until he could only hold on to the edge of the boat with one hand, gasping in agony, as with the other he attempted to raise the gun to his shoulder and kill the moose.

All the time, of course, the moose was running wildly. Pursued by this strange, heavy, screeching, banging, booming thing, it fled in dull terror through bush and slough. It ran and continued to run. Those who saw Nanapush as he passed all up and down the reservation stood a moment in fascinated shock and rubbed their eyes, then went to fetch others, so that soon the predicament of Nanapush was known and reported everywhere. By then, the moose had attained a smooth loping trot, and passed with swift ease through farmsteads and pastures, the boat flying up and then disappearing down behind. Many stopped what they were doing to gape and yell, and others ran for their rifles, but they were all too late to shoot the moose and free poor Nanapush.

One day passed. In his moose-drawn fishing boat, Nanapush toured every part of the reservation that he'd ever hunted and saw everyone that he'd ever known and then went to places that he hadn't visited since childhood. At one point, a family digging cattail roots was stunned to see the boat, the moose towing it across a slough, and a man slumped over, for by now poor Nanapush had given up and surrendered to the pain, which at least, he said later, he shared with the beast, whose rump he'd stung with bullets. The moose was heading now for the most remote parts of the reservation, where poor Nanapush was convinced he surely would die.

"*Niijii*," he cried out to the moose, "my brother, slow down!"

The animal flicked back an ear to catch the sound of the thing's voice, but didn't stop.

"I will kill no more!" declared Nanapush. "I now throw away my gun!" And he cast it aside, after kissing the barrel and noting well his surroundings. But as though it sensed and felt only contempt for the man's hypocrisy, the moose snorted and kept moving.

"I apologize to you," cried Nanapush, "and to all of the moose I have ever killed and to the spirit of the moose and the boss of the moose and to every moose that has lived or will ever live in the future."

As if slightly placated, the moose slowed to a walk, and Nanapush was able, finally, to snatch a few berries from the bushes they passed, to scoop up a mouthful of water from the slough, and to sleep, though by moonlight the moose still browsed and walked toward some goal, thought Nanapush, delirious with exhaustion and pain. Perhaps the next world. Perhaps this moose had been sent by the all-clever

75

Creator to fetch Nanapush along to the spirit life in this novel way. But, just as he was imagining such a thing, the first light showed and by that ever-strengthening radiance he saw that his moose did indeed have a direction and an intention and that that object was a female moose of an uncommonly robust size, just ahead, peering over her shoulder in a way that was apparently bewitching to a male moose, for Nanapush's animal uttered a squeal of bullish intensity that he recognized as pure lust.

Nanapush, now wishing that he had aimed for the huge swinging balls of the moose, wept with exasperation.

"Should I be subjected to this? This, too? In addition to all that I have suffered?" And Nanapush cursed the moose, cursed himself, the fishhooks, and the person who so carefully and sturdily constructed the boat that would not fall apart. He cursed in English, as there are no true swear words in Ojibwemowin, and so it was Nanapush and not the Devil whom Josette Bizhieu heard passing by her remote cabin at first light, shouting all manner of unspeakable and innovative imprecations, and it was Nanapush, furthermore, who was heard howling in the deep slough grass, howling, though more dead at this point than alive, at the outrageous acts he was forced to witness there, before his nose, as the boat tipped up and the bull moose in the extremity of his passion loved the female moose with ponderous mountings and thrilling thrusts that swung Nanapush from side to side but did not succeed in dislodging him from the terrible grip of the fishhooks. No, that was not to happen. Nanapush was bound to suffer for one more day before the satisfied moose toppled over to snore and members of the rescue party Margaret had raised crept up and shot the animal stone dead in its sleep.

The moose, Margaret found, for she had brought with her a meat hatchet, had lost a distressing amount of fat and its meat was now stringy from the long flight and sour with a combination of fear and spent sex, so that in butchering it she winced and moaned and travelled far in her raging thoughts, imagining sore revenges she would exact upon her husband.

In the meantime, Father Damien, who had followed his friend as best he could in the parish touring car, was able to assist those who emerged from the bush. He drove Nanapush, raving, to Sister Hildegarde, who was adept at extracting fishhooks. At the school infirmary, she was not upset to see the bare buttocks of Nanapush sticking straight up in the air. She swabbed the area with iodine and tested the strength of her pliers. With great relief for his friend and a certain amount of pity, Father Damien tried to make him smile: "Don't be ashamed of your display. Even the Virgin Mary had two asses, one to sit upon and the other ass that bore her to Egypt."

Nanapush only nodded gloomily and gritted his teeth as Sister Hildegarde pushed the hook with the pliers until the barbed tip broke through his tough skin, then clipped the barb off and pulled out the rest of the hook.

"Is there any chance," he weakly croaked once the operation was accomplished, "that this will affect my manhood?"

"Unfortunately not," Hildegarde said.

The lovemaking skills of Nanapush, whole or damaged, were to remain untested until after his death. For Margaret took a long time punishing her husband. She ignored him, she browbeat him, and, worst of all, she cooked for him.

It was the winter of instructional beans, for every time Margaret boiled up a pot of rock-hard pellets drawn from the fifty-pound sack of beans that were their only sustenance besides the sour strings of meat, she reminded Nanapush of each brainless turning point last fall at which he should have killed the moose but did not.

"And my," she sneered then, "wasn't its meat both tender and sweet before you ran it to rags?"

She never boiled the beans quite soft enough, either, for she could will her own body to process the toughest sinew with no trouble. Nanapush, however, suffered digestive torments of a nature that soon became destructive to his health and ruined their nightly rest entirely, for that is when the great explosive winds would gather in his body. His *boogidiwinan*, which had always been manly, yet meek enough to remain under his control, overwhelmed the power of his *ojiid*, and there was nothing he could do but surrender to their whims and force. At least it was a form of revenge on Margaret, he thought, exhausted, near dawn. But at the same time he worried that she would leave him. Already, she made him sleep on a pile of skins near the door so as not to pollute her flowered mattress.

"My precious one," he sometimes begged, "can you not spare me? Boil the beans a while longer, and the moose, as well. Have pity!"

She only raised her brow, and her glare was a slice of knifelike light. Maybe she was angriest because she'd softened toward him during that moose ride across the lake, and now she was determined to punish him for her uncharacteristic lapse into tenderness. At any rate, one night she boiled the beans only long enough to soften their skins and threw in a chunk of moose that was coated with a green mold she claimed was medicinal, but which tied poor Nanapush's guts in knots.

"Eat up, old man." She banged the plate down before him. He saw that she was implacable, and then he thought back to the way he had got around the impasse of the maple syrup before, and resolved to do exactly the opposite of what he felt. And so, resigned to sacrificing this night to pain, desperate, he proceeded to loudly enjoy the beans.

"They are excellent, *niwiiw*, crunchy and fine! *Minopogwad!*" He wolfed them down, eager as a boy, and tore at the moldy moose as though presented with the finest morsels. "Howah! I've never eaten such a fine dish!" He rubbed his belly and smiled in false satisfaction. "*Nindebisinii*, my pretty fawn, oh, how well I'll sleep." He rolled up in his blankets by the door, then, and waited for the gas pains to tear him apart.

They did come. That night was phenomenal. Margaret was sure that the cans of grease rattled on the windowsill, and she saw a glowing stench rise around her husband, saw with her own eyes but chose to plug her ears with wax and turn to the wall, poking an airhole for herself in the mud between logs, and so she fell asleep not knowing that the symphony of sounds that disarranged papers and blew out the door by morning were her husband's last utterances.

Yes, he was dead. She found when she went to shake him awake the next morning that he was utterly lifeless. She gave a shriek then, of abysmal loss, and began to weep with sudden horror at the depth of her unforgiving nature. She kissed his face all over, patted his hands and hair. He did not look as though death had taken him, no, he looked oddly well. Although it would seem that a death of this sort would shrivel him like a spent sack and leave him wrinkled and limp, he was shut tight and swollen, his mouth a firm line and his eyes squeezed shut as though holding something in. And he was stiff as a horn where she used to love him. There was some mistake! Perhaps, thought Margaret, wild in her grief, he was only deeply asleep and she could love him back awake.

She climbed aboard and commenced to ride him until she herself collapsed, exhausted and weeping, on his still breast. It was no use. His manliness still stood straight up and although she could swear the grim smile had deepened on his face, there were no other signs of life—no breath, not the faintest heartbeat could be detected. Margaret fell beside him, senseless, and was found there disheveled and out cold so that at first Father Damien thought the two had committed a double suicide, as some old people did those hard winters. But Margaret was soon roused. The cabin was aired out. Father Damien, ravaged with the loss, held his old friend Nanapush's hand all day and allowed his own tears to flow, soaking his black gown.

And so it was. The wake and the funeral were conducted in the old way. Margaret prepared his body. She cleaned him, wrapped him in her best quilt. As there was no disguising his bone-tough hard-on, she let it stand there proudly and decided not to be ashamed of her old man's prowess. She laid him on the bed that was her pride, and bitterly regretted how she'd forced him to sleep on the floor in the cold wind by the door.

Everyone showed up that night, bringing food and even a bit of wine, but Margaret wanted nothing of their comfort. Sorrow bit deep into her lungs and the pain radiated out like the shooting rays of a star. She lost her breath. A dizzy veil fell over her. She wanted most of all to express to her husband the terrible depth of the love she felt but had been too proud, too stingy, or, she now saw, too afraid to show him while he lived. She had deprived him of such pleasure: that great horn in his pants, she knew guiltily, was there because she had denied him physical satisfaction ever since the boat ride behind the moose.

"*Nimanendam.* If only he'd come back to me, I'd make him a happy man." She blew her nose on a big white dishcloth and bowed her head. Whom would she scold? Whom would she punish? Who would suffer for Margaret Kashpaw now? What was she to do? She dropped her face into her hands and wept with uncharacteristic abandon. The whole crowd of Nanapush's friends and loved ones, packed into the house, lifted a toast to the old man and made a salute. At last, Father Damien spoke, and his speech was so eloquent that in moments the whole room was bathed in tears and sobs.

It was at that moment, in the depth of their sorrow, just at the hour when they felt the loss of Nanapush most keenly, that a great explosion occurred, a rip of sound. A vicious cloud of stink sent mourners gasping for air. As soon as the fresh winter cold had rolled into the house, however, everyone returned. Nanapush sat straight up, still wrapped in Margaret's best quilt.

"I just couldn't hold it in anymore," he said, embarrassed to find such an assembly of people around him. He proceeded, then, to drink a cup of the mourners' wine. He was unwrapped. He stretched his arms. The wine made him voluble.

"Friends," he said, "how it fills my heart to see you here. I did, indeed, visit the spirit world and there I saw my former wives, now married to other men. Quill was there, and is now making me a pair of *makizinan* beaded on the soles, to wear when I travel there for good. Friends, do not fear. On the other side of life there is plenty of food and no government agents."

Nanapush then rose from the bed and walked among the people tendering greetings and messages from their dead loved ones. At last, however, he came to Margaret, who sat in the corner frozen in shock at her husband's resurrection. "Oh, how I missed my old lady!" he cried and opened his arms to her. But just as she started forward, eager at his forgiveness, he remembered the beans, dropped his arms, and stepped back.

"No matter how I love you," he said then, "I would rather go to the spirit world than stay here and eat your cooking!"

With that, he sank to the floor quite cold and lifeless again. He was carried to the bed and wrapped in the quilt once more, but his body was closely watched for signs of revival. Nobody yet quite believed that he was gone, and it took some time—in fact, they feasted far into the night—before everyone, including poor Margaret, addled now with additional rage and shame, felt certain that he was gone. Of course, just as everyone had accepted the reality of his demise, Nanapush again jerked upright and his eyes flipped open.

"Oh, yai!" exclaimed one of the old ladies. "He lives yet!"

And although everyone well hid their irritation, it was inevitable that there were some who were impatient. "If you're dead, stay dead," someone muttered. Nobody was so heartless as to express this feeling straight out. There was just a slow but certain drifting away of people from the house and it wasn't long, indeed, before even Father Damien had left. He was thrilled to have his old friend back, but in his tactful way intuited that Margaret and Nanapush had much to mend between them and needed to be alone to do it.

Once everyone was gone, Nanapush went over to the door and put the bar down. Then he turned to his wife and spoke before she could say a word.

"I returned for one reason only, my wife. When I was gone and far away, I felt how you tried to revive me with the heat of your body. I was happy you tried to do that—my heart was full. This time when I left with harsh words on my lips about your cooking, I got a ways down the road leading to the spirit world and I just couldn't go any farther, my dear woman, because I had wronged you. I wanted to make things smooth between us. I came back to love you good."

And, between the confusion and the grief, the exhaustion and the bewilderment, Margaret hadn't the wit to do anything but go to her husband and allow all the hidden sweetness of her nature to join the fire he kindled, so that they spent together, in her spring bed, the finest and most elegantly accomplished hours that perhaps lovers ever spent on earth. And when it was over they both fell asleep, and although only Margaret woke up, her heart was at peace.

Margaret would not have Nanapush buried in the ground, but high in a tree, the old way, as Ojibweg did before the priests came. A year later, his bones and the tattered quilt were put into a box and set under a grave house just at the edge of her yard. The grave house was well built, carefully painted a spanking white, and had a small window with a shelf where Margaret always left food. Sometimes she left Nanapush a plate of ill-cooked beans because she missed his complaints, but more often she cooked his favorites, seasoned his meat with maple syrup, pampered and pitied him the way she hadn't dared in life for fear he'd get the better of her, though she wondered why that had ever mattered, now, without him in the simple quiet of her endless life.

A PIECE OF THE TRUE CROSS

1

M y sister, Darla, was struck by lightning the summer we bought the house on Block Island.

She wasn't killed, and, now, twenty years later she is married to an investment banker named Tad and has two healthy sons. She complains of deafness in her left ear and a residual ache in her left elbow and shoulder. She is apprehensive when storms approach. She claims sometimes to see auras around peoples' heads. A lot of people claim to see auras, but I generally disbelieve them. Darla, I believe.

I was thirteen that year, and the world seemed an ineffably sad and lonely place to me. Our father had founded a chemical company with plants in Georgia and Louisiana. He had come from the South, those were his roots, but he had never taken us back for so much as a visit. Summers we usually went to Nantucket or Provincetown — until we bought the old Waring place on Block Island. I spent my falls, winters and springs at a boarding school in the Berkshires.

I was standing at my bedroom window watching storm clouds advance over the sound when the lightning struck our house. More distant bolts were etching maps in the sky. I had just spotted one that looked so much like the Mississippi River I could pinpoint where the family fertilizer factory stood, down by the delta.

I imagined the delta heat and humidity; I imagined elderly black men with floppy-eared dogs sitting before ramshackle clapboard houses, spitting and nodding to me as I rode by on my bicycle; I imagined fishing for catfish in the bayous on long mosquito-filled evenings. But I failed to notice at once that the Mississippi of my imagination had struck dangerously close to the house. It hung there a moment, illuminating everything in a brilliant chiaroscuro, until the clap of thunder broke over my head.

Almost at once a second clap erupted through the ceiling of my room. A ball of fire the size of a tennis ball hovered over the metal bedstead, then split in two and traveled along the frame and across the painted plank floor before climbing the pipes of my bedroom sink. With amazement and delight, I watched it recombine and spiral into the sink, disappearing down the drain hole. With a loud pop, the sink suddenly exploded away from the wall, dangling free on its pipes, a cloud of plaster dust mushrooming up from the floor.

From elsewhere in the house, there came the sounds of splintering glass and wood. On the floor below, Mother began to scream, filling me with irritation and dread.

I was so confused I could only turn again to the window to watch the play of light and dark on last year's dead leaves swirling above the broken stone walk, the skewed croquet pins in the lawn, and the dying elm tree next to the mysterious octagonal carriage house with the revolving floor and the garret apartment where St. John Waring's mistress had once lived in luxury and car fumes.

Just below, the gardener's elderly black lab, Sukey, raced her sinister shadow, her tongue lolling in fright, past the juniper bushes.

Then, hearing Father's grumpy, short-winded imprecations and his heavy feet on the stair, I finally ran to the hall doorway and peered out. The house was dark, the electricity having failed when the storm began. Lightning struck again, bursting white from the hall-end window. The pungent odors of smoke and singed hair penetrated my nostrils.

I saw Mother standing at Darla's door, her face a pale mask of horror, her mouth open, everything white and black.

The old Waring place was to be our summer home from then on.

The Warings, who had once been very rich, built the house with the intention of establishing a permanent family seat on the model of the old English country home, a refuge and retreat for succeeding generations of Warings stretching into the millennium. But Grace Waring, the widow, had closed the house after St. John's death, mostly because of that mistress and her bitter memories.

When she died, a son sold the estate for taxes and for a time it had served as a tuberculosis sanitarium, hence the metal bedsteads and the chipped enamel wash basins in every room.

The basement and attic concealed more macabre vestiges of those sad years: kidney-shaped bed pans and spit dishes, musty cardboard crates of patient records, bales of blank admission forms, a pyramid of unexposed x-ray film, the frame of the old x-ray machine, and neatly stapled files of invoices (for fresh vegetables from the local farmers, a keg of nails and a dozen copper pipe elbows from the hardware store in the village, gas and per diems for a doctor's trip to a medical convention in New Haven—homely things oddly unconnected with thoughts of death).

These parts of the house were considered closed-off by my parents, who seemed to have gotten an idea from their real estate agent that doors had been nailed up or bricked over, that whole wings had been condemned (this is why, they congratulated themselves, they had been able to buy it so cheaply), though, in fact, Darla and I wandered in there for days on end, alternately chilled and fascinated by each grisly discovery.

The last owners before we moved in, the summer the lightning struck Darla, were a French-Canadian family called the La Douceurs, a madcap bunch, by all accounts, who, when they abandoned the place, left behind a large assortment of beach furniture, a roomful of fake Japanese screens bought at a sale when the 1967 World's Fair closed in Montreal, a fieldstone and concrete shrine on the front lawn with a statue of the Virgin Mary in a niche, and their grandmother's ashes.

We only learned about the ashes a week after our arrival when Mr. La Douceur telephoned from Quebec City in a panic.

Mother sent me racing upstairs to a room marked LINEN where, in a back corner of a wall cabinet, I found a copper urn about the size and shape of a bowling pin. The urn smelled vaguely medicinal, as did almost everything in that house. The ashes made the sound of sand shifting.

When I looked up there was a stranger, a gaunt, young woman, wrapped in a sheet, like a mummy, I thought, standing in the doorway watching me. She had black eyebrows like bits of charcoal, and wide, feverish eyes that gazed at me with startled affection. When she saw that I saw her, she smiled slightly, wearily, it seemed, then turned and vanished down the hall. Clumsy with the weight of the La Douceur family ashes, I ran to the door, but the woman was nowhere to be seen.

Reluctantly, I returned to the wall cabinet where, just as she appeared, I had noticed something hidden on the shelf behind the urn. I reached up and fished out a clear plastic plaque with a jagged splinter of wood embedded in it. On the plaque backing, behind the splinter, there was an illustration of the Sacred Heart. Turning the plaque over, I found a legend printed in gothic script: A PIECE OF THE TRUE CROSS.

Later, when I told Darla about the woman in the white sheet and showed her the relic, she seemed unsurprised.

Darla was two years older than me, and it was about this time that she tried to have sexual intercourse with me in one of the eight bathrooms distributed amongst the upstairs bedrooms. This was our one and only attempt at physical intimacy, and it was unsuccessful (to be precise, I did not attain complete erection, and my bladder sphincter relaxed out of nervousness just as I entered her vagina, causing us both a good deal of embarrassment).

Mr. La Douceur arrived a week later alone in the family station wagon to retrieve his mother's ashes, sweaty, self-important and evincing little embarrassment at forgetting such an important item. Though there were several Japanese screens in evidence (Mother having decided she liked them as an interior decoration for breaking up the vast spaces and sight lines of the living room), he did not mention them. And he drove away quickly without a nod to the Virgin Mary.

Once a year Father had the basal cell cancers removed from his nose and forehead, his face becoming a pattern of red skin and flesh-colored bandages. ("Quite a sight," Darla would say.) The last time I saw him was at the opening of a show of my paintings at Verna Walter's gallery in Soho when he came through the door with his face bandaged, wearing a dinner jacket and carpet slippers.

Offering him a glass of champagne, I whispered huffily, "You always have to make yourself the center of attention."

He blinked but did not reply, though I believe he understood what I meant, the whole depth and breadth of my lifelong accusation.

He was blind by then and chronically depressed. He wore thick spectacles and read, with difficulty, with the aid of a magnifying glass. This blindness contributed to his death three years ago when he spilled something in a lab and the whole Louisiana factory went up. What was left of him could have fit easily in Madame La Douceur's urn.

I have his glasses, though.

Mother was mesmerizing, energetic, directionless and hysterical. When I was sad, Mother tore her clothes. When I was angry, Mother punished me. She was forever exhorting me to *do* things with the accent and enthusiasm of a girls' school field hockey coach (a tone I notice Darla suddenly acquired when it came to raising her own sons).

I would never have skied, played softball or ice hockey, sung in the St. John of the Apostle's choir (where I was fondled, pleasantly enough, by one of the lay brothers named Peter McNab), gone out on dates, or learned to paint, if it hadn't been for Mother. I wouldn't have lived without her, Darla says, meaning "lived" figuratively.

Yet when my father died, she became a spent force.

Now, like me, she lives in the city. Once a week she telephones to ask what she should do, redecorate the living room or buy new china, go to Jamaica or take a tour of English pubs?

"Sell the old Waring place," I say.

But, like me, she never does anything.

Both my parents refused to see ghosts or anything else unusual about the summer house, or themselves for that matter (I was twenty-five before I realized there was nothing normal about my upbringing). They thought it was a sign when Darla did not die of lightning bolts. A miracle, Mother said, with her usual melodramatic flare.

I remember the three of us converging on Darla's door, the odors of singed hair, dry rot, and ancient dust (since house dust is mainly sloughed off skin cells, Darla and I assumed we had been breathing dead TB patients the whole summer), and the sounds of glass breaking, clapboards tearing themselves from old square nails in agony, and Mother's muffled shrieks.

Darla lay amidst her smoldering bedclothes, the hair on one side of her head burned down to the scalp, her window frame smashed in and dangling from the wall, shards of glass glittering on the floor and blankets every time the lightning flashed. Her left breast was bare, the nightdress torn or burned from her, and her nipple stood black and salient against the whiteness of her skin.

She looked like a queen of the dead, with her startled eyes, the black and white strobing of the lightning, the terrible music of the breaking glass.

88

Unable to see, Father stumbled forward with his arms out-stretched (his magnified eyes peering everywhere, trying to identify who was a friend and what was dangerous).

Mother flung herself at his neck, crying inanely, "Oh, darling, I'll save you. I'll save you. Don't go near her."

Pushing past them, cutting my bare feet on the glass, but feeling nothing, hypnotized by the beauty of the scene and the sense of strangeness, I touched Darla's forearm where it lay across her belly, half-expecting it to be cold in death, half-expecting it to jump with high voltage and drop me in my tracks. It was only then, in a flash of lightning, that I saw she was still breathing and that in her hand she clutched the La Douceur relic, the plasticized piece of the True Cross.

2

I am thirty-three now. My private life is a disaster.

A year ago I gave Mother's Irish claddagh ring, the one my father gave her on their engagement (signifying love, friendship and loy-alty), to a twenty-year-old leather boy who let me masturbate him in a peep show on 42nd Street. I did not know his name but believed, apparently without foundation, that we were in love.

For four years, I shared my loft and bed with an aspiring poet from Cleveland named Vicky Wonderlight, and though we kissed and cuddled and masturbated each other, we never made love (to be fair, this must reveal as much about Vicky's capacity for intimacy as mine).

I design and build museum exhibits for a living (growing up in my family, I had become accustomed to making old dead things the cen-ter of my life), traveling around the country, sometimes sojourning for weeks in comfortingly anonymous motel rooms while I do my work.

Nights, I linger in my loft (now all my own) painting huge can-vasses that look, at first, almost preternaturally black. Yet, when held under a bright light, they come up in a dozen hues of electric blue-white and red.

The subjects are all the same, a naked man (self-portrait) falling in space. Around him swirl a number of objects, ash urns, thick wire-rimmed spectacles, croquet pins, old Daimler automobiles (of the kind that St. John Waring used to park beneath his mistress's apartment), iron bedsteads and enameled bedroom sinks, choirboy vestments and lightning bolts and tennis ball-sized balls of light that dance upon his fingertips.

Always half-hidden somewhere in the chaotic background there is an object that resembles a plaque of clear plastic containing a splinter of wood (like a lightning bolt) to signify the miraculous quality of life, our slim hope of redemption.

These naked male figures are like ghosts. You can see through them, and their faces wear hurt expressions of puzzlement and nostalgia.

Darla always claimed to remember nothing of her near brush with death by electrocution. A doctor examined her, gave her a sedative by injection, and closed her eyes with his fingers. She slept for three days, and when she awoke she was deaf.

The deafness lasted a month, and then gradually abated—though for years Darla was haunted by mysterious pops, grindings, clangs and echoes. My mother and father never noticed, except insofar as they grew irritated with her inattentiveness. I managed to cover for her most of the time, answering their questions, giving her furtive hand signals and exaggerating my lip movements when I could get away with it. Alone, we seemed to communicate telepathically. By touching hands and pointing, or looking into each other's eyes, we knew at once each others' most complicated thoughts.

Mother cut Darla's hair so that the singed areas did not seem so obvious, but for several weeks Darla drew stares when she ventured into town on grocery-buying trips.

Because of her deafness and the hair, and a certain timidity caused by her fear of storms (at first she had only to look up at a clear sky to be overcome with terror), she grew to depend on me completely.

One day I found her in the bathroom next to my room, naked, stinking, and moaning, covered with her own feces which she had retrieved from the toilet and rubbed on herself. I cleaned her up and helped her to bed, where she slept an afternoon away, only to appear for dinner, clean and fresh-smelling, silent and inattentive.

That summer I lost my virginity to the gardener's son, Billy Dedankalus, a pale, thin young man who was terrified of the ghosts (though he had never seen one). I think now that I was in love without really knowing it. Sometimes I think that this was the one great love of my life, the pattern for all the rest. For Billy quickly fell in love with Darla and left me with my memories.

In the days following Darla's accident, while she was still confined to her room, I began wandering in the gardens, sometimes following the aging Sukey on her habitual rounds, or in the abandoned hothouses where old Dedankalus, the gardener, kept a few beds for starting vegetables and a collection of rare cacti, huge in red earthenware pots on the rough wood tables.

At first silently and at a distance, I watched him work, admiring the ritualistic precision with which he dug, planted, weeded and pruned. Soon I began to help, working alongside him with my sleeves rolled up and sweat rolling down my flushed cheeks.

He was a lean, sinewy man, with a sun-browned, cadaverous face and thin, white hair cropped close like a convict's. He carried a rifle, wherever he worked, to shoot stray cats, groundhogs and rabbits that threatened his plantings. His intensity and off-hand cruelty both repelled and fascinated me.

He had first worked there as a boy, assisting a Japanese gardener the Warings imported from the city to lay out their estate. He had helped put in a pool where fat-cheeked goldfish swam and where the La Douceurs' Virgin Mary now stood contemplating her feet. Behind the house where the shore dunes met the lawn, there were dwarf cedars Dedankalus had learned to trim and bind into agonized shapes, now run mostly wild, or dead.

During the years the place had been used as a hospital, he had turned the ornamental flower beds into vegetable gardens. His greenhouses forced hothouse tomatoes and melons for the dying patients. Now he tended the place mostly out of love, or the memory of love.

Neither of my parents knew what a superb gardener he was; they only complained about the cost (though he charged for part-time work and supplemented his income doing odd jobs and caretaking for several other summer residents).

Darla joined us when she was out of bed, not because she loved gardening, but to be close to me. She was pale and, with her singed and cropped hair, looked touched in the head. She would sit at the edge of a flower bed, pulling up tufts of grass and watching. Sometimes, she would wander away a few yards and stare at the ocean, or one of the contorted cedars that separated the grounds from the sandy shore dunes.

Dedankalus was kind to her because (this is what I believe) she reminded him of the patients who had once lived in the house and similarly spent their wan convalescence watching him garden.

It was on one of these hot working days, while Dedankalus and I sweated in the rock garden below the back patio, that Billy came home on leave from the army base in Georgia where he was stationed. He was twenty-two, fearful of ghosts, in awe of and hating his father. He wore jeans, a dirty T-shirt, a wallet on a chain, and down-at-heel cowboy boots.

These memories are painful, let me tell you.

And I would not write them out this way except on the advice of my therapist who has come to understand that I cannot speak what I feel but that I can hint at it in my art or in a diary that will be destroyed, in letters that will not be sent, or in stories that will not be read.

The secret self is the real self, and I make my paintings difficult to understand because I am afraid that what I really have to say will be met with apathy and stony silences, or a sigh and a quick change of subject. This would be devastating—so I make difficulty the subject of my paintings. The images adumbrate a soul whose unique activity is concealment. It is highly adept, it has made an art, a whole aesthetic out of concealment, while yearning, aching, straining for some other connection.

"Why did you let them rob you?" asks Darla.

I don't know what she means.

I am the empty man, I have no feelings left because my habit of concealment has hidden me from myself.

When I started therapy, she said, "This will do you good only if you don't turn it into another technique."

Remembering Billy makes me think of Vicky—the truth is I fell in love with both of them because they rejected me. In bed at night, Vicky would hiss at me in the dark, "Faggot! Queer! Shit-lover! Art-fraud! How many times did you take it up the ass today?" and I would spurt come on my pajamas, weeping and melting at the same time.

Then she would come by herself, shouting "Mamma? Mamma? Save them! Can't you save them?"

What she meant by this was a mystery.

That summer, working with Dedankalus, watching his rough hands delve in the soil and fondle the tender plants, watching him casually raise his rifle to kill small animals (so cold and stiff within minutes), observing him unzip his pants and urinate in the junipers, being aware of the ghosts, or the sense that always there was someone watching,

93

and that so much was hidden, I began to have sexual feelings that seemed unconnected with any particular person.

I began to masturbate out of doors, hidden in the dunes, or in the old sanitarium morgue, imagining someone tall and lank and beautiful coming upon me like that, stripping and joining me on the dune grass or the loose cool soil or on the padded gurney.

One day Billy did find me, or (and this is what I think) perhaps he had been watching me all along and only chose then to reveal himself. I pulled up my shorts and started to weep with embarrassment. When I tried to run away, he grabbed my shirt, tearing a button off, and laughed.

It was strange to see him laugh, a combination of a grimace and a sneer. I could see the self-loathing in his face, the strange compulsion to do the worst thing, to seek danger, to put himself in jeopardy. His carelessness propelled him into some zone of freedom, and our sex became a composition of fear, violence and abandonment.

It was Billy who told us stories about the men and women who haunted the rooms of the old house, about the doomed patients, old and young, or the young nurses recruited with danger pay to care for them, and who, as often as not, fell stricken with the same disease and died on the premises. About the babies born to patients lonely for love, babies born with the disease, who died almost at once, buried without names. About the doctors who lived in cottages in the village, their uproarious, drunken parties, their balls, their black-tie bridge tournaments.

It was Billy who told us about St. John Waring's mistress and her apartment over the garage and who also showed us the machinery beneath the garage floor that turned the cars around.

Nights, Billy told us, his father had trundled the plain pine coffins from the morgue and buried them in the lonely, unmarked graves. It was the memory of this time, of all the anonymous dead, that had rendered him so inward, silent and cruel. The gardener had a recurring dream that he awoke tied up, wrapped in a sheet, cradled in the frozen earth. A gaunt, skeletal man with red cheeks and shining eyes bends over and beckons him.

Old Dedankalus had finally married one of the patients, that was the romance of Billy's life. She was a fortyish, unmarried Italian woman from New York who had come to the island to die. No one had ever visited her, so Dedankalus had brought her fresh vegetables and flowers smuggled from his hothouses. When she was allowed outside, he would wheel her invalid chair to the row of contorted trees, explaining about the shapes and the Japanese gardener.

She had died a week after Billy was born, and Dedankalus had dug her grave.

Billy showed us her admission forms, her death certificate, and, most chillingly, her autopsy report. He even had a chest x-ray, showing the lesions and scars on her lungs, the enlarged heart, the tangle of arteries like the contorted limbs of her husband's trees.

His mother, Billy believed, haunted the house, and whenever I or Darla came across one of the ghosts (in time, it seemed, we saw them as often as real people—they grew to accept us and went about their business as though we weren't there), he would cross-examine us, hoping that we had spotted her.

I never told him about the woman in the linen closet the day I found the piece of the True Cross. With those eyebrows and the pale, gaunt cheeks, they could have been twins.

The worst is that this will go on and on without changing, that my father's heavy, depressive presence and Mother's melodrama will define me to eternity. I am happy only when I can lose myself in my paintings, which are really nothing more than elaborate messages, as Darla says, to the world outside.

It is as if the paintings are myself, and I am this oddly constructed and inept instrument for expressing them. Yet I also stand in the way of my paintings; yes, it is I who obstructs, inhibits, corrupts, and deforms them.

For me, the task was always to liberate myself from love.

3

Darla telephoned me at my loft a week ago.

This was twenty years to the day (I checked the wall calendar next to the phone) since she and Billy tried to elope, stealing his father's car and driving as far as the ferry landing before my father and the gardener caught up with them.

"Why did you let them rob you?" she asked. Perhaps, I thought, she is only asking herself, though she seems to have everything any normal person could desire.

Hearing her voice, I remembered Father, Billy and Vicky and all the other losses and betrayals that seem to comprise my destiny.

One day Billy said to me, "The minute someone tells me they love me, I start planning my escape as if he had taken me prisoner of war."

"I didn't say I loved you," I pleaded, but by then it was too late.

Sometimes out of loneliness I would crawl into bed with Darla in the mornings, and she would be fully dressed, the ankles of her jeans damp with sand and dew from the dunes.

Sand everywhere.

Darla had finally talked Mother into letting us sell the Waring place. She wanted me to drive up with her to meet the real estate agent, who was, it turned out, a cousin of Dedankalus.

She went on in a tone of voice I found surprising but also oddly familiar, a tone that was at once breathless and frightened.

Without pausing, she told me that Tad had gone into a corporate drug rehab clinic near Lake Placid, that Lonny, her youngest, her baby, was having nightmares, horrid dreams of dark men cutting off his genitals and throwing him off buildings, that her own life was falling apart. She had had two abnormal pap smears in a row, and was scheduled for a biopsy. No one else knew.

After a moment's hesitation, I said yes, remembering the way she looked in the weeks after the lightning struck, her pale vacantness, her cropped hair and the outsized clothes she borrowed from me or Billy.

I said I would pick her up with the boys in the morning. We would make a family outing, complete with a picnic lunch and seafood dinner at Renaldo's on the ferry pier. I would pack the picnic, she should bring the wine from Tad's cellar.

"Don't pretend," she whispered. "You can't even take care of yourself. This terrifies you."

I hung up, wishing she did not know me quite so well.

I thought, these things that happen to us have no cause nor reason. It is as though we are not real at all but being written by some ghostly hand. There is no presence, only a vast nostalgia and, on every page, just the shadow of something which never appears and is never named.

I could not paint any more, just stared and stared at my canvas, a black vortex of images, falling boys, a bloated face covered with moth-like twists of gauze, Japanese screens, bowling pins, a jagged crucifix of light, a girl with blazing hair, Billy Dedankalus slumped in his chair with his rifle propped against his forehead, the way we found him, and myself as a grown man, standing to one side, watching in horror.

That night the black dog visited, by which I mean that I dreamt of Sukey, the gardener's aged black lab. Waking, I heard the distant rumble of a thunder storm, an occurrence which, for obvious reasons, always sets me on edge. Though it was 3 A.M., I tried to telephone Darla and kept getting a recorded message telling me to hang up and dial again.

We made the trip in silence.

I asked Darla once when Tad was coming back and then tried to remind her of Mr. La Douceur and his mother's ashes. But she was lost in thought, her fingers working nervously at her pocketbook. She was wearing jeans and one of her husband's checked workshirts. Her hair was done up at the back in a ponytail—such informality has long been completely out of character for her. The boys, in the backseat, seemed crabby and tired, and promptly fell asleep before we left the city.

Ray Dedankalus, the cousin, met us at the ferry dock and drove with us to the house, stopping for hamburgers along the way.

Darla maintained her reserved silence, staring out the passenger window. I could not help wondering if, somehow, she were reliving those long-ago events. After all, she had driven this road with Billy the night they tried to escape, only to be dragged back from the pier in Old Dedankalus's car. Billy had ridden just ahead of her, in the backseat of Father's station wagon.

She remembered Father driving exceedingly slowly all the way back to the house, sometimes stopping for minutes at a time, then jerking forward again. She had had the feeling, she said, that something terrible, something truly evil, was taking place in that station wagon. And she strained her eyes in the dark for any sign of movement. But there was none. The car would stop, and then creep forward.

In the morning, we found him dead.

"How did they know?" she wailed. "How did they know?"

I shrugged helplessly, and burst into tears at the sight of Billy's body slumped over the rifle.

. . .

98

When we finally pulled into the drive of the Waring place, the boys leaped out and ran ahead, rested, excited to be out of the car, taking turns pretending to be accident victims needing an ambulance. We shook hands with Dedankalus and told him to give us a few hours to look around.

I went to switch on the lights and water and returned to find Darla gone, the boys shying rocks at the water just past the line of contorted cedars. When I was a boy, the place had seemed big enough to get lost in, much too big for us. Now it startled me how little had changed, with the smell of decay everywhere, the crumbling gatehouse, the dried-up lawn and peeling paint and the ivy growing across the windows so that the rooms were suffused with a dim, green glow.

I thought, if there are ghosts, this is somehow what they must feel, as though they inhabited a reality more vivid, familiar and substantial than they themselves were.

I called Darla's name, and went hunting over the grounds, past the tennis courts and octagonal garage and through the greenhouses now open to the elements and littered with shattered glass. Old Dedankalus's cactus pots still crowded the wooden tables, but nothing grew in them. The earth was desiccated, cracked.

They had buried Billy in a regular graveyard, not on the grounds. We weren't allowed to attend the funeral. Darla stole a bottle of bourbon from Father's cabinet, and we drank it in her room till night came and we knew everything was finished.

"How did they know?" she asked again and again. Though I believe the truth had already begun to clarify itself like muddy water gradually becoming clear as the sediment settles.

I found Darla in the morgue, now used as a storeroom for years of accumulated summer furniture, boxes of Christmas ornaments abandoned when we no longer put up a tree, stacks of Father's business records in exploding file boxes, trunks bursting with childhood toys and old photographs—all the detritus of a family we no longer remembered, no longer felt part of. She was leafing through a photograph album which she held up as I walked in.

"Do you remember the puppy you had when you were three?"

I shook my head, feeling the weight of all the things I did not remember. She jabbed a finger at a snapshot of a smiling toddler struggling to hold a miniature dachshund in his pale arms. The dog had a sharp, wet nose and charming little eyes fixed knowingly on the boy's face.

"You only had him a couple of months. Daddy couldn't stand the noise and the mess."

"I don't remember," I said. "I look happy though."

"Mamma called him Romeo. But you couldn't say that. When you said it, it came out Vemeo." Her face had gone dead, expressionless, yet there was some steely desperation underneath, some determination to assert the truth at any cost.

I handed her back the album and began rummaging, finding a torn Bloomingdale's bag with our remaining croquet mallets and, at the bottom, the plaque that once held a chip of wood from the True Cross. Someone had sawn through the plastic to remove the relic. There was only an empty space where it had been.

"You must remember the night Romeo shit on your bed and Daddy kicked him around the room till he couldn't walk and then said he was taking him to the vet. It was after midnight. We never saw him again."

"I don't remember much," I said.

But I did remember the morning Billy Dedankalus died.

It was in this very room, the place of the dead, that we found him, purely by chance, since no one yet knew he was missing, and we only came here to hide out. It was our secret place, which, of course, Billy knew.

He had shot himself with the gardener's rifle, nesting the muzzle in the soft V of flesh just beneath his chin and firing up through the back of his mouth into the brain.

Blood had drained from his throat and mouth, soaking his T-shirt and jeans and pooling beneath the chair. But his face was unmarked and bore, partly because of the wide-open eyes, an expression of mild astonishment.

Darla dropped to her knees in the blood and gagged and tried to embrace him, and he fell over onto the floor, awkwardly, like a marionette. The impact of his fall compressed his chest, forcing air suddenly out his lungs, so that he sighed, or seemed to sigh.

Or maybe this was my imagination.

Darla's teeth began to chatter, an inhuman rattle. And I noticed that she was staring into the shadows beyond the x-ray frame.

There seemed to be something there, a shadow within a shadow, a trace of movement.

I don't know now what I saw. But everything had taken on an air of seeming, and what was real was Billy and the blood and the details of the hole in his throat which I have never forgotten—the jagged line of skin, yellow fat, darkening clots of blood, that awful exhalation of breath, as though he had been waiting for us.

I was only thirteen.

I went down beside Darla and tried to touch her, not to comfort her, but to try to stop that chattering, which I knew would drive me insane. She mistook my motive and grasped my hand and began to weep, smearing me with blood.

From where I knelt I could finally see what she saw, the gaunt face in the shadows, the pale dome of the woman's forehead above her charcoal eyebrows, her fevered eyes darting with anguish, tears glittering on her cheeks, her silent chest heaving.

As soon as I saw her, she began to fade, her eyes fixed on Billy. Love and pain fused in that look. I have never been able to separate them. There is no such thing as love without betrayal. You hold the thing that kills you as close as you can and watch it die, all the time whispering, Love me, Love me, Don't go.

Darla took my hand and pressed it.

But her voice was harsh, that tone of desperation. It rasped out the words.

I said nothing. I meant my silence as a confession. Her words were like a burst of light. I held the empty plaque in my hands. Her words went through me like blue fire. Choked with sadness, I remembered how she had looked with her smoldering hair and burned bedclothes.

But I quickly realized that whatever I had to confess was old news. Now she was going to die, and the story had taken on fresh meaning because, like Billy Dedankalus, her boys would always be alone.

We were in the morgue, and I suddenly felt like the only living creature in a room littered with corpses. I stumbled about among the corpses looking for signs of life.

I said nothing—more confession, it was pouring out of me, meaningless. I wanted to weep, but it came out a dry sob. For ages, I have been all dried up inside. I thought what I always think, How am I going to get through this? How am I going to endure such pain? It seems impossible that a human being could suffer this much and live. And just when you think you can't stand any more, it gets worse and you discover new possibilities of living.

This is the reason I have never owned a gun. There is only one person I would shoot and, like my father, I have always found it easy to kill.

Telling it, remembering the intensity, it seems impossible that we could get out of that room alive, that the ordinary world would let us back in. But Darla finally let go of my hand, and her voice began to return to normal. And the past receded until it was nothing but a presence and a dull ache, like a tumor.

I dropped the plaque to the floor. We had somehow agreed to take nothing, to leave everything for the next owner to deliver to the holocaust.

On the stairway, Darla paused. We were brother and sister again, leaving the intolerable splendor of the scene in the morgue for a lesser ecstasy.

She said, "I haven't seen them for years."

I nodded.

"But Lonny does. They're in his dreams."

I shuddered and glanced back, praying for a sight that would sear my eyelids shut forever, but the room was empty.

There was nothing there, nothing as terrible as the future.

A TROLL STORY:
LESSON IN WHAT MATTERS, NO. 1

No, don't turn on the lamp; who I am is not important. The lamp wouldn't work, anyway. If you shout for your parents, they won't hear you. Are you afraid? There's no need, I'm here only to tell you a story. If you wish you may pretend I'm a figment of your imagination, product of a fever dream. Oh, yes, I know about your fever. Your mother thinks you're coming down with something, but it's not that, is it? It's guilt. You feel bad and there's no one to tell. Such a small thing, too, to punch a boy on the nose and make it bleed, and in a noble cause, for what else can a person do but step in when a bully is hurting the weak? Unexpected though, the sound of breaking bone, eh? That noise, that meaty creak makes it all real. Tomorrow you'll pluck up courage to tell your mother, and she will wipe away your tears and snot and tell you it doesn't matter, to forget it, that you did the right thing. Which is why I'm here. It does matter, you see, and nine is not too young to learn these things. Everything you do is a step towards who you will become. We are born in blank ignorance, a kind of darkness, if you will, and every act, every thought is a little piece of knowledge that illuminates the world and leads us farther from the nothing of our beginning. We don't always like what we see but it is important that we look, otherwise the steps mean nothing, and we become lost.

I see your hand by the lamp switch once more. Very well, try it if you must. You see? I told you the truth. Everything I will tell you is true, at least in the ways that matter. There's no need to scrunch up in a heap like that, no reason to fear me. Perhaps the light bulb simply needs replacing.

But light can be such a comfort, can't it? There are some times and places, some circumstances which only make it more so. I am here to tell you about one such time and place. Listen carefully; it matters.

In Norway a thousand years ago, all dreaded morketiden, the murky time of winter when the sun hides below the horizon for weeks on end and the very rock sometimes stirs to walk the steep fjell in troll form. Families lived in lonely seters, and in winter, trapped by snow and darkness, the only comfort was to lift a burning twig from the hearth and touch it to the twisted wool wick floating in a bowl of greasy tallow, to watch light flare yellow and uncertain, and to hope the wind that howled down the fjell would not blow it out, leaving nothing but long twisting shadow from the fire, whose coals were already dying to deepest black tinged with red.

In the Oppland lived one such family, a hard-working man called Tors and his strong-minded wife, Hjorda, and their sandy-haired daughters Kari and Lisbet, better off than most. They had a fat flock of sheep and fine cows for milk, their seter was large and well-covered with living sod and surrounded by sturdy outbuildings, and in addition to their bond servants, they could afford a shepherd in winter, two hired men to tend the fields and mend the walls, and a dairymaid. At this time it was the end of summer and the livestock were fat, the grass green and the storehouse full, but Tors and Hjorda were worried. Oh, it was not their daughters, who ran about the fields like little plump geese, not a care in the world. Nor was it the hired men or the dairymaid they both mooned after. No, it was that even as the nights began to draw in, Torsgaard did not have a winter shepherd.

Hjorda decided that Tors must go to the All-Meet, the Thing, that year. "For while it is not always true, more heads may on occasion lead to greater wisdom."

So Tors went to the Thing, and he and his neighbors from Gjendebu and Leine and other places as far away as Dragsvik talked of fields and sheep and the price of oats. On the last night they drank vast quantities of mead. "Last winter trolls came to walk the fjell," Tors said. "Our shepherd disappeared and no local man will be persuaded to watch the sheep this year." This was very bad, and no one had any advice to offer. Eventually, many horns of mead later, Grettir, a farmer from the richer lowlands of Leine, stroked his beard and said, "There is a man, a strange, rough man, Glam by name, who might watch your sheep. But I would not want him watching my sheep if I had daughters." Despite the mead, Tors was not a stupid man, and he agreed that it is better to lose one's sheep than one's daughters. Especially if you have a woman like Hjorda to deal with at home.

The next day, he woke up feeling as though his head were seven times too big for his hat and his legs three times too weak for his body and, to top it all, his horse was gone. None of his neighbors could spare him even a nag; he would have to walk the long, long path home. Mid-morning found him tramping the springy turf of a narrow valley between two hills. Autumn berries grew bright around him but the air was chill, and he worried about what Hjorda might say when he returned to Torsgaard not only without a shepherd but without his horse. And then, crossing his path, was a man, a huge bundle of faggots on his back. If the bundle was huge, the man was more so.

"What is your name?" asked Tors in amazement, looking up at the massive brow, ox-like shoulders, and the muscles of his bare arms which were plump as new-born piglets, but white.

"They call me Glam." His voice was harsh, like the grinding together of granite millstones, and he tossed the bundle to the ground as though it weighed less than his hat—a greasy leather thing. His hair, too, was greasy, black and coarse as an old wolf's. The face under it was pale and slippery looking, like whey, and his eyes were a queer, wet dark gray-green, like kelp.

"Well, Glam, I need your help." Tors had been about to ask for directions to a farm or settlement where he might buy a horse, but his head ached, and he felt out of sorts, and thought perhaps if he didn't tell Hjorda about Grettir's warning, all might be well. "Grettir tells me you might be persuaded to work for me at Torsgaard as my winter shepherd."

"I might, but I work to please myself and no one else, and I do not like to be crossed."

His harsh voice made Tors' head ache more. "Name your terms."

"Where is your last winter shepherd?"

"We are haunted by trolls. He was afraid." No need to mention the fact that he had disappeared on the fjell, where the trolls walked.

"A troll will provide me with amusement during the long winter nights."

They bargained, and Glam agreed to start work on haustblot, the celebration that marks the first day of morketiden. As soon as they spat on their hands and shook, Glam slung his bundle up onto his back without even a grunt, and though his walk was shambling and crab-like, it was fast, and he was gone behind a stand of aspens before Tors could think to ask about a nag. But scarcely was Glam out of sight when from behind the very same stand of aspens came trotting Tors' very own horse. Its eyes were white-ringed and it was sweating, but it seemed pleased to see Tors, and it was only later that he began to scratch his beard and wonder at the odd coincidence. So he went home a hero, with his horse and his promise of a winter shepherd, and waited for morketiden.

The people of Torsgaard and the surrounding farms went to the hov to celebrate haustblot: to welcome the winter season and implore Thor to protect them against disease, sorcery and other dangers, and Frigg to ensure warmth and comfort and plenty in the home during the time of dark and bitter cold. With all the fine white beeswax candles lit, the strong light showed men in their best sealskin caps and women with dried flowers woven into their hair. All made merry, for soon the dark would come. Amidst the singing and laughter and drinking came Glam.

He wore the same greasy hat and despite the cold his arms were still bare. All his possessions were bundled in a jerkin and slung over his back. He walked through the suddenly quiet people toward Tors, and Tors' two hired men stepped in front of the dairymaid, and Tors himself looked about for Hjorda and his girls, and people moved from Glam's path, from his queer gaze and hoarse, ill breath. Hjorda appeared from the crowd and stood at Tors' elbow. "Husband," she whispered, "tell me this is not our shepherd."

Glam stopped some distance from them and folded his arms. He shouted, so all could hear, "It is morketiden and I am come to look after Tors' sheep." A murmur went up in the hov, and Hjorda said privately, "Husband, look how the very candles sway from his presence. Send him away," but Tors did not want to be gainsaid before his neighbours, so he turned to Hjorda with a ghastly smile, and said, "Hard times need hard remedies." Raising his voice he called to Glam, "Welcome to Torsgaard. Now our sheep will be safe." And it was done.

The rest of haustblot passed uneasily, with Glam tearing into a great ham and draining horn after horn of feast mead, and Tors telling people Glam would no doubt be on the fjell every day with the sheep and manners after all were not everything.

And, indeed, the next morning Glam left with the sheep before Tors woke and did not come back until the evening fire was dying. And as the days passed, even Hjorda had to admit that Glam was a master of sheep herding: they seemed terrified of him, and all he had to do was call out in that terrible hoarse voice and they huddled at his direction. Days turned to weeks, and he lost never a single sheep. But not a man or woman or child would go near him, except as they must when he called for meat and drink, and even the dogs slunk away when they heard his tread.

Many weeks passed in this fashion and the days drew in upon themselves and the nights spread until even noon became just a thin, pale dream of daytime and nothing seemed real but the cold, the howling wind, and the red flickers of firelight. And still Glam called for his sheep in the dark of every morning and led them up into the hills to find grass, and every night he came back in the dark, face white as clabbered milk despite the cold.

Midvintersblot was a day sacred to Frey, when all the people of Torsgaard gathered to beg Frey to ensure fruitfulness for people and animals and crops during the coming year. It is a day of fasting until the evening feast, when holiday mead is brought out and the plumpest hog roasted, and the people feast by torchlight all night and don't sleep until dawn. That midvintersblot, Glam rose as usual in the dark and called for bread and meat. The noise woke Kari, the eldest daughter. His shouting grew louder—no one seemed to be attending him—followed by a great thump as if he had sent a man flying with a casual blow with the back of his hand.

Kari rose from her bed. "Today is midvintersblot. We fast until the evening to honor the gods."

Glam sneered. "I have never seen a god and I have never seen a troll. And who are you to say whether I should eat or drink? Now go get my food!" And he stepped aside so Kari could see the bondservant lying senseless by the cold hearth. Kari, frightened, brought his food. When he stepped out into the dark, shouting in that horrible voice for his sheep, she went to her mother and spoke of what had happened.

Hjorda saw to the bondservant, then sought Tors and told him of events. "Glam must be paid off and turned out, husband."

"But what of the sheep, wife? Besides, the man was probably just hungry."

"The servant's cheek is broken, and he is only now recovering his wits. He would have done the same to Kari, had she not obeyed."

"Nonsense. No doubt the girl misunderstood, frightened by his loud voice." He turned back to the warmth of his wolfskin coverlet and slept. He didn't hear the rising note of the north wind, the first flurries of driving snow. He didn't hear Glam roaring above the wind for his sheep, the shouts getting fainter and fainter and further off. By the time he rose, Glam could not be heard and the snow was settling in fat white folds on sills and stoops. The hours slipped by, with all the servants and the women of the house working over spits and ovens and Tors working over his tally sticks. The flurries became a blizzard and the dairymaid, when she went to milk the cows, could not see her hand before her face.

The scents from the kitchen grew more delicious; the wind climbed to a high-pitched howl. The trenchers were laid on the board, and still Glam did not return. The hired men and several male servants came to Hjorda. "It's cruel outside, but if you asked we would venture into the cold and dark and wind, as some misfortune might have befallen Glam."

"No, no," said Hjorda, thinking quickly. "Glam is strong and wily. No doubt he can look after himself, and the sheep have fine wool coats. See that you don't bother Tors with this."

"Certainly not, mistress," they said, knowing full well that Tors might take them up on their offer—and the bondservant with the addled wits and broken cheek being a friend of theirs. And so the feast was laid out and eaten without Glam, and not a soul missed him until it was long past midnight and Tors asked, "But where is our winter shepherd?" By this time, the snow lay hipdeep and the wind was cold enough to freeze the breath in one's throat, turn eyeballs to ice and crack open one's very bones. Tors declared no man could step forth and live, so they turned their back to the door and drank barrel after barrel of ale, cask after cask of mead, and sang loudly enough to drown out the terrible noises and deep vibrations that rolled down the fjell—though Lisbet, the youngest daughter, who had fallen asleep on a bearskin after her third horn of mead, had strange and awful dreams of dark shapes battling on snow. Not long before dawn, sodden with celebration, they slept.

They woke after noon. Headaches and guilt are fine partners, so Tors did not have to urge the men to put on their boots and fur capes and caps and set off up the mountain. The pale winter sun shone brilliant on the new-fallen snow and the air lay still. Snow crunched and one of the hired men could be heard groaning softly to himself every time his boots thumped down. They walked and walked, and eventually they heard the faint bleat of a sheep, and suddenly sheep were all around them: some nothing more than frozen woolly mounds in the snow, some bleating pitifully, some standing lost on crags or caught in bushes. Past the sheep they found a place where great boulders and trees had been torn from the ground and the snow beaten down in some mortal struggle. They walked faster now, and found a bloody, leveled place where Glam lay on his back, his strange seaweed eyes open to the sky and covered in snow, which did not melt. His skin was mottled and bloated, as though he had been dead a long, long time. Huge tracks, the size of barrel hoops, filled with frozen blood, led off to a deep and narrow gully. Something had fallen and splashed blood—hogsheads of the stuff—all about but there were no more tracks so the men could not follow. The hired man stopped groaning long enough to peer into the gully, look at the blood, and say, "Nothing, not even a troll, could have survived that." There was general agreement, and the hired men and bondservants returned to Glam's body.

The bolder among them tried to move him, but it was as if his bones had turned to stone and he would not shift. Nor could they close his eyes. They herded up the sheep and returned to Torsgaard. "Glam is dead," they said to Tors. "He killed the troll and most of the sheep are living. We tried to bring him down but his body is strangely heavy."

"Well, take a yoke of oxen up the mountain and drag him down if necessary," said Tors. "We must bring him back to the hov for a proper send off."

"No," said Hjorda, "take faggots and tallow to the gully and burn him there, like carrion."

"Yes," said Kari.

"Yes," piped up Lisbet, whose dreams still hung about her.

"No," said Tors, and the men tried not to sigh. They took the oxen up the mountain, and some rope, but even with the oxen Glam's body, black as Hel now and bloated as a bladder, would not move even along level ground. After hours of this, with his men surly and tired and his own fingers and toes going white with cold, Tors unyoked the oxen. "He seems to want to stay here, so let him. We will cover him with stones."

So it was done, and they walked back to the women and a warm hearth.

Three days later, Lisbet woke in the middle of the night and ran to her mother. "Glam walks in my dreams!" Hjorda cuddled her close and they both fell back to sleep. They were woken in the morning by a shriek from the dairymaid, who had opened the door and tripped over a dog—or what was left of a dog—on the stoop. Later that morning, the haunch of mutton on the spit was found to be green and black on one side and the servant who tended the ovens was clean out of her wits: "Glam came down the chimney, Glam came down the chimney, Glam came down the chimney," was all she could say, over and over.

Glam did not lie easy in his grave. He came again, and again and again, driving more people mad, sending one hired man—who had taken the sheep out—headlong down the fjell, falling and breaking his neck, and the dairymaid running away to another farm, snow or no snow.

Hjorda found Tors. "You must burn him, husband."

But upon toiling up the mountain with faggots and tallow, and heaving aside the stones, they found nothing. When he returned, Tors told this to his wife, who nodded. "The troll lives in his bones and walks abroad wearing his skin, even under the sun."

While Glam could appear during the day, it was at night that he spread true terror: he ran on the rooftops until the beams buckled, he rolled great boulders down the fjell, destroying some outbuildings entirely, and he laughed. His deep horrible laughter ground over Torsgaard and the farms of Oppland, crushing the spirit of men, driving cattle mad and women to weeping in their terror that Glam was coming for *them*. The dairymaid who had escaped to another farm was found by a barn, used and torn and tossed aside, like a broken doll. The still-living hired man ran mad and took an axe up the mountain, foaming at the mouth, vowing to chop Glam to pieces. His head, and pieces of his torso, rained down on Torsgaard all that night. The whole countryside felt disaster looming. Hjorda bade her daughters to sleep in her alcove, and they carried eating knives in their belts that were a little too long and a little too sharp for manners.

But as the days grew longer and the sun stood higher in the sky, the hauntings lessened.

"Summer sun is not kind to trolls," Hjorda observed. "But when winter comes he will be back, and no one in Oppland will be safe."

Tors did not want to hear it. He hired more men and a new dairymaid and worked to rebuild the broken outbuildings. His wife insisted that he strengthen the doors and roof beams of Torsgaard. And when this was done she sent him to the Thing, only this time she sent Kari with him. "Find a good strong man," she told her daughter, "one who can do more than tend the sheep during winter.

Spend your portion to hire him if you must—for what good is a dowry to a dead maid?"

Now it happened that at this time, a ship came into the fjord and Agnar the Strong, who was tired of adventuring in foreign lands, came to the Thing and heard that Tors of Torsgaard needed a winter shepherd but that no man would take up his offer. He sought out Tors and asked of him, "Why will no one take up this offer of yours?"

"The last shepherd, Glam, died on the fjell and there is some superstition attached to his name," said Tors evasively. "Have some of this mead." Now Tors was generally an honest man, and his shame at speaking false would have been apparent even to a lesser man of the world than Agnar. Agnar declined the mead and watched thoughtfully as Tors walked away, ashamed.

"Sir, allow me to offer you the mead again," came a woman's voice from behind him. He turned to face the maid with bright blue eyes. "I am Kari Torsdottir. Drink the mead and I will tell you of Glam." He did, and she did, leaving nothing out, and finishing "—and so if you would look after our winter sheep and keep them safe, you could have my marriage portion and welcome."

"Money is no good to a dead man."

"My mother says that if you are but a strong man, good and true, and willing to listen to her, you will prevail, for trolls, even trolls who wear a man's skin, are stupid, being made mostly of rock."

And so Agnar the strong agreed to come to Torsgaard and be the winter shepherd, but instead of waiting for morketiden, he returned directly with Tors and Kari, for he was curiously unwilling to let Tors' daughter out of his sight.

His open face, clear blue eyes and ox-wide shoulders were welcomed by all. He noted the great gashes in the doors and the rents and holes in walls and gates but kept his own counsel. All through the summer, Agnar helped at the farm. He repaired stone walls and cut huge trees to reinforce roof beams, he helped herd cattle, and walked with Kari and Lisbet when they went berry-picking. As the evenings drew in, he held their yarn while they span and Hjorda did not fail to notice that he was always willing to fetch a cape for Kari, or pump the bellows to coax the fire hotter when she sat by it. A good man.

On the eve of the first day of morketiden, Hjorda drew him aside. "Glam will return, perhaps as soon as tomorrow."

"Glam doesn't frighten me!"

"Then you are more of a fool than I thought. He is more stone troll than man, and more heartless. Alive he was twice as powerful as a brace of bulls. Now even bulls would flee. And he wants to destroy this farm and all the people in it, only this time he is stronger and will be after choicer fare than the dairymaid." Hjorda noted Agnar's quick glance at Kari, combing her hair before the hearth. "Yes. Glam will come for the eldest daughter of the house. If you wish to save her, you will listen to me." But Agnar knew in his heart he needed nothing but his own strong back, and he laughed, and walked away.

That night, the ground shook as Glam stalked the farm, his bones so heavy his feet sank ten inches into the turf. His awful, grinding laugh filled the dark as he tore off chunks of wall and gate. A rending crash and a high-pitched scream split the dark, followed by the terrible sound of a large animal being torn limb from limb, and the splash and patter of blood on the iron hard ground of the barn enclosure. Then with a roar of satisfaction he ran up the mountain and was gone. When the people crept from the hearth hall the next day, they found Tors' poor horse ripped into quarters and its guts arranged in a rune of challenge.

The next night, Agnar the Strong, who had been a-viking as far as Novgorod and the shores of Ireland, who had burnt priests and fought the hordes of Rus, who was famed for his strength and bravery from Oppland to Hordaland to Rogaland and beyond, sought out Hjorda, the woman of Torsgaard. "If you speak on this subject, I will listen, and do as you say."

And so as the sun went down that evening, Tors found himself strangely sleepy and while the great fire still roared in the hearth, he fell sound asleep and snored on his wallbed by the inglenook. Hjorda directed Agnar to pick up her drugged husband and bundle him into the bed at the far end of the hall, away from the passage that led to the door. Then she dressed Lisbet in her warmest clothes, and the two of them stole out to hide in the barn, cozy in the straw with the cattle. Then there was only Kari and Agnar. They stood opposite each other by the hearth.

Agnar, forgetting himself in his fear for her, took her by the hand. "It's not too late to hide with your mother and sister."

"You will need me," she said. "We must bring Glam inside."

When the embers began to die, Kari, still wearing her clothes, left the curtain between the passage and the hall open, and lay down on the wallbed by the inglenook, and Agnar, similarly dressed, wrapped himself like a sausage in an old, heavy fur cloak so that one end was tucked tightly under his feet and the other securely under his chin, leaving his head free so he could look about. Then he settled himself on the wall bench opposite Kari's bed. In front of the bench lay a bench beam, a huge ancient thing set into the floor when the farm was built. He set his feet against it and straightened his legs so he was firmly braced between the beam and the wall. And then he waited.

The embers glowed then dulled then sighed into ash. Kari's breath grew soft and slow and regular. Once, there was a rattle as a gust of wind shook the only gate still standing. Far, far away he heard the lonely howl of a wolf. But Agnar's heart did not beat soft or easy, it hammered like a smith beating hot iron into an axe-head, and he touched the sword at his belt constantly. The hilt was cold as only iron can be, and he could no longer quite feel his feet.

Sudden as an avalanche, something leapt onto the roof and thundered about, driving down with its heels, until the new beam buckled and splintered and the roof almost fell in. Glam. The walls shook and Glam jumped down, and the earth trembled as he strode to the door. A sharp creak as he laid his huge horny hand on the door and suddenly it was ripped away, lintel and all, and moonlight briefly lit the hearthroom. But then Glam blocked out all light as he thrust his huge head through. The whites of his strange eyes gleamed like sickly oysters, and Agnar's heart failed him. Glam's head brushed the roof of the passage as he came into the hall.

"Glam," said a soft voice, and Kari stood there slim and brave by the door, her hair silver in the moonlight. "I will come with you, but it is cold outside and I must have a bearskin to lie on. Bring that old cloak on the bench by the fire. I'll wait for you outside." And Agnar's heart filled with admiration for her and there was no room left for fear.

Glam strode to the sausage-shaped bundle of fur, and tried to pick it up with one hand. Agnar was braced and ready. He made no sound and the fur did not move. Glam pulled harder, but Agnar braced his feet all the more firmly. He was sweating now. Glam grunted, and laid two hands on the bundle, and now a titanic struggle began, Glam hauling up, Agnar fighting to push against the bench beam with all the strength of his muscle and sinew yet make no noise. But then Glam put his back into it and the old cloak tore in two. He stood there, the fur in his hands and his horrible eyes staring, and Agnar flung himself at the troll, gripped him around the waist and set his feet. With a massive grunt, he squeezed tight and started to bend the monster backwards. It would not be the first time he had snapped a man's spine in a wrestling match.

But Glam was now more, much more than a man, his bones were made of the rock of the mountain, and with a single heave he had Agnar off his feet and was flinging him about. But Agnar had been in many wrestling matches and he did all he could to brace his legs against roof beam or hearth edge, bench or wall. In the passageway he strained until the veins stood out in his neck and sweat sprang out on his forehead, and always he avoided the ruined doorway. It was bad enough in the enclosed spaces of the hall; outdoors, it would be seven times worse. Closer he was drawn to the door, and closer still. Sweat poured from him. With a furious wriggle, he eeled around in Glam's grip until his back was to the awful face and bull-like chest. He dug his heels against the threshold stone and with a strength that was equal parts fear, determination, and desperation, he leaned in towards the last breath of warm, indoor air. As Glam hauled backwards with all his might, so too did Agnar thrust *backwards*, and his last strength and the inhuman force of Glam's heave hurled them both outside. Glam, with Agnar still clutched to his breast, landed spine down across a rock. The spine parted with a loud *crack*, a sound that would live in Agnar's mind for the rest of his days.

Agnar could not rise; all he could do was lie like a gasping fish in the dying troll's grasp, drained not just by the effort of fighting a monster, but by the awful touch of its skin against his own. His strength ebbed and ebbed, until his muscles were made of lead and his bones felt like lace and he could not even touch the hilt of his sword with his fingertips. And then Glam spoke, hoarse and horrible in his ear.

"You will live, Agnar the Strong, but you will never be the same. You will always look into the dark and see my face, hear my voice, and know yourself." And the troll laughed, dark and full of wickedness. At the laugh, Agnar felt the strength flow back. He sprang to his feet, pulled free his sword, and swung. Once, twice, three times, and the muscle and sinew and bone of Glam's neck parted, and the head, like some vile rock, rolled free, and Agnar did not laugh, but wept.

The moon tugged clear of its cloud, and Kari ran to his side, and Hjorda and Lisbet emerged from the barn. Even Tors stumbled up from his drugged sleep and stood blinking and beaming with happiness on the soiled turf. "Agnar the Strong! You can have anything of mine you name!" And Kari took his hand and kissed it, and laid it against her cheek. Agnar held her close but could not meet her gaze.

He stood, numb and tired, while Kari wrapped him in the wolf-skin and the servants brought him mead warmed by the hurriedly stirred fire, and while Hjorda ordered in a great voice that the hired men bring faggots and tallow and waste not a minute.

They burnt Glam right there, outside the hall. And then they burnt the ashes. And when the ashes were cold they were gathered in the torn cloak and wrapped tight, and Hjorda saw to it that it was thrown into a chasm, and huge boulders hurled down on top of it.

Torsgaard celebrated all day and into the evening, with men and women arriving from all over Oppland to share the good news. In all that time, Kari remained at Agnar's side, and she noted how he shook with fatigue. Eventually the fire dwindled and the torches were doused. Everyone slept. In the middle of the night, Kari was woken up by a strange noise, like a child crying. It was Agnar, trying to light the torch and rocking back and forth. "He will come for me. He will come for me."

"He is dead, beloved."

"I am all alone and he will come for me!"

"You will never be alone again." But he would not hear her, he just rocked and rocked, back and forth.

And the story goes that though Kari stayed by his side every living minute, much to the disapproval of the very traditional Opplanders, and married him not long after, his fear grew worse and he began to rock back and forth and light torches even in the daytime. In the end, they say he ran out, barking mad, and Kari was left without a husband and the hall at the Oppland farm gradually declined. No flowers ever grew on the chasm where they had thrown Glam's ashes.

And that's the end of the story. Agnar was a hero. He saved a household from Glam, the man who became a troll. But before that he was called a hero for slaughtering women and children, roasting priests on the spit, and burning down churches while he drank the altar wine and laughed, and "Never mind," his father would have said after that first trip a-viking, "forget that sucking sound your sword makes when you pull it from a woman's stomach."

And so you punched a bully on the nose and broke it, and some will call you a hero, and some will think you a beast, and you feel so confused you have worked yourself into a fever, and it's not something your mother can kiss away in the morning. Nor should she, for if you pretend it never happened you will never bring it into the light to examine and it will fester there in the dark and grow strong, as a troll does, and one day when you are grown and you punch a man on the nose, the weight of all the things you have done and tried to forget will rise up and eat you up from inside.

There, now, you're sweating; perhaps the fever is breaking. In a little while you will sleep, and your mother will wake and come sit by your bedside, and in the morning she will be the first thing you see. You may pretend that this never happened, that I was never here, that this was all a dream. If you like. It's your choice, weigh it carefully before we meet again.

ORDER

I am orderly. Annabelle thought this.

She had told him when they met: I am orderly. A place for everything and everything in its place. If a job is worth doing it's worth doing well, he had answered, feeling them kindred spirits. They had kissed and shortly after decided to marry.

She was orderly and he was thorough. The two were in no way related she had discovered, later. It was as if she had said, I'm hungry, and he had said, I'm a banker. But then, she was hungry, when they met; and he was a banker. So maybe the statements parallel after all.

She was like a blind person who has to know where every piece of furniture is, each chair, each rug, each bar of soap. If a thing is moved, there is panic: how can it be located in the darkness? That was because at her house, her mama and daddy's house, nothing had a place. Where is a comb? Where is a needle? For God's sake, where are the scissors? Are there any clean socks in this house?

She had made a home where for nineteen years the couch had sat in the same spot, its legs wearing slow caves in the carpet. Pictures once hung, permanently straightened, lived out their colors on that spot. Summer linen slips could cover velvet chairs; summer white could bloom in pots beneath glass windows, instead of Christmas reds. But that was sequence, not disorder.

It was because her father belonged to a forty-million-member con-spiracy not to pay taxes, because what you got for wages had not been Money since we went off the silver standard. It was because her mother crocheted pot holders, one hundred every month, and spent the rest of the hours of the day imposing the surplus on orphanages, rest homes, rummage and garage sales. (Annabelle had set aside a small closet off the pantry for pot holders. So that they would stay in their place. Not take over. Annabelle's husband paid taxes on what he and the government agreed was money.)

I am terrified, she thought.

She had a house with a red-tiled roof, a lawn planted with white caladium and blue plumbago. She had an expertise in gardening. (She liked to line up her small areas of expertise like so many spools of thread in a sewing basket. Since her marriage, she had become proficient at: Dinner Party, Potty Training, Jogging, Flirting, Orthodontics, The New Republic, and, now, Gardening.)

The terror had not to do with an area of weakness, but with today, and the fear that it would all come apart, that nothing would stay put: jogging shoes would end up in the library, potting tools in the bed-room, *The Saturday Review* propped by the mixing bowl in the kitchen. Pot holders on every surface. And unpaid 1040 forms. Nothing in its place.

In San Antonio, Texas, there were only three things you had to do if you were female. The rest you might do, perhaps should do, were a little set apart if you did not do, but still were not required. You had to marry, have children, and have a surprise fortieth birthday party You might also pledge, make your debut, graduate, join the Junior League, but excuses could be found for omissions from this list. You could go to Wellesley instead of pledging; be in Spain the year of your debut; marry before you finished school; be too creative for vol-unteerism, having, perhaps, a gallery of your own. But you had to marry, have children, and have a surprise fortieth birthday party.

Annabelle was forty today.

She had tried to talk to Ed.

(She hated his name. Her mother called him Eddie, like a car salesman. When she, Annabelle, was somewhere they would not know her—a Laundromat if her washer was broken, an airport ticket counter in another city, a Shell station—she would refer to him as my husband Ted, or Ned. Edwards could be called either, couldn't they? Ned must be from Edward, what else could a Ned be? Ethelned?)

None of that was true. She called her husband Ed to herself, to put him in his place. He called himself Ted. As did his mother. Her mother called him the banker.

Her three best friends had already had their fortieths. Susan had had a surprise trip to Bermuda. She thought they were going to the airport to pick up his mother (the irony of that) and lo and behold forty people with suitcases were there, Supper Club en masse; and they all spent the weekend on the clean white birdless beaches of Bermuda. Anita had got a brand-new house as a surprise, completely furnished, even dish towels. She had thought they were going to dinner at a new friend's house, someone Susan and Annabelle had known in school, and, surprise, on the door was a brass nameplate that said Anita. Mary Virginia had been surprised with a face-lift. She had thought she was going to sit with Anita while Anita's son had his tonsils out, and, surprise, there was Frank the plastic surgeon of Supper Club, with pictures of her already, and a little soothing chatter to go with the eye tucks. She looked almost thirty-seven again when he got through.

Annabelle had tried to talk to Ned. (Ed.)

"Don't," she had said.

"I'd rather not," she had told him.

A place for everything and everything in its place. No trip, no move, no sleight of jaw. "Please. Let things be as they are. Surprise me with no surprise."

She had spent this morning in dilemma. Also, in the Saltillo-tiled kitchen, drinking a lot of coffee from a series of white china cups. Out her window past the tile patio she could see white snaps, blue iris and agapanthus lilies. Gardening, she thought, fingering a spool of expertise with her mind.

If I stay here, they can do nothing; or maybe it's if I go they can do nothing.

She decided, finally, that if Susan had not agreed to go to the airport, or Anita out to dinner, or Mary Virginia to sit a spell at the hospital with a friend, none of them would have been caught unaware.

At ten o'clock she packed her suitcase and left him a note on the blue kitchen counter: I have surprised myself and gone to see Mama and Daddy for my birthday. Don't wait up. Feed the boys. She wrote To Ed on the envelope, in her anxiety forgetting which was his real name.

Her daddy told her that they had got four thousand lawsuits on their way to the Supreme Court supporting the fact that this paper was not Money and could not be taxed. Four thousand. Law suits. Her mama showed her five hundred pot holders in a new style she was doing which used many-colored yarn so that they were variegated as a rainbow. My rainbow holders, she called them. Variegated. Five hundred.

The next day she went home. Ed (Ted?) had called. He said she was right; she had pulled the surprise herself. She could come back.

When she got there—late afternoon, before the boys were due, in time for two, perhaps three, cups of coffee from white cups in the Saltillo-tiled room with its border of caladium out the window past the overhanging red-tiled roof—she opened the front door, anticipating herself back in her place: to find the rooms empty.

Nothing.

No couch set where it belonged, only deep leg-caves in the carpet.

No pictures, only neat punctures in the white walls. No white cups. No fresh ground French-blend coffee in no five-year-old refrigerator.

Telephone?

She found a phone, in what had been a bedroom (Ned's) in the west wing. She called his office. Alamo National, the woman said. Ted, she asked for him. "We have no one here in our trust department by that name," the woman told her.

She called the school. Those being the only two numbers she knew by heart.

"Eddie, Freddie? I'm sorry, ma'am, we have no one registered in sixth grade by those names."

She went out into the yard. Gardening, she thought.

Someone had set out pink petunias and lavender calendulas.

She began to sob.

"Surprise!" They were all there, hiding in the trees in the back. Susan, Anita, Mary Virginia, their husbands Ted, Ned, and Fred. Her husband Ed. Her twins. All of Supper Club. The plastic surgeon, the dentist, the lawyer, and their wives.

"Weren't you just amazed?" he asked later, after the moving company had brought everything back and put it in its place.

"I wish I could have seen your face when you walked in that door. What a sight that must have been. I got the idea because of that call referral trick the phone company has. Where you can have any number switched to any other number. I guess you couldn't tell, but that was Susan's house you got when you thought you were calling the bank, and Anita's when you dialed the school. They nearly cracked up. What a twist. This guy at my office, he had his switched to his dad's, and his brother who hasn't spoken to his dad in ten years kept dialing his brother and hearing the old man's voice. It's amazing. It took a lot of coordination, to get all the stuff out and the phones switched, just for an hour. But I wanted to do it up right. If a job is worth doing, it's worth doing well."

"You're thorough," she said.

Disorder began to grow, slow as mold. "Where are the scissors?" Ed asked on Tuesday. On Wednesday one twin hollered to the other: "Are there any clean socks in this house?" On Friday, the couch moved.

THE DAY GHOST

What happened was I'd forgotten my wallet. It was a sunny morning, Indian summer. I felt good. My work wasn't pressing me. So I walked back home. Three blocks of downtown, then three of fresh air, blue sky, serenity, and the front yards of my neighborhood. Once I unlocked my back door and walked inside the house, I realized I wasn't alone. At the foot of the stairs I stood listening. Wafting softly down was my wife's voice—*Oh, oh, oh,* as if she were surprised or crying or pleased . . . or crying over a pleasant surprise . . .

Those were sex sounds!

Standing there, I experienced a little sexual jolt of my own. A twitch of the old gristle. It must have been chemical—my wife making those noises setting off the corresponding apparatus in me. In a moment like that, you realize what a funny guy God is. And don't give me that kaka about She. He isn't a She. A she-God wouldn't let a wife get found out the way I'd just caught Suzanne.

Whom is she fucking? Another husband might have been less grammatical. I loathed my education. The nerd shall be known by his pronouns. Even in realizing cuckoldry, correct usage remains his priority. No wonder she snuck home from work to break her vows in the middle of the morning. To prove myself a man, I supposed I'd have to murder this homewrecker. Another gem of a question arrived at my station by the newel post: *Could she be by herself?*

Unlikely, I replied. Demeaning enough to think of Suzanne up there with a man. Was there more dignity in masturbation? Was that something I really thought? Nevermind the spouse, the mind betrays us every ten seconds. Nevertheless, to gather the essential data, I had to keep standing still. Then I heard him. Or I heard male noises. Disgusting, really.

In the very room where they were committing their biblical acts, on my dresser, lay my innocent wallet. Screaming curses, flailing and slashing with the carving knife from the kitchen, I could have burst in upon them. *I forgot my wallet!* I'd bellow. More likely was that I'd tiptoe in, murmur *Excuse me,* smile my nerdy smile, snatch up the wallet, and scuttle back downstairs.

I departed my household. Better to go quietly. Like Death. Like electronic crime. They couldn't know I knew. In my own time, I'd plot revenge. At that moment I did not begin to hate God; however, the weather I'd adored five minutes earlier infuriated me now. All that sunlight and blaze of red and gold leaves—I wanted to kick it in the teeth. Whoever walked past me on the sidewalk got a good glare. Grand in my anger, I gave it right to them.

Approaching my office building, though, I had to keep wiping the tears off my face. What is a man that he can be reduced to emotional pudding?

My wife is an art historian, which has always placed her somewhat beyond my reach. The spiritual G-spot of someone of that inclination is permanently located in the Sistine Chapel. Until now, I had appreciated how untouchable she was. Suzanne could wear the same underwear for a week, and it would come off her body smelling of bath soap and Chanel. I had even liked it that when she came, all she did was shape her lips into an O and just say it like that, a soft, definite "Oh." To the bricks of my building I turned and sobbed aloud.

Then, to make my way into my office, I faked an allergy attack. As a boy I learned always to carry a handkerchief. When I sat down to my desk and tried to envision the future, unhappy words came to mind: *Oh yes, I'm the great pretender.* Four Negro men in powder-blue tuxedoes, smiling and gesturing in unison, serenaded me. I hadn't even liked that song in high school. Now the lyrics plummeted into my mind. *I pretend to be / what I'm not, you see—oh yes.* . . .

It's nothing to sing about. The Noble and Intricate Science of Pretense is my profession. Last year my income from Nelson Consulting Associates was two hundred and forty-five thousand dollars. That's in Burlington, Vermont. In Atlanta or Houston, they'd name a building after me. Around here I'm Guru to the Bucks-Makers, Weather Man to the Rain-Makers. Who starts a business checks with me first. Who wants to know what's ailing his business asks me. I cost three hundred dollars an hour, more than the city's best lawyer. I'm the man to put the right face on what you're up to.

My mother taught me manners and taste in clothes; my father instilled in me an appreciation of the King's English. As an eight-year-old I took tennis lessons because my mother thought I looked striking in white. By the time I was twelve, my father had me looking up words in the dictionary for entertainment. That's how I was raised. Even people who can't stand me respect my vocabulary and my backhand.

Suzanne has always had her reservations. On the evening she agreed to marry me, she said, "You do have a heart, Jack—I'm fairly sure of that. But you certainly don't wear it on your sleeve." She was a young Ph.D. of chilling beauty. She had very little choice as to whether or not to accept my courtship. Cultivated women have a major difficulty—men being so far behind them in terms of refinement that almost none are compatible. A few years before we met, I'd spent a summer touring Europe. At least I could talk to her about Giotto and the quality of light in Venice in March.

In my office, after I buzzed Eva to tell her that I wished to take no calls, I began to carry out a ruthlessly basic inventory. I made myself sit at my desk with my hands steepled at my chin. My theory is that everyone ordinarily functions with a lot of self-deception in the system. To make important decisions, however, you break down the delusion. I had put quite a number of my clients through this exercise. Before this morning, it hadn't occurred to me that I'd need to do it.

That I'd never considered the possibility of Suzanne's taking a lover was gross hypocrisy, I saw that now. I'd had a few involvements of my own. But before I so much as lifted an eyebrow at a woman I had to know that she valued discretion. I'd made no errors. Which is to say that my involvements began and ended with no one but the woman and me knowing what we'd been up to. I had a skill for this kind of thing. Suzanne's coming home for her rendezvous was, by my standards, an unpardonable blunder.

What was she thinking? What, for that matter, had I thought in seeking congress with those women? Ellie Jacobs, Jennifer Barnes, Kate Wetherall, and Monica Greenberg—one of my most dreaded fantasies involved a luncheon where the four of them discovered that each had taken a turn with me. The actual sex with them seldom lived up to its pre-intercourse promise. Reasonable enough, I'd thought at the time, a fair penalty. And in no case had the sex been atrocious. Spending time naked in motel beds, telling each other one little thing and another, had been sufficient reason to pursue it.

So was that it for Suzanne?—was she merely claiming a module of extramarital intimacy? That's not what I thought I was hearing in those *Ohs*—unusually spirited *Ohs* now that I thought about them!—wafting down from the master bedroom. They had the tone of authentic, major-league lust. Suzanne was in it because the guy who was doing the sex thing for her up there did it better than I did.

There it was—irrefutable.

I know people who are polite and funny and sometimes even

shockingly candid, but who have something about them that makes you wonder where they really live. There's a dimension of consciousness to which they deny you access—like they were raised in the forest by wolves. That's Suzanne. Not that I've ever caught her not paying attention to me—when we're together, she can probably repeat back the last eight sentences I've spoken. She's like that, too. Disturbingly alert. But occasionally I've suspected that for whole evenings we've spent together, Suzanne's true mind has been elsewhere. So now I wondered if maybe she'd just located a soul brother. Somebody who lived where she did. Maybe it had nothing to do with what the man had below the waist or how he was using it.

But did I like it better that she found him more *simpatico* than that she liked how he was hung? Which hurt the least? It was at this point in my self-interrogation that Eva buzzed me. I touched the button but said nothing to let her know how irked I was. "I'm sorry, Jack," she said, "but Suzanne's on line one. She says it's urgent."

Like heat lightning, my cardiovascular system blinked. In any circumstances a call at the office from Suzanne was unusual; this was a Pearl Harbor of my interior life. Summoning my resources, I made myself breathe deeply and evenly.

"Suzanne," I said. My tone sounded so light and witty I got a flash of what Cary Grant must have felt like in one of his early movies. "To what do I owe this honor?"

"Jack, I think somebody broke into our house this morning."

So I hadn't been as slick as I'd thought. She'd seen or heard something. I tried to imagine how this might play out. Clearly she was ready to admit that she had come home this morning. Clearly she was fishing to see if I'd let it slip that I was the one who'd been there. To make this phone call, Suzanne must have been desperate to know whether or not I knew. My neck burned. I was intensely aware of how much our future depended on the sentences we were about to utter.

"Why do you say that? Did you get a call from the police?" These words seemed to come from some source other than my own mind. It was as if my subconscious decision-makers had secretly deliberated and, without even checking with my conscious mind, decided to bluff it out with Suzanne.

"No, no. Nothing like that. There's not even anything missing that I can see. It's just that I came home this morning—I'd forgotten my lecture notes for this afternoon's class. Then while I was up in the study, I started reviewing them, and I lost track of time. When I came downstairs, I found the back door wide open. I distinctly remember closing that door behind me when I came in. It was the strangest thing—like a break-in occurred while I was upstairs, and I didn't even know it. But they didn't take anything. Apparently they just walked in and walked straight back out."

She was right about the door—she had closed and locked it. And I had left it open. Now that she mentioned it, I remembered it clearly. What was I thinking when I walked out without even closing that door, let alone locking it? What part of me wanted her to find *me* out? "Very strange," I murmured. "A ghost maybe."

"A daylight ghost," Suzanne murmured back. She kept quiet then, and I did, too. That silence had more content than four or five sentences. I could actually tell that Suzanne was feeling remorseful and tender toward me. I felt oddly remorseful myself. I'd had no business walking in and eavesdropping on her like that.

The emotional texture of the moment took me back to Suzanne's and my discussion last year when I came home from my doctor's appointment. I had decided to play the occasion as comedy. "It's not a mystery any longer, my dear," I announced when I walked into her study. She turned away from her computer to look up at me. Already she knew what I was about to tell her. She was already feeling the hurt of it. I went on with my charade anyway—I had no choice. "Doctor Lehman says I have the lowest sperm count of any healthy male he's ever examined. I thought he was going to award me a plaque with the inscription JACK NELSON — MAN LEAST LIKELY TO GET YOU PREGNANT."

"Oh, Jack," Suzanne said. Her voice was awful with pity.

"He says our options are to adopt or start looking for a stud." I didn't seem able to stop myself. "He says you and I are a true couple of the '90s. He says what with the world being the way it is, maybe I'm living evidence that the human species knows when to put the brakes on. He says he's proud of us for making our contribution to population ex—"

"Jack, please stop." Suzanne stood up with her face so contorted I had to look away, but I still couldn't shut myself up.

"He says men like me are the way of the future. He says you probably don't realize how lucky—"

That's when Suzanne slapped me. She didn't really slap me — she just patted her palm against my cheek to get my attention. "Shush, Jack," she said. Then she reached for me, placed my arms around her shoulders and pressed her forehead against my chest. "Just you shush," she said. We stood like that, in her study, with her computer humming along behind her. The snaky lines of its screen-saver danced while she squeezed me with her arms.

Suzanne and I had been married five years. By then I'd already had a couple of involvements, and she and I had even started up a very abstract discussion about the "viability of long-term childless relationships." That seemed to me a conversation we'd probably have before we began the conversation about whether or not to get a divorce. But in her study that day I knew Suzanne wasn't about to unclasp her arms any time soon, even though she wasn't ordinarily a hugger. It came to me that she actually felt something very similar to love for me. Then I wondered why I hadn't known that before. I supposed I hadn't been equipped to know it. But I wasn't about to worry the question of whether the shortfall was hers or mine. Right then she felt what she felt, and I did, too.

On the phone with her, though, in our silence, it was a different matter. Still feeling tender toward her, I nevertheless had this impulse to hang up. I actually moved the receiver away from my ear. I wasn't angry, I just had a momentary desire to give it all up, to let everything go. There was way too much pain.

"Jack," she said. Or rather the receiver I was holding between my face and my desk said. I could feel it coming—Suzanne's news. She was about to tell me she was having an affair with Barry Kitchner. So *he* was the bastard! I should have known Kitchner would be the one—her department chair. Mr. High-and-Mighty Spanish Renaissance Specialist. Such an obvious case of power-abuse! My God, the man must have propositioned her during their mandatory salary-evaluation talk! Suzanne always said Kitchner made her uncomfortable during those talks, the insinuating way he closed his office door before the two of them sat down.

"Jack," the receiver said again. This time I had it pressed right to my ear. "Jack, I know I'm not an easy person to live with."

All right, I knew what she was telling me. So she knew about my involvements after all. I'd always suspected that she did. That didn't mean I hadn't been impeccably discreet. She had no proof, I was certain of that.

"I just want you to know that there's a lot that doesn't get said. I think it's the same with you, Jack—we don't say everything we feel. I do appreciate you. I know it doesn't always seem that way, but I really do."

My God, so the affair with Kitchner was over! This morning was their last meeting. I was truly shocked. I wondered which one of them had put an end to it, I wondered how long it had been going on, I wondered what she had told Kitchner about me and what she'd told him about our marriage and whether or not he'd tried to talk her into leaving me. But then I supposed none of that mattered. If it was over, that was the crucial fact. That was it. She was finished with Kitchner, and I still had a wife.

"Jack, are you still there?"

"Yes, I am, sweetheart. I'm just a little distracted right now. Sorry. You know how it is down here. Way too much action for a normal man."

"Jack, by the way, did you leave your wallet here this morning?"

I moved the receiver down so she could hear me slapping my hip pocket. "My God," I said with just the right measure of panic in my voice. "I did! Is it there? Do you have it?"

"Even as we speak, I'm holding it. I have it right here in the palm of my hand."

"Yes?" I said. "Yes?" I wasn't faking the relief I felt—I knew I was inspired by the Day Ghost, which wanted nothing more than to give me back my life. "Can you tell me more, my dear? Can you tell me which hand?" I asked her. "Which palm?"

THE TRAIN, THE LAKE,
THE BRIDGE

We save this story for only the darkest winter nights, the thickest snows, when we know we cannot dig out for a few days, and so are guaranteed each other's company.

Sure, there are plenty of stories we pass back and forth among us. There is the story of Elder Hosmer, dead these one hundred years, and the Hosmer place, about the light that passes from window to window early midsummer mornings. There is the story of the Indian, one of King Philip's men, and how he screams certain evenings from the top of Greenscott Hill, his foot snapped in a saw-toothed bear trap generations ago. And there is the Provost (maybe he set the trap the Indian was caught in, we often speculate) and the story of how he walks our creeks and streams autumn nights, his wife's scalp in one hand, his own bloodied hatchet in the other. These are all stories we tell indiscriminately when we are hunting, rifles crooked in our arms as we stand before a blazing campfire at dawn, or walking home nights after town meeting, or after large suppers.

But the story of the train is irrefutable. It happened. We were there, three boys, but boys with enough sense and enough fear to know when not to tamper with the truth. It was the truth that frightened us the most.

As was often our habit during the Great Depression, and as we still do today, our families had gathered together for dinner. It was a night much like this, a night of snow, and by 10:30 there was no chance of anyone leaving. There had not been much snow that winter, not until that night, but there had been bitter cold, and Shatney Lake had already frozen clear and thick. We were assured of having nothing to do the next day: no work, no school, only the giant task of digging ourselves out, and even then there would be no hurry. The snow was there to stay, and we had no idea when it would let up. We started to bunk down for the night, the men and boys in the front room and kitchen, the women and girls in the bedrooms. We boys settled into our quilts and blankets and waited for the stories our fathers used to tell. They did not fail us. There was nothing more pleasant back then than to be warm, full, and have a frightening story in our heads before falling off to sleep.

And, like every night, we waited for the last train through, a train that made no stop in our small town, but which we counted on every night to rock us gently to sleep, the rhythm of the boxcars like the soft roll of thunder in a summer storm. The train came by, and we closed our eyes, imagining we were on it, riding the rails to destinations unknown, the train rolling along the ridge and slowly curving toward deep, frozen Shatney Lake, then crossing the old trestle, disappearing until the next night, when we would imagine the same things all over again.

But as soon as the rocking of the boxcars disappeared, there came a scream of metal on metal that seemed to last hours, as though Satan had wanted to wake the world on that peaceful night. The scream shuddered up and down the valley until surely every household within four miles had been awakened.

We got up and looked out the windows but could see little, the snow was falling so heavily. Something had happened, we all knew, something terrible. Our fathers decided to go have a look, but our mothers decided otherwise. They would not let the men outside, not in that storm, not in that cold, not in that snow. While they argued the point, we boys climbed out the kitchen window. We were going whether our fathers did or not. We waded through the snow up to the crest of the ridge and to the tracks.

Once there, we looked back to the house and saw a faint yellow glow from one of the windows. All else was white, save for the tracks cleared of snow by the train only a few minutes before. Our fathers would be out there soon, we knew, either to find out what happened or to take us home.

From the crest we could see nothing around us, but we knew the track from summer days, following it out to Shatney and the bluffs, walking the gravel and rock bare-footed, skipping every other creosoted tie. The tracks slowly curved to the lake, and once there on those hot days we would climb down somewhere on the old trestle, drop our fishing lines in, and spend the rest of the day. But these thoughts were far away. We wanted to find out what in God's world had happened.

We reached the lake and stopped dead. There in the white darkness we saw the broken timber of the trestle and the twisted rail torn from the edge of the bluff overlooking Shatney. Had the snow been falling any more heavily, had it drifted any more, had we not been looking where we placed each step, the three of us would have stepped off the edge and fallen to the ice forty feet below.

Look, one of us said, pointing off into the snow. He was pointing down. There was something dark there on the lake. We climbed a few feet down onto the ice-covered rocks and stared hard into the swirling, blowing snow. There was something huge and dark and awful down there, something that took on more and more detail as we stared at it, until we realized it was a boxcar. It was a boxcar planted halfway into the ice, hammered into the lake like a spike. It was silent, a dark leviathan in a sea of white snow. We said nothing, only watched the terrible thing standing on end.

And there in the howling wind, the snow stinging our faces, our bodies shivering, the boxcar started to move, slipping slowly down, down, silently into the ice. At first the movement was imperceptible; we imagined it was our eyes or the cold or the play of the snow, but before we could say anything, the boxcar disappeared into the ice, swallowed into the lake as if it were a snake returning to its hole.

Our fathers arrived a few minutes later to find us still there on the rocks staring into the white, none of us having yet spoken a word. We said nothing on the way home, said nothing until we were back inside and near the fire. Our mothers scolded us for having gone, while our fathers looked out the windows, speaking quietly to each other. We were sent to bed after we drank some coffee, but we could not sleep. The snow continued.

The next morning was bright and clear, and the three of us, having not slept all night, watched the sun rise over the ridge. Our footprints out into the snow had long since disappeared. The snow had drifted so that it took us a good hour just to clear a path from the house to the barn. We fed the horses, which stood in the darkness of the barn, their breath shooting from their mouths like great clouds.

We came out of the barn and saw that our fathers were leaving for the trestle, snowshoes on, daypacks on their backs. We came running at them, yelling and crying about wanting to go—it was our right, we reasoned, as we had been the first ones there and had seen the last boxcar slip into the ice. In the morning light, the sun banging up off the new snow, the awfulness of that huge black car was wearing off, and the idea of that sunken train in the lake seemed more like an adventure. It was a novelty, something out of the ordinary. We wanted to go down there and look again. They decided to let us go.

Damage to the trestle was greater than we had seen the night before. The bridge had fallen from the bluffs to midlake, and the wooden structure looked like some great animal bowing down on its knees. Ice had collected on all the crossbeams and had broken many of the struts in half. We figured that when the engine first moved out onto the trestle, the added weight then broke in two the already ice-laden crossbeams. The engine and the cars following it had fallen in line into the lake.

We stood at the top of the bluff and looked off to where we had seen the boxcar the night before. All that was left to indicate anything had happened at all, that anything had ever been near the lake surface last night, was a sunken area of snow about thirty feet off the edge of the rocks and a little to the right of the bridge. Snow had covered the skim of ice which had already formed in the hole.

Suddenly we heard a whistle blast break clean across the valley, carried across the snow. We turned from the lake to see an engine coming around the last curve before the lake, moving slowly, the prow scraping snow from the tracks as it moved along. The railroad people had arrived.

Only two men had been aboard the wreck, the maintenance supervisor told us. The supervisor was a clean-shaven man and wore blue overalls and shiny black boots. He had on a wool cap and a heavy coat slick with machine oil. Two engineers, he told us, and four empty boxcars coming down from Canada. He told us they had known for a long time that this bridge was a hazard, and that sooner or later the worst was bound to happen, and that they were going to have to close the route anyway, what with the Depression and all. He said it was a terrible shame that it had happened at all, and that it had been these two men in particular. We looked at him for a few moments, then looked at each other.

Then the supervisor broke out several shovels from inside the cab and asked if we didn't mind giving him and his assistant a hand down there on the ice. Railroad policy, he told us, demanded that all accidents be verified, and he had an idea that if we dug away some of the snow from the ice he might be able to verify the engine number, just to make double sure the right train had gone down. The right wives had to be notified of their husbands' demises, the supervisor said.

We took the shovels, as did our fathers, and climbed down the rocks onto the ice. The lake had been frozen a month or so, and we had no fear the ice would not support us. It seemed a foot thick.

We started clearing, keeping a safe distance from the hole where the train had entered. We dug into the snow, clearing an area where the supervisor imagined the engine must have been resting, but all we could see through the ice was the cold dark water below. No train. He had us dig in a wider area, enlarging the borders of the original area, and then we stopped digging again. He saw nothing. He asked that we clear a little larger area, nearer the hole, and we did. Our fathers shoveled snow with less and less enthusiasm, but we boys thought it great fun, and with each request of the supervisor dug even more furiously. Still there was no sign of the train.

After an hour and a half of digging, our fathers quit, saying that the railroad should be damned for sending out good men on a dangerous bridge in the first place. Down on his knees, his hands cupped around his eyes, the supervisor was oblivious and only stared down into the ice.

And then he screamed.

He stood up quickly, and slipped on the ice, then tried to stand up again.

"What is it?" we asked. "What is it?"

But before he could answer, if indeed he had ever had any intention of answering, we looked down to where he had been searching and saw a man under the ice, frozen, gray, his arms out to either side in perfect silence.

He wore blue jeans and a red and black plaid jacket. He had no face, only a blurred gray area where we expected to see his face.

We all stood there on the ice, none of us moving any closer to what was there under the supervisor. He still screamed and slipped on the ice, calling for our help, for anyone's help. He could not move from his spot above the frozen man.

Then they appeared, first one, then three, then five, all around us, beneath the ice. It took a moment, and then we recognized these men.

They were hoboes, bums catching rides on a southbound train, the same men who hung out of empty cars on summer days and hooted at us fishing from the trestle below them. But these men below us did not move and kept floating to the ice like swimmers seeking air. They appeared from nowhere, and we could not keep them from coming, a dozen, twenty, thirty of them, all bobbing to the surface in different positions, some curled up like stillborn animals, others stretched out straight. They wore overalls and caps and flannel shirts and coats, but none had faces, only the blurred, undefined patches above their shoulders. And still they came.

We tried to run on the ice, to get away, but slipped and fell over one another, falling to the ice, our faces meeting the formless faces of the dead. We screamed, the railroad men screamed, our fathers screamed. We struggled to make it to the snow, to get off the ice and those dead men, those derelicts who had no family except those around them, and who would never receive any burial except that which the lake had given them. We struggled to the snow, almost diving in head first when we finally made it off the ice.

And then, just as suddenly, the bodies disappeared, first one, then another, then another, all sinking back to the lake bottom and the train, their home. They seemed to peel away from one another, and fell slowly back into the blue.

We did not stay there to figure out what had happened, but moved as quickly and as silently as we could up onto the ice-covered rocks of the bluff, back onto the tracks, and home. The supervisor and his assistant climbed into the cab without a word, the shovels still down on the ice, and backed the engine along the tracks, first slowly, then faster and faster.

They were gone from the valley by the time we made it home.

. . .

The story is finished. There is silence in my living room as everyone here thinks over matters: the train, the lake, the bridge. There are no ghosts to speak of in this story, and it is precisely this fact that frightens us. We have no legends to create around this tale, no stories of old Indians or Provosts we can exaggerate. There are no ghosts, except the trestle, still torn and twisted after fifty years, a reminder of our childhood. The train stopped coming through this valley the night of the wreck and has not been back since.

We are no longer rocked off to sleep by the rolling train, but now must put ourselves to sleep, drinking warm milk, reading, or simply staying up all night, assuring ourselves we are alive in this frozen wilderness.

And there is the ghost of the lake, the silence that is taken there. There are no screams at midnight, no candlelights in windows, no blood. We no longer fish there, no longer dare even to set foot in that lake for what we know is buried there. There is only silence.

DOORS

She closed another door. It must have happened while he was taking his afternoon nap. All fall, as the days nipped into dusk at an earlier hour, throwing shadows deep into the long second-floor hallway, Franklin had walked past the other doors without really thinking about them, without thinking *closed*. Until today when he noticed that the light had changed once again, that there was less of it. Now, of all the various bedrooms, adjacent bathrooms, and attic, their bedroom and his wife's sewing room were the only rooms whose doors were still open.

Tonight his wife was out, meeting with the Library Board to plan the town's Halloween events. "Children are so difficult to scare these days," she said, as she was leaving. "They think ghosts retired with the horse and buggy." Old red draperies were folded over her arm. "How about a few sinister elements in the school's drinking water," he'd joked, anxious for her to go. He needed to know what she was up to here at home.

When he was sure that she wouldn't return for some forgotten item, he'd climbed the stairs to the second floor, followed by a panting Zeus, their aging setter.

Tall and narrow with molded panels and faceted glass doorknobs, the doors had particularly pleased his wife when they were looking for a house years ago. She had scraped and painted them with a creamy high gloss lacquer and they had gleamed in the hallway like windows. With age they'd acquired a dull patina and now their glow was the experimental quavering of candlelight.

Tentatively, he put his hand on the cool glass knob of the first door she had closed. It had been their oldest daughter's room, with pink-ribboned wallpaper and a pink vanity table. Of course he was defeating his wife's purpose by opening it, but he resented the authority of her purpose anyway.

He turned the knob. When the door didn't yield, he twisted it back and forth, then rattled it. Surely it couldn't be locked?

He gripped the doorknob harder and pushed against it with his shoulder as Zeus looked on in bored disbelief. When his wife had closed the first door, Zeus lay on the carpet outside, his scraggly head between his paws, eyes mournful, and whined all night. "Just let him in for a minute so he can see that Frannie isn't there," Franklin said from his side of the bed. "Oh, I don't want to do that," his wife had said. "He'll just have to learn that the room isn't there." Well, Franklin would see about that soon enough. Except that clearly the door was locked. This possibility had never occurred to him. He hadn't even known the bedroom doors had locks, though of course that special sharp-waisted opening beneath the knob was a keyhole. Where was the key? He pictured it dangling from a chain attached to a belt circling his wife's ample waist. Surely not. Annoyance gnawed in his chest like a caged rodent he might have operated on at the lab—one of those hapless creatures he sometimes named and later regretted.

Ever since their youngest daughter had married, he talked of moving to a smaller house, less yard to mow and to protect from moles, closer to his work. "Leave? Leave our home?" his wife said, the first time he brought it up. He had tracked her down in the kitchen where she was drying herbs. Abruptly she stopped stripping the thin twigs of dried sage and thyme and stared at him. "How could you even think of selling this house."

Perhaps his response—that he could leave it quite easily and that maybe he'd call in a real estate agent for an estimate—had been a bit hasty. She'd gone on to say that they'd reared their three children here, that four cats, three dogs, and two gerbils were buried in the field beyond the barn, and that her greenhouse was a second home, not to mention home to her extensive orchid collection and herb garden. Impatiently, he waited several months before he'd asked the realtor to stop by.

"You have a gem of a gold mine here," the realtor said, his small eyes promising huge profits he would no doubt share. "Classy old farmhouses with architectural detail are hard to come by. Just enough land. Good location."

"We'll let you know," his wife said, ushering the realtor and his paperwork toward the door. When he'd gone she turned to Franklin. "Gold mine!" The next day she closed the first door and at dinner announced, "I've closed the door to Alessa's room. Don't go in there anymore. You'll see. Pretty soon the house will seem smaller."

Several months later, he brought home spec sheets for the apartments in the new block of condominiums near his lab, and the next day she closed the second door. "It won't just seem smaller," she said. "It *is* smaller."

When the realtor returned with two eager people from his office and papers awarding his firm an exclusive listing for the first two months, his wife retreated to the greenhouse till they were gone, and then set about cleaning out the attic. She hired the teenage son of the neighbor who farmed their land and together they unpacked and repacked boxes, and sent it all off to the three children or Good Will. Franklin took it as a hopeful sign that she'd come round to his point of view, but when the last box was disposed of, she didn't acknowledge his talk of summer as a good time to sell at all. She merely firmly closed the attic door. Looking back, he suspected she'd emptied out the attic so she could close that door too.

He moved to the second door, that of their son, who was overseeing the installation of a colossal oil rig he'd designed for Australian waters. The walls of his room were covered with posters of the world's tallest buildings and drawings of the most improbable bridges. Franklin sometimes wondered if they'd ever been built or not.

He tried the knob. Locked, too.

He moved along the hallway, surprised to find the door to their younger daughter's bedroom also locked, its shelves of delicate music boxes silent and still. His wife used to go in there of an evening and set two or three music boxes going. "They miss singing," she'd say, getting into bed. And he'd turn his back to her, his head deep in a pillow, grumbling that he didn't miss their puny tinkling at all. Just as he admitted to himself he didn't really miss the children. But actually locking these rooms was going too far. He now pictured six keys dangling and clanking on his wife's belt, above stiff black skirts and tightly laced shoes that only a nun should wear.

Once again, he gripped the glass knob of his daughter's room and tried in vain to force the lock, an old-fashioned cast-iron rectangle. "God damn it," he said, kicking the bottom panel hard. A slight tinkle came from inside the room, then silence. "Be damned," he said. Another kick to the door sent Zeus panting to the top of the stairs, clearly hoping the fuss would not flush a rabbit he'd be obliged to track. Frustrated, Franklin nudged the dog down the stairs ahead of him and waited for his wife. Damn it, it was his house.

He'd never liked closed doors anyway. He could vaguely remember, as a child of three or four, watching his parents open the front door and disappear into the dark night. "For an evening out," his mother would say, waving cheerily to Franklin and the sitter, then she'd pull shut the door. For years he'd thought that "out" meant they were just outside on the porch, on the other side of the door, standing still, breathing quietly, until whim would bring them back long after he'd cried himself to sleep.

He must have dozed off because he woke with a start at hearing his wife's merry voice in the entryway, murmuring the praises of her prize orchids. Soon she set the teakettle on and then looked into the study where he'd been working the *Times* daily crossword. "Tea, Franklin?" she asked, her sweatered arms around her arms. "The library is almost ready for Halloween. Just a bit more atmosphere — cobwebs, infrared lights in the stacks, the carrols closed off into tiny hidden rooms — the kids will love it." She bent to the fireplace and reached up to open the damper. "I think I'll build us a fire — the first of the fall." Zeus padded over and nudged her shoulder.

"Locked," Franklin said, his jaw so locked itself that it was all he could manage to say.

"Ah, the doors," she said, scratching Zeus behind the ears.

"Why? Why did you lock the doors?"

She looked up, surely in genuine surprise. "So you wouldn't open them."

"Why shouldn't I open them?"

"But you want a smaller house, Franklin. How can I make the house smaller if you insist on keeping it large?"

How had their children survived her logic? "There are only a few condominiums left," he said. "I'm stopping by for floor plans tomorrow. If you won't go look at them, I'll bring them home to you." The teakettle began to whistle.

"Oh dear," she said, patting Zeus's head, then rising. "Please, Franklin. It feels like such a loss. Just give us a little more time."

"Loss," he said, throwing the crossword into the fire. "Don't be so melodramatic. We're merely downscaling our living arrangements."

The next day, unbelievably, the door to her sewing room was closed, the place where she'd sewn curtains for the forty-four windows he cursed each spring and fall as he prepared to put up or take down the summer screens. Wisely, he'd hired someone to do this job the last ten years. This fall, as he'd followed the hired man around from window to window, calling instructions from the bottom of the long aluminum ladder, the task oddly had seemed to take less time. But her sewing room—how could she abandon it! Now only their bedroom was left.

He felt so queasy that it took him five minutes to find the right kind of chisel to open such locks. Zeus lumbered after him to the basement and back to the sewing room where Franklin knelt in front of the door. He imagined dust settling on the long library table where she cut out patterns and on the white cloth torso of the mannequin she fitted and pinned the fabric to. Years ago, he'd had erotic dreams about that padded torso, and now it was as if he were going to visit a woman he'd once flirted with at a party. Didn't his wife miss the whir and turn of the sewing machine? When was the last time she made something for their home?

Finally the door swung open.

Still on his knees, he had to grip the doorframe to keep from falling into the night. Zeus whimpered at his side.

The room was gone.

There was at least a twenty-foot sheer drop to the lawn below. Franklin could smell the fertilizer from the back paddock and the Harvest moon showed golden on the horizon. A chill wind blew against his face. Breathless, he pulled closed the door and leaned against the wall. It couldn't be. He set the chisel in place on the attic door.

Absurdly, it too was gone.

Where there had once been a steep curving staircase, the door to the attic now opened onto a view of his wife's slumbering greenhouse and the gnarled orchard stretching as far as the eye could see. The same chill wind, this time carrying the scent of marjoram, made his chest ache. What had she done with the rooms? The furniture?

Franticly, he peered around for something—anything—to throw through the open doorway. Zeus obliged by dropping a slobbery fake bone at his feet. It sailed, glistening, out into the night and landed with a soft plop on the wet grass. Real grass.

He hadn't the courage to open the other doors. Instead he put new batteries in the flashlight, pulled on a heavy sweater and went outside, feeling oddly safer there. Crickets sawed in the dewy grass. A coyote howled a mating call. Slowly, Franklin prowled the perimeter of the house, squinting up at the flashlight's beam playing over the white clapboards as he located each bedroom, indentified the corner windows of his wife's sewing room. The house's dimensions were unchanged.

"Where's your bone?" he whispered to Zeus beneath the attic window, and stood there shivering in the cool night while Zeus reluctantly zigzagged back and forth, sniffing the wet grass. "Find your bone," he called. But Zeus returned without it, tail drooping. "What are you good for," Franklin said, but after five minutes of pacing back and forth, he too failed to find the bone. A cloud passed over the moon and Franklin gave up. He didn't know if he was more frightened or relieved.

On the way back to the house he stopped by the car for the condominium plans. He'd been patient long enough. In wide swipes, he spread the rolled pages on the table in his study. They glowed invitingly in the dim light of the moon. Zeus came by to slobber over them and Franklin pushed him away. He knew exactly which apartment he wanted— four rooms with a generous storage room in the basement. Bringing the plans home for his wife's approval was only a formality. They'd move sometime after the new year. Sad, but condominium rules decreed that Zeus would not be able to make the move with them.

He sat in the deep shadows of the corner near the fireplace, in his old leather chair, and waited, his eye on the door, too angry to turn on a light. About ten he heard her foolish murmuring in the hall, flattering her orchids, then heard her solid footsteps on the kitchen tiles. Finally, she stepped into the library and glanced around. Zeus stood and stretched and when she said his name he padded over to her, his tail swishing loyal and low.

Franklin smiled furtively to himself. Let her turn on the light, let her find the plans for herself.

The dog padded out into the hall and after a moment's hesitation she followed him. Seemingly as an afterthought, she turned and closed the door. Then she locked it.

ACHILLES' GRAVE

Around them then, a great and blameless mound
We built, the sacred host of Argive spearmen,
Upon the jutting strand by the wide Hellespont,
So bright a monument as to be seen by men sailing afar,
Those who live now and those yet to be born.

(Homer, *The Odyssey*, XXIV, 82–86)

T he smell of the trenches rose as from rotten veins in the earth.
And it wasn't so much the heat of day but the anticipated inter-
minable length of it that made me sick with hopelessness. The broken terrain—ravines, gullies, sandy escarpments and measly bushes of
wilting grass—sketched all around a planet of known yet unknown
character, and the way back was not as easy as retracing my steps.

It had happened before to others, even though by now, July's end,
1915, things ought to have changed. Yet here I was, lost past the
reach of my own, brought forward by the heedless impetus of the
battle for Gallipoli, when after hours of bombardment we could
barely hear ourselves think, and like automatons rushed forth just to
escape the noise. Achi Baba, the Tree Hill, loomed before me
stretching its infamous arms across the width of the peninsula.
Between those rocky limbs thousands of men lay dead from the
most recent attacks, and the Turk was still entrenched at the foot of

the mountain, as exhausted and dazed as we were, but not flushed out yet. Never to be.

And the loss of my patrol was not unique but soon to be unbearable, when the shock of battle should wear off me. At this hour I was still numb past the reckoning of my own wholeness — the fact that, at least, I was physically unhurt. Sitting on a rock I kept my head low to the knees and dully began to ache, not my first time for exhaustion in Gallipoli. Ears still ringing with the shrapnel fire and fusillade, at first I did not take notice of the clicking sound to my right. It was as if small rocks were misplaced and made to roll upon others, a metallic noise nearly, without echoes. There hung great weariness for killing in me, still when I looked up the nozzle of my gun followed, and it was the slender, long nozzle of another gun that met it. Our pistols fronted one another for a time through their single, dark, cyclopean eye, then the one held by the newcomer swayed briefly and swung down, to rest at the end of his arm.

His uniform was different but not alien, not really. Khaki-colored, dirt-encrusted, boots made opaque by sandy loam. Even the tropical cork helmet, though not a Wolsey, wasn't that different at all.

"No ammunition," the German said. Not regretfully but as a statement of fact, letting the useless pistol dangle from his hand as if to prove that he didn't need it to confront me.

I sought my holster also. "Same here," I said, and there wasn't much more to do in terms of hostility.

One hand in his belt, the German stood with an air of dismayed fatigue.

"I became separated from my group," I admitted. He looked around. "Lost all my men," I added.

He said nothing, but came closer. "So have I." There was blood from one of my soldiers on my clothes. "Are you wounded?" He nodded towards the stains. If my face was as chalked with dust, we must both have looked like death.

"No."

But I had a sudden great need to cry with the denial. His being here outraged me, when he was the one who had been shooting at us since daybreak. Yet he didn't look more composed than I. An aghast expression of loss stayed on his face, and I knew he was starting to mourn also, too acutely to conceal it. There came between us a revolting and anguished communion of pity for the dead, and for ourselves, who had survived them.

Meanwhile we stared at one another, looking deep for the possibility of deceit, although it didn't seem feasible that we should be playing games in the felling heat of day. Noon had rolled into an afternoon so ablaze, the crop of the earth seemed to tremble as if with inner vapors.

The German crouched, finally, hands loosely twined between parted knees. He was a young company officer, bearing a couple of long thin scars on a cheek, such as student duels afforded those days in military school. I knew the *Mensur* to be a not-so-innocent proof of a man's character. He smiled briefly in apology, his face in the shade so that his teeth stood out white as bones. "You are grieving," he said.

My first reaction was to strike him for having said it. And I could, indeed. A blow in the face and then take my chances at fighting it out with him on the rocky dirt. Would it accomplish anything? I ended up by not replying.

"We may as well be civil to each other," he said. "There's nothing else to do for now."

It was true enough. We had been shooting at each other like madmen until a moment ago, inciting our own—my Britons, his Turks— to destroy the wavy line of the adversary, and likely we had. We had killed each other's resources off. There lay the measure of shared dismay in it, I knew. This is what he meant.

"We ought to find some shade," he suggested. At that I rose, walked off and found my way to a small *nullah*, steep-sided, whose bottom promised coolness. The stench of the blown-up trenches did not get here as strongly. I could hear the calm pace of his boots following, and the small clank of stones as he began to come down too.

We sat there for a time, and as the shell-shocked numbness of the afternoon wore thin in us, grief came. It made me once more bury my head in my folded arms, and the German passed one hand across his face until the fingers rested against his mouth, looking away. He was weeping when I glanced through the corner of my eye, shoulders rigid, tears running over his hand. In his place I would have scrambled away not to expose my weakness. But there he sat, knees drawn up, going through his own helpless grief. The sharing of it embarrassed me.

"You speak English well." I threw the words in eventually, just to fill the void. He had by now composed himself and was uncorking a cloth-covered canteen. He paused and offered it to me. I refused, and he drank from it.

For a minute, perhaps, we sat with our legs cramped at the bottom of the *nullah*, flies buzzing above us, and an eery silence that swept the broken plateau where men had died. The German made fast his canteen again, though it was pointless to replace the stopple. There was no water left in it. In excess of mine, it seemed, total control had returned to him.

"It'd be impractical to walk back now, for either one of us." He tilted the helmet forward to rest the nape of his neck on the dirt wall. "Tonight, we can."

Nothing could be opposed to that. I sat gloomily, and closed my eyes to shield them from the glare cutting like a blade upon us. Soon a rustle of paper told me the German had taken something out of his knapsack. By the repeated soft sounds I assumed it must be a book. I looked over, and he was indeed leafing through a pocket-size edition of Greek poetry.

"*The Iliad?*" I asked.

"No, no. Not *The Iliad. The Odyssey.*" He showed me the bilingual text, Greek on one page, German on the other. Both languages were remote but not obscure to me.

So, like us, the young German officers were living the Homeric nightmare in this narrow peninsula facing the plains of Troy. I know *we* were. Homer in our pocket, we had traveled here much like Byron had, and Xerxes, the great king who sat on a throne on the highland to watch his two million bronze-clad warriors invade Europe.

"This area is what they called the Thracian Chersonesus," he volunteered.

"I know well what it is."

"What I meant is—never mind."

We sat at arm's length, myself brooding, he reading the graciously curving Greek characters, accents afloat on the verses. Was he pragmatically killing time, or did he seriously read the poetry? And what did mill in his mind anyway? Was he planning to take me prisoner— this was more Turkish than no man's land, by all accounts—as soon as fresh troops came? And why didn't I just clamber up and go my own way, and find another *nullah* to sit in?

The truth is that I could not. Whether it was weariness of limbs or an undone laxity of the soul, there I sat, and felt I had to stay there, next to a man from the ranks of those bent on destroying us. They well nigh had, too. So what? He was right, I was grieving, but not for my men alone.

I craned my neck to see. "What part are you reading?"

"*Amph' autoisi d'epeita megan kai amymona tumbon,*" he read.

It was the verse where the building of Achilles' burial mound on the Hellespont is described.

"They raised it just across the Strait," I said. "It's bizarre, I was thinking about it this morning before the attack: *a great and blameless mound.*"

He nodded. "That's whom I'm grieving for."

"Achilles?"

"For all Achilles represents. For us. You understand."

"Yes." I did. *"This is the stone of a man dead long ago.* Christ, this is a horrible war."

He put down the book. "You see, you should let go of *The Iliad*. It's *The Odyssey* that holds the key."

"What key?"

"To grief. To the resolution of grief."

"And do you think I would miss my dead less if I read some three-thousand-year-old poetry?"

He looked away. "Of course not."

"What, then?"

"I'm thinking of the *nekuya*."

I asked him what he meant by that, and he said, "The meeting Odysseus had with the dead."

Had he not looked so unaffected, I'd have sneered in his face. "It's nothing but a tale."

"Maybe. But I don't see why it couldn't be done."

For a fleeting moment the doubt crossed my mind that perhaps he was not in his senses. Flushed with the heat, but otherwise composed, he did not trouble himself with convincing me, and went back to reading. As for me, I stood up to climb over the *nullah's* wall and regained the godawful plateau, run by a hot wind like an oven that opens in your face. It hissed in my ears, and the misery of the blown trenches and the dead came back to me with the stench. For an hour or more I sat on the upper crust of the land, uselessly seeking comfort in the scanty shade of a rock, so narrow it afforded no reprieve. When I looked over, I saw the German walk towards the Achi Baba with measured steps, now and then finding his way among the rubble, over the torn bundles of barbed wire. Without turning he gestured at me. "If you want water, it's this way."

We walked a stretch in silence, and before long found ourselves in a deep ravine, narrowing at the bottom into a reduced track between steep walls, fringed with vegetation.

"The spring is just to the left."

It was. We filled our canteens with icy water that trickled down and soon became lost in the heat of the ground, like a snake that slithers away. I thought of the Greeks, who gave names of swift animals to creeks and rivers. It felt good to drink.

It still amazes me why, or why at this point, I thought the true core of my grief should be admitted, one that otherwise I warded closely.

"My brother died two months ago, " I said.

The German stared at me. And now that I had foolishly spoken, there was no stopping me. It was as when one starts drinking water and will not let off even though he knows the excess will make him ill. Why should I tell an enemy, I wondered. I spoke nonetheless, in a jumble of words, and ended up confessing, "Before we left England someone told him he'd die by a large river."

The German had been pouring water from the canteen on his head. He stopped. "Such was not the case, then. Not at Gallipoli."

"You forget the landing off Cape Helles. The name of his ship was *River Clyde*."

Stockstill, the German looked at me. With the sun at his back, the moist halo of short blond hair on his head reminded me of my brother. He was tall and wide-shouldered, even as my brother had been. "I am very sorry." And then, absentmindedly, "I should think you would want to speak to him again."

That carelessness sounded like blasphemy. Without warning I hit the canteen he was still holding, knocking it off his hand. It flew off far behind him. He struck me back, hard, so that I was thrown against the wet wall of the spring. He pinned me down with his boot. The Luger came out, and from the sound it made when he handled it, I realized the magazine was in it, and it was loaded. Had been loaded when he first saw me and did not shoot. Without letting go of it, he offered me his left hand to help me get up. I wriggled instead from under his relenting hold, and rose on my own, too angry to be intimidated by the pistol.

"I don't even know where he's buried, damn you!"

"But you could find out."

"You're insane."

"Do you know your way out of here and back?" He grinned. "If not, *you*'re insane to be here. I know this plateau well. I can find my way back before dawn, and not be killed on a mine." Now that he had washed off the grime, his face was tanned and smooth, bearing a cruel youthfulness entirely unlike my brother. "I have been thinking of the *nekuya* for a time. And I'm going tonight. You may join me if you wish. The dead will gather."

The dead will gather. As sometimes happens, a pattern of thought is upheaved by some outwardly innocent addition to a phrase. It was what he said last that made me fling the impossibilities off, and be hopeful against hope even if it was mad.

"Going where?" I asked.

"To the slope of Achi Baba, and up its right side trail. Absurd though it sounds, it is in the strength of the sacrifice and the intent of it that the difference lies. And the place is perfect. Odysseus would like it, even, or Achilles."

I gaped. "Why would you want someone with you then, an enemy at that?"

"You are grieving hard. Your grief will also make the difference."

It was then that I started thinking of what strategic insight could be gained by climbing the mountain we had failed to take in every other way. "What guarantees do you give me that I will not be taken prisoner if I come along? Your redoubts are that way."

"I will *not* show you our redoubts, be sure. As for the rest, you will have to trust me."

I wavered, but the absurdity of the task somehow scored better than the anxiety of waiting here for the Turks to come searching for survivors. Entering the wolf's mouth was quicker and less unnerving. "I don't recall the poetry as well as you do."

He took the book out again, and put it in my hands.

"Why are *you* doing it?" I inquired.

"Because I don't think I'll get out of here, and I mean to find out when it will come. And I grieve for Achilles, of course."

"Is that all?"

"I think it's plenty."

We found a protected place to sit and read the episode where Odysseus describes to his host his sacrifice and dialogue with the dead. We pored over the text, considering the words—his knowledge of Greek was excellent—and soon I had to ask how he meant to do what he planned.

"Simple. I already set aside the things necessary."

"Down to sheep and barley?"

"Of course. And the drinks, too. The prayers are not described, but I imagine the words will come."

"And the dead?"

"And the dead."

"Just like that."

"No, not just like that. It has been long in preparation, and long in grief. This is the right time, that's all. You may come if you wish, or I will go alone."

He truly knew his way around. We went up and down the upheaved terrain, avoiding this or that expanse of land that seemed to me no more dangerous than another. We clambered into shell holes and out of them, taking in stride the horrible presence of death everywhere. Through what remained of shelled hamlets, now heaps of refuse run by meager dogs, along hastily built stacks of bodies charred to stumps, we walked, and I wondered if the dead were supposed to come as they were now, burnt or rotting under a veil of dirt.

The sun was arching down when we reached the foothill of Achi Baba.

I never thought I would get as far as this low massif, against which Britons had been battering themselves for months. Here I was, and on my way up to its sides. Before the climb we could have had a brief dinner of bully beef and tack, but chose only to drink water—in case it should make a difference to the dead, I suppose, or to our stomachs, should the dead come.

The German said we should wait until nightfall, and we did, under a light that gilded us less and less as an immaterial tongue lapping low.

"Are you really grieving for Achilles?"

The German sat on a rock, splitting measly blades of grass lengthwise with his fingers. The flimsy strips he let go between his legs to his feet. He looked over at my question as if amused by my doubts. "Yes. I always did, and I always wanted to come here."

"To Gallipoli?"

"Yes." The blades in his left hand were fragile, thin. I didn't know why I felt anxiety for them as he resumed slicing them. "Haven't you?"

"God, no."

He smiled. "So, I'm luckier than you are."

It had taken us long to reach this point because he carefully led me away from the Turkish lines, as if the confusion of the terrain were not enough to protect them. Now that the day was nearly done we began to climb. A clear glaze of topaz dressed the air, cutting out the crags above us as stenciled forms and giving us glimpses of the empty sea as we gained altitude. With night ahead of us the enterprise did not seem so absurd anymore. Certainly not ridiculous. I looked up at the forbidding goat trails that darkness began to flatten and jumble here and there, and felt apprehension instead. The German was coolly beckoning from a place where the land surged not so sheerly. We kept going up, with night adrift at us from above. Soon the fires from the Turkish camps could be seen below, to the left. I screwed my eyes for the British lines, but could not identify them in the growing shadow, and was glad of it.

The German walked securely ahead of me, soon to clamber up a rocky side that was high and more precipitous. "There isn't much to go after this," he said when I warned him that I could not keep my footing.

"I'm going down a bit," I insisted. "I don't care for heights." As I spoke, he slid down and joined the place where I crouched. "I can't very well rest here!" I protested.

"Why not? It's perfectly safe." He stood, anchoring himself somehow with his heels to roots or rock stays, careless of the crag's pendency. Only a shade of daylight remained. Still, the diminished sense of space did not help my vertigo. I dimly saw the German rummage his left front pocket and take a cigarette case out. "Do you want one?" he asked.

We smoked, and it was the most precarious smoking I ever had, flicking red points that flared as we inhaled to reveal brief sights of our faces.

"Will the dead really come?"

"Yes."

"I don't see how you can be so certain."

"We're all dead, in relative terms. Why should they not come to their own?"

"We're *not* dead, in any terms."

He flicked away the cigarette, to tumble in the windy dark. "How do you know that I am not?" But he laughed.

It was a lucid and perfectly wrought night when we reached a flat extension, adjutting from the flank of Achi Baba like a terrace. Stars garlanded the horizon and it seemed as though we were at the top of a bloody and forgotten world. Wind wrapped the mountain with the briny scent of the sea. As we climbed the last stretch, words had become slow and fewer between us.

Too far gone into them, I no longer wondered at the bizarre turn of things. My companion found his way to the wall of the ledge, looking for things, I supposed, in the luminous dark of the summer night. Low bleating indicated where the animals were kept; their weak, tender voice was archaic and familiar to my ears, because I had known the country and the mild sounds of it.

The German rejoined me, carrying something. "Honey and milk," he said, "and wine. You have the water." He put in my hand a satchel with the barley seed.

"We need a pit. Has it been dug already?"

"To your right, yes."

Some steps off, I discerned two sheep tethered to a stake. Behind them I could also see the blackness of the pit dug as a squarish trough. A chill searched my spine.

Standing or kneeling to one side of the pit, we would be facing the mountain wall, where the shadow was now perfect and uninterrupted. This hole, too small to be one grave, should be our channel to the other world? I ran between my fingers the dirt piled at its rim, wondering whether Odysseus really had dared this, if he had ever even lived. This may have been

Gallipoli, but it was not 1915 anymore. Or not yet, and we were in a suspended hiatus of time.

The German stood behind me, undoing his holster.

"Do the same."

At his words something like panic took me for the part expected of me in this. He might have sensed it, because he crouched alongside me then.

"Now remember your brother," he said. "Do not just think of

him: remember. It's different if you remember, the dead know. Do not pray. Remember. How you will honor him when you return to your country. Remember those plans, too."

I felt tension in his voice for the first time.

"And you?"

"I know what I have to do."

Like him, I undid the strap of the holster and laid it aside. "I'm not ready yet," I said.

He stood up. "You're confusing readiness with lack of fear."

"So I am. It amounts to the same."

He walked off and went to wait on the ledge, I presumed, where the night must have been an endless bowl of whirling stars. While he was gone I groped for his holster on the ground, found it, took out the Luger and substituted it with my empty gun, which fit perfectly in its place. Then I sat and prayed, and *remembered.*

We were unarmed and bareheaded as we brought the flask of mixed honey and milk to the pit and poured it in. Then came the wine, from an earthen bowl. I could smell its heady sweetness gulping down to the earth. Gestures were spare, ritual in their essential brevity. Some of the stars were so huge when I turned to reach for my canteen, they seemed a hand-reach away. I looked down from them and hastily went about my business, which was letting the water into the hole. It braided down like swift metal, and was gone. The German followed by widening the mouth of the satchel and sprinkling the white small barley over all. We held our breath, I know, aware of the power of night and place on us—of what circumstances made that power pulse with dread. It had been a windy evening, and it was odd that the wind should fall now, where we were most exposed to crosscurrents from the coasts. Silence grew high like a fence that enclosed us and shielded us somehow from the bitter reality beneath.

Now the German stepped back to untie the first animal, whose bleating became alarmed as he carried it over. At the pit's edge, the sheep resisted, and he had to force it down with his knee even as Odysseus must have, and Achilles when he slew the victims for Patroclus. His hand held it by the wool of the shoulder, arching its back. Skillfully he cut across the side of the sheep's neck and there was a gurgle and hiss and a warm odor of blood, sickening memory of the trenches, a useless thrashing and death. Silence was now higher than the mountain. I numbly watched and heard things happen. The German led in the second sheep and killed it. He left the carcasses draped with their heads down the pit, to drain into it. My heart felt ill.

Both of us knelt on the rocky dirt, no longer even glancing at each other. Silence climbed over the stars. The thick trench knife was now held by the German with blade downturned, even as Odysseus had, ready to plant it in the earth to keep the dead from drawing too close. I felt I could have run away long ago, but not now: the knife kept me here, and not by threat.

I had never before known of Time stretching out and magnifying itself. As if it were a folded, compacted kind of Time which is known to us and we live by, and this was the same Time but it had opened, yawned and lay flat, and incommensurable space was covered by it, so that it was an eternity gaping around us.

Bodily laxitude would have kept us kneeling for our own dead, whether or not the darkness should spew them out again.

The pit, filled with the sinister mixture and dressed by the emptying bodies of the sheep, was like a mouth that had been fed and stayed hungry, dangerously agape. And we so close to it. I was awed by the simple horror of it, as obscene a symbol as I can find even today for war and men in it—the German and myself exposed to the same dark gulf, by choice.

Would the dead come to this? The jaws of death had chewed them already. Long digested, would they be vomited out again?

How long we waited, I cannot tell. Time gaped endless, as the night glided around us and constellations wheeled above and sank behind us. Yet without moving we waited, neither one of us able to bear the thought of letting go and then regretting it forever. We had to wait. I know I did. I was past being mesmerized by the absence of sounds, or the strange presence of the man who had brought me here, still I did not quiet my mind enough to fully remember. I held the key, and stolidly toyed with it.

The past flowed back eventually as Time reached that corner of reality, even as eddies fill the bend in the river, not through my doing. But with sore thoughts of my brother it flooded me: our childhood together, hopes, war, the news of his death, and absence even of the poor knowledge of his burial place. Memory broke through like a dam, a levee of regret. An unmeasurable rush of unhappiness streamed over me, and all the while I knelt on the ledge of Tree Hill, before the bloody offering.

The pit yawned dark and sharply smelling. I was staring down at it when I heard the sudden stab of the knife in the earth. With a start I looked up.

From the opposite side of the pit, close to the ground and emerging from it as one who wades through high water or grass, a man was coming toward it. He wore a uniform, too battered to tell which. His arms were raised forward but not stretched, as if he were blindly groping for the food. My hair stood on end, my entire body bristled in the way animals cringe in fear.

He seemed one drowned and left in the water to float supine under the surface, there and not there, blindly groping. The eyes in his face, dull, jellylike, were horribly open and as spoiled drops of milk, pupils curdled and void.

My heart had sunk so deep in the chest, I could not hear it draw blood. I was too frozen to tear myself away from the sight, as though my bones and muscles had been disconnected from one other and without structure I were lumped on the ground in a heap. My tongue clung to the roof of my mouth. Had I found the strength to shout, I'd have howled inarticulate sounds like madmen do.

"Is he your brother?"

I don't know how the German could find the courage to ask. He was still holding the knife down, like a rock hewn at my side and unwavering.

My eyes riveted to the hideous shape from the dark, I could only shake my head in denial. All I hoped for was enough energy to beg him to quit this place, but it was too late. Already it was a crowd of half-figures wading toward the pit from nothingness, pale and luminescent as the tucking of the waves at night. Here and there they swayed through one another, shuffling places. Their motions were fettered, pleading, yet hideously familiar to me. These were faces I had known. Those of my men who had died just hours ago, contorted as at the point of passing, bloodless, their clothing upheaved and stained and torn. And like cripples, from their belly down there was nothing, only the black earth from which they rose. How many could assemble in one place, it seemed incomprehensible. Shifting and fading, the faces superimposed as reflections in dark mirrors— now they were my men, now they were long-jawed Germans and Turks with big staring eyes.

And how many of them had we killed, my companion and I? How many had I sent to this swamp of darkness unthinking that I should ever see them again? It curdled my blood to think that they knew. Fear ran unchecked through me. There was no safety on this ledge, and none to be sought next to me. I could sense the revulse of the German beside me, but the knife stayed down. Whatever kept me here, it was lack of strength that rooted me.

Then I saw my brother in the fishlike pale mingle. As one in an inexorably moving throng makes out a face and it becomes the center of a now inexpressive fluidity, all other shapes lost value to me.

Even fear. I found my heart again, and control of my sinews enough to kneel up.

It *was* my brother, feeling his way towards me in a tentative, halting gait. The face was his, my brother's face, though I saw now how much of his features had been expression, and how without it there was an alien cast to them—a frightening and despair-breeding estrangement, as if no longer we might know each other when we had been so close. I must have called out to him, such surge of agony seized me for seeing him there. I lunged forward and stumbled with my foot in the pit, where it sank in the squelch of blood and mixed liquids. The hand of the German reclaimed me harshly.

"Get back! You will talk to him when I let you!"

And I'd have fought his command, except that I longed to speak to my brother. I drew back. Only then the knife was pulled out of the earth, and what I witnessed next I tremble to repeat even after so many years. My brother bent over the pit and seemed to fish down with his hand to drink from it.

The German kept motionless at my side, knife resting in his lap, but I was shaking so violently, it was like a seizure that rattled the teeth in my head. Disgust and love tied slimy knots in me as I watched my brother feed from the repulsive trough. If only I had not so closely recognized the way he parted his hair, the freckles on his neck, the motion of his shoulders as he pulled up from the pit. This was no dream. Tears welled in my eyes and made him waver in my view while he looked up, mouth fouled from the drink. I found myself grasping the dirt with my hands, because I knew he would speak now.

"Why did you come here?"

I didn't see his lips part, though they must have. His face gained no expression, nor did he attempt to wipe the blood from his chin. It was his voice, the voice I knew so well, and thought I should never again hear while in this world. All reserves collapsed within me at the sound of it and I was too convulsed to speak back, but he must have known what I sought, or someone else asked for me, because, "It is by the *wadi* north of our first landing," he said. The voice was hollow as though heard through a tunnel, expressionless like the rest of him, unmoved. It was his, but how the familiar ring was gone. "You may ask the corporal, he put me there, and will remember if you tell him my tag had been blown off."

Oh, God. I could see why. There was a gaping hole in his tunic, black with blood and wide enough to have blasted life out of him. It was the sight of the wound that made his death too much for me to withstand. I cried out and stretched my hand to him across the pit. I met with nothing, my fingers met with nothing but the night air.

That was my mistake, as it had been Odysseus's. Fingering the empty space I had broken his fabric, immaterial though it may be, flimsier than web spittle. I searched with my eyes and fumbled uselessly until dejection doubled me over, because he was gone.

Not so the hazy crowd of others rising from the hard soil to draw only so close: Britons and Germans, Frenchmen, gangling Anzacs, the small, angry-looking Turks, and we facing them. But how my heart was sour by now. I felt my soul had poured itself in the pit and would be drunk by the earth, never to be returned to me. All I had meant to gain from this was over, since my brother had been swallowed back. I cared to see no more.

The shades afloat in the dark were hungry. They wanted brief sustenance and the means of speech, all of them, for all had died with unsaid things, as we likely all will. But I cared no more to witness the ghosts of their lacerated selves, flesh hanging as beggars' cloth, hair matted by the ooze of blood and brains. Fear rose and ebbed in me only because no excess can be maintained, and I had seen enough horror.

I became aware of the German again, whose stiffness was yet vigilant. Insensible to the reach of hands to him—they knew he held the power—he still warded our space by the jagged length of his knife, waiting for one more face to appear.

Slowly I tried to crawl back from him, but he held me by the arm until I resumed my slumped kneeling alongside the pit.

"Let me go," I begged. "Let me go."

"Why?"

"Let me go."

His fingers relented so that I cowered away from the hole, and at a distance crouched hiding my face in my arms, where I could weep.

Another long interval passed, until the presence he awaited came forth. I did not look, but I'm sure it was unknown to me, and I would not recall it. He must have taken the knife out then, and there followed the grim feeding into the pit and an exchange of words. All I could hear was his whispered voice, not the other's. Eyes shut behind the childish protection of my hands, I would not look over, but he did ask a question, and I caught the word *sterben*, to die, in it.

I knew that in a pale luminous curtain the dead must be facing him, and how he could speak to them with any measure of control was loathsome to me, because those bloated, hollowed faces, those gaping mouths and eyes drifting up to him should terrify him as they had me.

Let him face them alone, I cringed to myself. Shredded out of life, torn from it, let them wade to him from the hard swamp of death— my men and his alike, men we had never known, men long dead and Achilles himself, were his goodly shade able to raise itself and come bronze-clad to give answer.

When I looked up, God knows how much later, the German had replaced the knife in the soil, deep to the hilt. Across from the pit, the slow tide of the shadows pressed on and was checked, no longer wading. Pleading still, but he had no mercy on them.

There was good reason. Time was folding up again around us in the brief summer night. As a fan that closes, its creases gathered nearer and more arduous to slip through. An awareness of twilight already drew a nacred reflection on the eastern horizon. The German kept fast until the curtain of shades grew thin and faint, less and less visible, until there was nothing left beyond the pit but the bare wall of the mountain.

After he pulled back we sat as men fallen from undiscovered heights, wondering, I am sure, whether we were alive. I could not speak, and at first neither could he. His face was stark and white like a chalk stain in the fading dark—mine surely no less, judging by the way I felt.

The stars had begun to burst like bubbles in the sky when the German tucked the sheep in the hole, and began sweeping dirt on them with his hands. It amazed me that he could move.

"They ought to be skinned and burned, but there's no time."

Even his voice was efficient again. He buried the knife with the sheep and the containers, pressed the dirt over them with his boots. I still simply sat. I watched him reach for the holster belt and without check or hesitation wear it about him.

"I'll take you back to your lines," he said.

I stirred, no differently from one who is awakened and slowly gathers his wits. How cold the hours before morning were, and moist. I stood shivering, with the acute renewed knowledge that I was wearing his loaded gun, which gave me an entirely different advantage from yesterday.

"I think you will," I stammered, to which he said nothing. It was still too dark to see his expression clearly, but he must have wondered at my words. I felt drunk with fatigue, and otherwise empty inside.

All that had passed made us incapable of speaking of it, so a makeshift trite logic ruled over our motions as we set off from the ledge. The day was near breaking, an immense cosmic egg whose fracture could no longer be amazing to us after this night. Colors began to be distinguishable in it, emerging from the gray to help define shapes, distances.

My sense of balance was gone. The German had to help me find my footing down from the ledge. And it was all I could do—haltingly following him along the precipitous path, more perilous in descent, until we regained a less plunging ground and eventually the foothill. I needed to stop, but he would not let me. The way we had followed here with growing expectation and tenseness unfurled in reverse, and there was nothing left of those emotions. He drove me on, for my safety and his, giving us no time to think.

Once more we avoided trenches and redoubts, while the light of day stole upon us clear and unmarred by clouds overhead. Birds called in it. Like any other day at Gallipoli, this might have been a time to die. Shelling was likely to start any minute, we both knew: my tired steps gained machinelike sprint from the thought, while his gait drew long and easy. And comfortingly at my side was the holster, filled with its potential of death.

Past the entrenched piedmont, we trailed back the calvary through destroyed hamlets, abandoned posts, the German two steps ahead of me. His back and the nape of his neck were exposed to me, and when he turned once or twice to see if I followed, the bony and shatterable youth of his face.

We came out to the broken plateau finally, with its jumbles of twisted wire, mined fields. The sun was on the horizon. Orange red, squat, it created shadows endless and blue under rocks, tufts of grass, ourselves. Ravines and *nullahs* lay still filled with night. Whenever we passed a body we both looked away.

In absolute silence the German led, two steps ahead, bareheaded and vulnerable. I planned to undo the flap of the holster before long. In my imagination my fingers had done so many times already, sending him to join the fishlike throng of the dead, so that he should foul himself to drink blood and dirt as my brother had, were anyone ever to summon him. It was vengeance on our impiety, and my own renewed grief. I knew his mind was a captive—even as mine—of the time we had spent by the bloody pit. He could not help it any more than I could. We did not *think* of it: it was in us. And I would kill him as soon as he asked the question.

So we walked extraneous to each other, more than enemies now, myself waiting for a word, he not pronouncing it. Across the embattled ground he chose our steps for us and I accepted that choice, grudgingly, until it occurred to me that he didn't dare ask. Fear or reticence, or even just restraint, kept him from it, or canny wisdom.

And anyway, were I to kill him here and awaken echoes first and other guns right after, who should lead me back to the lines? The thought, until now secondary, came to the fore. And no solution to it. I walked with hand trembling in the belt, anxious to hurt him, impotent before my own danger and unwilling to risk my life to bring him down. Our time grew shorter like our shadows. And this is why I did what I did next, and it is unforgivable perhaps, but took the place of killing him.

"I saw nothing." I prevented his question, more calmly than I could tell the truth.

He looked back at me over his shoulder.

"There was nothing there," I added. "Just the pit and the two of us, and the dead sheep."

He turned his back to me again. His pace hesitated, then resumed the speed he had kept until now to avoid search parties and bombardment. But now he had to escape my doubt as well. I knew how fragile he must feel inside, how dazed and insecure my words must make him.

"I have seen nothing, I tell you."

He would not look at me. I was alerted that we were close to danger when he indicated to me silently what trail to take ahead. We heard Turkish voices to our left from a protected place, and came down to our hands and knees in the dust. I did not stand again until he did.

I should have killed him. Shame for lying tugged at me already, but it was done, and was less honorable than killing. I can justify myself today, and say that unless I were ready to face what I had seen, the truth was too frightening to be shared. I was not ready—would not be for years to come. What I said then was, let *him* kill his doubts for the rest of his days. My mental safety came first. Inner refusal could only feed on open denial. I saved myself thereby, in self-defence. Catching up with his pace, I lightly inquired, "And you, have you found out when you'll die?"

"I didn't ask."

I knew he had. He was aware of my game and played by the rules, without amusement. Now we were lying to each other for good. He told me in the next breath, with a neutral lack of concern, "There was no need to take my gun. You will please give it back now."

The sentence shook me from pretended apathy, because it was impossible that he should know. I had been watching him closely, and not once had he checked his holster, not even felt for it with his hand. How did he know? I swallowed hard at being discovered.

He faced me, so I handed the Luger to him, and he checked the magazine of it and then gave me back my pistol.

There was no more possibility of an exchange between us. In complete silence he brought me back to the spot where we had met, giving me a clipped indication as to the shortest way to the British line. Save for the kinder sky overhead, we could be as we had stood the day before, and nothing have happened in the meanwhile.

"Good-bye," he said, and without delay began retracing his steps until he disappeared in a depression of the upheaved earth, to emerge again but very distant, bound for the hard-held Turkish line.

It took me just over twenty minutes to negotiate my paces to our most advanced post, where I had been given up like the rest of the patrol. Hot coffee awaited me, breakfast and the clumsy congratulations of my companions. I sat and ate, letting them talk me out of distress and anger with the recited list of my lucky circumstances. The triteness of their words paled before their blindness.

"Bloody lucky, Lieutenant, that's what you are!"

"We thought you were gone for good."

"My God, old man, you come back from the dead!"

I never saw the German again. I ignore whether he survived and left Gallipoli, as we Britons did. Beaten back and unable to wrest the peninsula from the Turk, we would be evacuated within four months of that encounter, and the last thing we should see on the shore at night was the high burning piles of material we destroyed not to leave it in enemy hands. They looked like funerary pyres on the waterfront, such as the heroes of old were cremated upon, such as Achilles had been rested over, on the other side of the Hellespont, "so bright a monument as to be seen from men sailing afar."

My brother lay indeed buried by the small *wadi*, and was eventually identified by some items on him, the tag having been blown off his neck chain. But often bodies are identified with delay. Was this enough to ascribe it to what I thought I heard over the bloody pit?

Nothing so great could take place on Achi Baba. What happened that night has ever since been fashioned by me into a near perfect dream. I spent years convincing myself of it: I was young, overwrought, under the pitiless strain of a losing campaign. Who the German was and why he should take me to his sacrifice for the dead, I cannot imagine, nor do I want to.

We were deluded, I have been telling myself these many years. Many strayed off in that war to the strange no-man's-land of illusion, afterwards to find their danger-fraught way back. The dead cannot be so close as to face the living by our offer of grim food, held at bay by the ancient taboo of metal: if they were, then man's existence would be at all times haunted by their silent hunger and hope to be fed.

And our intention was not pure enough for a miracle. The

German wanted power over his future—myself, I sought remembrance. Could we be so self-serving in prying open the frightful chink, and be allowed in? These questions I carry with me, knowing full well that not ever again could I be brought to find out whether it can be done.

What I truly would like to hear from the German is why he did not kill me when he first saw me crumpled on the boulder, because I would have in his stead. I did not kill him only because I meant to save myself through him. It troubles me that he left me in debt, possibly twice in debt. The grudge has only grown longer with time. There's no forgiveness when those we wronged do not avail themselves of vengeance.

And it's unlikely, but were I to return to Gallipoli, the ledge on Achi Baba would be all that I wish to see once more. I'm not sure why. I shouldn't go there by night, but with the light of day it would somehow fill my soul to catch a view of the terraced edge of the mountain, and the copper-bright sea lining the Strait across from Achilles' grave.

COME FLY WITH ME

Before the washing and the spraying, Jerry Bright looked like Woody Allen preparing to play Conan the Barbarian. A tangle of steely-gray hair fell from above his left ear to his shoulder and ran like a curtain around the back of his head to a spot just behind his right ear. From there forward, the hair was trimmed short and neat. The top of Jerry's head was as smooth as a McIntosh apple. Each morning, with his hair still damp but not dripping, he combed the hair above his left ear across his bald spot to the tip of his right ear and hair-sprayed it in place. Next, he combed the hair on the back of his head forward, over his eyes, and sprayed it in place. When the spray set, he placed the index finger on his left hand at his former hairline, swept back the hair hanging over his eyes into a Grecian Pompadour and sprayed it in place. He checked the mirror for skin showing, adjusted as needed, and sprayed again.

The technique had flaws. Wind, rain, and sweat were its greatest enemies. Young punks called Jerry "helmet head," and bald men glared at him, saying with their eyes, "You are so embarrassing."

But Jerry knew he deserved hair, and two days after his fiftieth birthday he decided to get some. He found Biotic Hair, Inc., in *The Miami Herald* sports section, between an ad for a businessmen's health club and a baseball card shop. The ad read: "Biotic Hair, Inc.

Burmese Breakthrough! It's Alive! Call Now!" Jerry did.

Biotic Hair was located on a side street off Hollywood Circle, between a travel agency and a bail bondsman. Jerry stepped from the street into a small reception room. The room smelled of fresh sawdust and carrots. A man he couldn't see sang a Sinatra tune, "Fly me to the moon and let me swing among the stars, let me see what spring is like on Jupiter or Mars. . . ." The guy had a voice. Jerry pushed the button below the handwritten sign, RING FOR SERVICE.

A buzzer sounded, the singing stopped, and a smoked-glass receptionist's window slid open. A round-faced man years younger than Jerry, with a luxurious head of curly brown, graying-at-the-temples hair and sleepy blue eyes looked out at him. "May I help you?"

"Jerry Bright," Jerry said. "I've got an eleven with Mister Anthony."

"That's me," the guy said. He stuck his hand out. "Call me Tony."

Jerry took the man's hand. "Call me Jerry," Jerry said.

"Okay, Jerry. Step back, let me see what we've got."

Jerry backed two steps from the window.

Tony smiled. "Grecian Pompadour. Very nice, except when the wind blows."

"Right," Jerry said. "Or in hot weather or rain."

"Don't I know it," Tony said.

If Tony was wearing a hairpiece, it was the best Jerry had ever seen. Gray temples. Small brown curls on top. No pads or creases showed at the hairline. "That a piece?"

"It's not a piece. It's *my* hair," Tony said, "But, without it, you'd think I was Wayne Huizenga or Uncle Fester from *The Adams Family.*"

"Wow," Jerry said.

"You could have this, too," Tony said.

"How much?"

"Jerry, you're bald. I'm bald. We're brothers. This is not about cost."

"Right," Jerry said, "we're brothers. How much?"

"What if I said ten thousand."

"What if I said three."

"I'd say you were insulting me and my business."

"Five?"

"Seven."

"Sixty-five hundred?"

"Deal," Tony said.

The window slid shut. Jerry heard steps on the other side of the wall. A door at the far end of the room opened.

Tony, dressed in a light blue, short-sleeved nylon smock, white trousers and white loafers with tassels, gestured at Jerry. "Come on, let's get you some hair."

Jerry followed Tony into a closet-sized room with a barber's chair, a mirror mounted on the wall. A neat pile of hair had been swept into one corner. Jerry patted his pockets, wishing for Tums.

"This is where we separate the men from the boys," Tony declared. "I have to cut off your hair."

Jerry looked at himself in the mirror. The Grecian Pompadour looked great.

"I know," Tony said. "It's tough. But to take the next step . . ."

"Do it," Jerry cried. "Do it as quick as you can." He jumped into the chair and stared down at his lap.

Tony draped a sheet over Jerry's shoulders and closed it at his neck. The electric trimmer snapped on. The trimmer's blades were cool and moved quickly across his scalp. He was about to shout, "Stop!" Just as the clippers did stop. He looked up. A hairless, frightened, middle-aged man stared at him from the mirror.

"Don't look," Tony said. "Look at this." He pointed to his own head, then whisked the sheet from around Jerry's neck. "Let's get you some hair."

Jerry followed Tony through another door. The smell of sawdust and carrots grew stronger. Small wire cages were stacked from floor to ceiling against the walls. Hair lay about the cages—shoulder-length red, a gray brush cut, midlength professional brown going gray, chocolate-colored dreadlocks, a jet-black Afro, an aging hip-ster's ponytail, a DA, three rainbow-colored mohawks, a pompadour, a blond shag, a black Caesar, and a brown Nero. Tousled hair, conked hair, permed hair—every style of hair Jerry had ever seen lay in those cages.

"My God," Jerry said.

"Burma," Tony said. "Rootstock captured live. Then bred like dogs. Go figure."

"Right," Jerry said.

A luminescent gold halo, large enough to encircle a man's head, floated in the corner across from the cages.

"Christ," Jerry said, "Is that real?"

Tony glanced over his shoulder and shrugged. "That's not for you. Too much responsibility. Believe me, Jerry—you want hair. Now, you can stick with a natural look. That's the way I went, or you could try something exotic. You Italian?" Tony asked.

Jerry shook his head. "Jewish."

"That's okay. We play each other in movies, and you could do this look. Or, like I said, something exotic."

"Exotic?"

"Yeah. Dreadlocks. An Afro. Ever think of yourself as a redhead?"

"No," Jerry said, "Natural. I want to look like me with hair."

Tony led him across the room to a cage where a steely-gray piece of hair lay on a bed of fresh sawdust. "What do you think of that baby?"

The mat of hair stirred a little.

Jerry whispered, "Is it sleeping?"

"No," Tony said. "It's being hair."

Jerry nodded.

"You want to try it?"

"Yes, please," Jerry said

"Put your hand here." Tony pointed at a bar adjacent to the cage door.

Jerry reached out with his hand and placed his fingertips on the bar.

"No," Tony said. "Hold on tight. Don't move."

Jerry squeezed the bar.

Tony opened the cage door and began singing, "Fly me to the moon and let me . . ." *Sotto voce*, between lyrics, he said, "They love Sinatra."

The hair moved across the cage, crawled out onto Jerry's hand, scuttled up his arm, and settled on his head. Its underside felt warm and soft like a puppy's belly.

Tony gestured toward the mirror. "What do you think?"

Jerry turned, saw his hair mussed and tousled as if he had just woken from a dream. "Can I touch it?"

"Touch it? It's your hair. Here, try this," Tony said, holding out a comb.

A tear rolled down Jerry's cheek. "Thank you, Tony," he said.

"What? It's my job."

Jerry stared at the comb. "How do I take care of it?"

"When it grows too long get a trim. Know any Sinatra tunes?"

"Yeah, sure."

"Sing some every now and then. Sinatra makes your hair happy."

INSOMNIA

Tripod in hand, Sandra Dillon strolls through her neighborhood, ready to take pictures in the dark. Her next show is less than two months away, and she's decided to dedicate the majority of it to night scenes. The gallery has been pestering her to come up with a title, and she's thought of things like "Twilight Dances" and "The Secrets of Night" and others that sound more like titles of supermarket paperbacks, but now she wants to call it "Insomnia." When her husband Jim is on the road to Gary or Indianapolis or Saint Paul, Sandra tiptoes outside with her camera, careful not to make too much noise for fear her next-door neighbor will mistake her for the cat burglar who's robbed two houses on their street in the past month.

"Cat burglar?" Sandra laughed after Jim made her promise to double check all the locks while he was gone. "I thought that was something they only said on old TV shows."

Sandra stands outside her house. The oldies station plays softly through the headphones of her son's Walkman. Above the line of maples and oaks looms a Texaco sign, a twirling red and white star to lure travelers off I-90. When the sign went up years ago, Sandra thought it made their neighborhood seem cheap, but now she no longer minds it; she figures no matter how bad the weather gets she can still see a star. She focuses on it and snaps a series of pictures before walking up the driveway that separates her house from the Millers'.

She gazes across her backyard. Pale moonlight shines on her garage windows and the clothes she's left on the line. A breeze lifts the arm of her husband's shirt. Like the wave of a ghost, she thinks.

"Leader of the Pack" plays through the headphones. Sandra hums along, remembering how she danced to this song when she was a teenager. She'd always thought the doo-wop words were silly, but tonight, the story of a misunderstood boy dying young only makes her sad. She turns the Walkman off and listens to the crickets and katydids instead.

Her son Tommy's grass-stained hightops lie on the patio, their tongues flopping over the laces as if words were frozen in their mouths. Last summer, Tommy cut lawns to put gas in the used car Sandra and Jim bought him for his birthday. Now Jim wears the sneakers to cut the grass even though Sandra wishes he wouldn't.

She steps out of her sandals and walks along the edge of the garden. A rabbit springs from the shadows and darts ahead of her. Every year she loses more of her vegetables to the rabbits. Jim wants to set traps for them, but Sandra has talked him out of it. "They're surviving the only way they know how," she says.

With the cool grass under her feet, she finds herself between the lines of her hanging laundry. She sets up the tripod and adjusts the shutter speed. Pillowcases and blouses bob gently on the breeze, brushing against her skin with the rhythm of soft whispers. From between the clothes, she catches brief glimpses of her neighbors' houses. She hears a muffled sound, like ice breaking on a winter lake, but she figures it's only her imagination. With the clothes fluttering around her, she takes the last shots on her roll.

She works in her darkroom while the rest of the neighborhood sleeps. She glides paper through the developer, watching as images awake in shadow and light. Beneath the red bulb hangs the picture of Tommy she took the week before he died. He stands by the garage, his hair still wet from swim practice as a Christmas Eve snow falls. Despite the closed-in warmth of her darkroom, the chill of that winter day settles in her bones, and she shivers reflexively. Most of the flakes are blurred streaks of white, but around his face a few are caught in perfect focus, like fragile stars orbiting his smile. Sandra stares at the picture, thinking perhaps she's missing something, some detail that might make a difference. Too late, she realizes her print has turned to a sheet of black.

"Happened last night," Kurt Miller says to the knot of neighbors gathered in his driveway. Sandra approaches, squinting in the morning sun. Kurt points to his shattered kitchen window. "Here's where he broke in. Took my new VCR."

Sandra studies the splotches of blood that cross the driveway and disappear into the grass.

"I saw him," Kurt says. His voice, booming the way it used to when he coached Tommy's Pee-Wee Football team, hurts Sandra's ears. "He bolted across the yard like a scared deer, but I gave a good description to the police."

"What did he look like?" Sandra asks.

"Young. Couldn't have been more than twenty. Skinny-like. Tall."

"What time did it happen?" Connie Anderson asks, turning her good ear toward Kurt.

"Just before midnight." He narrows his eyes. "We've got to stop him. We've got to get organized."

Sandra remembers the sound she heard the night before as she took pictures between her hanging clothes. She reaches toward the window and presses lightly on its jagged edge.

"Don't touch that!" Kurt snaps. Sandra's hand shrinks away. "He could have AIDS. Police said he's probably a drug addict. Said he could be dangerous." He turns to the others. "I'm having a meeting Thursday night, see if we can form a neighborhood watch." He places a hand on Sandra's shoulder. "Spread the word, will you? Thursday, seven-thirty."

"Sure," Sandra says absently. "Of course I will."

Later that night, Jim calls from a Holiday Inn in Muncy. "Have you been taking the pills the doctor gave you?" he asks. Jim worries that Sandra's sleepless nights are wearing her down.

"It's just the pressure of the show, Jim." She looks out the window. A grainy light filters between the thick clouds. An interesting night for pictures, she thinks. "I'll be fine once it's over."

After hanging up, she gathers her camera, tripod, and Walkman and strolls through the neighborhood. Honeysuckles perfume the air. Fireflies light the spaces above the wide lawns. Dion and the Belmonts sing "A Teenager in Love." Sandra takes pictures of the red mirrored ball in the Andersons' yard, snaps a close-up of the painted grin on the Gallaghers' lawn jockey.

The lights are out in Kurt Miller's house, and Sandra quietly approaches the window the cat burglar broke. In the moonless night, the blood stains have turned dark purple. Carefully, she eases a shard of glass from the pane. She cradles it in her palm and runs a finger over its dried teardrops of blood before sliding it into her pocket.

She looks toward the tree line. There's only one star left in the sky.

"See that, Mommy?" Tommy would ask when he was learning his alphabet. "That star has a 'T' on it, just like my name."

"Yes, it does," she'd say, scooping him up in her arms and brushing the hair from his eyes. "Mommy put it there just for you."

Sandra swims laps in the town's indoor pool, freestyle one way, a slow backstroke the other. Her new strategy for sleep is to exhaust herself, to deliberately grind her body down until it seizes like an oil-drained engine. She dives off the springboard, and underwater, she's aware of the absence of sound and the distorted images of parents watching their children from the wooden bleachers. When Tommy's team swam their meets here, she sat on the same bleachers, a program twisted tightly in her hands. During his races, she swallowed her self-consciousness and screamed until she went hoarse, synchronizing her cheers with each bob he took for air.

She showers alone in the locker room. Curtains of steam rise around her. In her darkroom, pictures emerge through a white fog like this. She imagines this is how sleep will finally come to her, as if it had welled up from inside, natural and undeniable.

A voice calls through the steam: "Mrs. Dillon?"

Sandra rubs her eyes. "Janet?"

Janet stands in the middle of the shower room. Janet was Tommy's steady, a delicate girl with swirls of teased blonde hair, now wet and tucked behind her ears. Sandra thinks she's beautiful.

"How have you been?" Janet asks. She tugs on a strand of hair. "I've been meaning to stop by, but things are kind of hectic and all."

"You must be excited to start at State." Sandra turns off the shower and reaches for her towel.

"I guess I'm excited," Janet says. "You still taking pictures?"

"Yes."

"That's good."

They nod politely. The shower heads trickle water onto the tiled floor. Sandra wonders if Tommy and Janet ever slept together, unable to make up her mind if she wishes they did or didn't. "Stop by before you leave town," Sandra says. "I've got some pictures of Tommy you can have if you want."

"I will," she says.

As Sandra towels off, she imagines Janet in the future. She will meet a nice boy at State, and on her wedding day, she'll be a beautiful bride. Her children will grow up golden-haired and precious. She will send Christmas cards until the weight of her life swallows Tommy's memory.

Sandra closes her locker and walks out into the bright sunshine, her hair still wet and dripping down her neck.

Sandra drives the lakeside road where Tommy was killed. The road rises and dips between rows of tall pines. From the hilltops, she can see the lake, the moonlight shimmering on its surface like a snowy highway. Fog banks collect at the bottom of the hills, and as she enters them, their wet coolness rushes over her skin.

When she worked for the town newspaper, she once drove out this road to take pictures of an overturned truckload of tomatoes. She couldn't get a sitter for Tommy on such short notice and she spent half the afternoon chasing him while he played among the tomatoes that spotted the roadside like strange wildflowers. Her editor threatened to fire her, saying her prints were too "artsy" for a local paper. Two years later, she used some of the shots in her first show.

Slowly, she approaches the crest of a long hill and pulls onto the shoulder, the loose stones crunching under her tires like broken glass. Moths beat against the headlights. She steps out of the car. The scent of pine reminds her of Christmas. She twists off her lens cap and takes a few shots.

The skid marks, what little there were on the icy road, are gone, washed away by snow and salt and the heavy spring rains. Onion grass tickles her ankles. She runs a finger over the pine with the section of missing bark. She still can't believe it's standing, not after the condition Tommy's car was in. The coroner said Tommy was thrown twenty yards through the windshield, that a seat belt might have saved his life.

Jim was on the road when the State Troopers came, and Sandra was the one who had to identify the body. She did this with quiet dignity, refusing to make a scene in front of the strangers who'd materialized into her night like characters from an awful dream. She asked if she could be alone with her son, and when the door swung shut behind the last nurse, Sandra clasped her hands over Tommy's chest and prayed for his soul. Warm tears streaked her face, but the prayers she'd hoped would bring comfort only made her angrier with a God who wouldn't give a boy so young a second chance.

She passes the Texaco station on her way back to town. Her weary eyes burn, and she tries to blink them back into focus. At the I-90 on-ramp, she slams on the brakes when she mistakes a plastic trash bag for a child darting into the road. The Platters come on the radio, and she calms her nerves by singing along: *Heavenly shades of night are falling, it's twilight time. Out of the mist your voice is calling, it's twilight time.* By the time she pulls into her driveway, the steering wheel is sticky with the pine sap that bled onto her fingers.

Damn him, she thinks as she watches the rabbits nibble in her garden. She throws a stone, sending them scurrying into her neighbors' yards. Damn him for not driving slower, for not wearing his seat belt. Damn the county for not taking care of the roads out there.

In her darkroom, she studies her latest set of proofs. Bathed in the dim red light, Tommy smiles at her from the wall. The shard of glass from Kurt Miller's window is propped on the shelf beneath his picture. As she begins to develop her prints, she has a memory so delicate she wonders if it ever really happened. Tommy was in the backyard, lying down and waving his arms in the snow. Then he started to cry, saying he was afraid that if he got up, he would ruin his snow angel.

"Hold your hand out," Sandra hears herself saying. "Mommy will pull you from the snow."

"I've had these printed up," Kurt says. He passes fliers to the neighbors gathered in his living room. The setting sun throws a brilliant orange on the bay windows. Kurt's wife circulates with a pitcher of iced tea, a tray of peanut butter cookies. The VCR's snipped cables dangle from the wall unit's empty shelf. Above it sits the photo of Kurt and his wife that Sandra took for their thirtieth anniversary.

Spiderweb cracks run along the frame's glass, and Sandra suddenly finds herself wondering why they never had any children.

"Remember this face," Kurt says when the last of the stragglers arrive. "This is the guy who's been robbing us."

Sandra studies the police sketch on the flier. The face is young, with wisps of hair hanging down in a pair of sad eyes. He's no more than a boy, she thinks. Tommy's hair used to get that long, and she suddenly regrets the time they wasted arguing about cutting it.

"I've got a volunteer roster here for a neighborhood watch," Kurt says. "Me and Stu Anderson are signed up for the first week."

Embarrassed, Stu stands and takes an awkward bow.

Kurt goes on, "We'll be patrolling from ten to two every night. We've got a car phone, I'll be handing out our number at the end of the meeting. If you see anything suspicious call 911 and then call us."

Sandra raises her hand. "What'll you do if you run into him?"

"We'll try to scare him off, but if he tries anything slick," Kurt winks at Stu, "we'll be able to take care of ourselves."

Outside, the sun goes down, and the first streetlights wink to life. Sandra's thoughts drift as Kurt continues, trying to imagine how the long-haired stranger saw Kurt's living room—his collection of Conway Twitty albums and the shelf of crystal knickknacks that must have glittered in the shine of his flashlight. "Cat burglar," Kurt repeats, the words snagging like sharp barbs in Sandra's daydreams. "Cat burglar" over and over until it seems as if the boy is here among them, his face just out of view but his presence as certain as the flowered breeze from Kurt's rose garden.

After Jim calls at eleven, Sandra tiptoes out of her house. A car eases down the quiet street, and without thinking, she retreats into the shadows until it passes. It's overcast, and her creaking knees tell her rain isn't far off. Stalks of spearmint sway against the side of her house. The Texaco star spins lazily above the tree line.

She hesitates by Kurt's window. The light from her back porch shines through the broken glass, patterning the curtains with jagged toothed shadows. She zooms in for a close-up and snaps a picture. For a moment, she imagines climbing inside, but instead she leans in closer and looks through the viewfinder. She holds the camera with one hand and touches the glass with the other. She snaps the picture. When she advances the film, she notices a thin stream of blood running across her palm.

Back home, she cleans her cut and wraps her hand in white gauze before going to the darkroom. She listens to the Walkman as she slides prints from the fixer and hangs them to dry. She's especially happy with the series she took between her clotheslines the other night. The forms are billowing and soft, and she decides they'll be perfect for her show. She mouths the words as Dean Parish sings "Tell Him," but she stops halfway through the chorus. Snaring a magnifying glass from the work table, she examines one of the prints, only now noticing the murky figure in the background climbing through Kurt Miller's window.

"Didn't see anything last night," Kurt says. He caulks a new pane of glass into his kitchen window. "What happened to your hand?"

"Nothing," Sandra says. "Cut myself on a broken glass doing the dishes."

"Jim back yet?"

"Saturday."

Kurt levels his finger as if it were a pistol and winks. "We'll be sure to keep an extra eye on your place then."

Sandra walks through the neighborhood, taking pictures of friends working in their yards. With their thoughts troubled by nothing more than crabgrass and slugs, sleep will come easily to them, an uncomplicated surrender that makes her jealous. Last night, she blistered her feet on a six-mile hike to County Line Road and back, but when she got home, she still couldn't rest. Instead, she lay awake until dawn, her muscles knotted and sore, her bloodshot eyes adjusting to the crumbling darkness.

A boy's voice calls out, "Watch it, lady!"

She ducks. A frisbee flies by her head. A boy no older than ten runs by her, picks it up, and hurls it back to his friends. Sandra wonders who these boys are, what parents they belong to. She wishes she could take their picture, but she knows boys are squeamish about things like that.

There was a time when she knew all the boys in the neighborhood. She memorized their names from Tommy's breathless stories and vacuumed the sneaker-patterned dirt clumps they left on her rugs. She was probably in better shape then than at any other time in her life. She was always chasing Tommy and his friends out of the house or away from her garden. Sometimes they came by because they knew she was a willing player if they needed an extra for stickball. She still sees Tommy's friends around town. They're older of course, some even have mustaches and beards, but Sandra still remembers them as children. Willy Strong pumps gas at the Texaco and Brandon Davis is getting ready for his first year at State. Whenever she sees them they always seem to be in such a hurry. They honk as they drive by, leaving her waving at a dwindling car with passengers she can hardly recognize.

That night in her darkroom, she destroys the print with the cat burglar breaking into Kurt Miller's house. Everyone deserves a second chance, she thinks. It will be their secret.

"Damn rabbits are ruining my garden," Kurt says. Dressed in shorts and sandals, he waters his roses. Rainbows shine above the red blossoms. "Pretty evening, isn't it?"

"Sure is," Sandra answers.

The gray of twilight filters between them, turning Kurt's features soft and out of focus. Sandra fears this is how Tommy will someday appear in her memories, as if he were falling away from her into a muddy pool, falling and fading until her only sure recollection is her Christmas Eve photo.

Kurt catches a firefly hovering between them. "No sign of the cat burglar all week," he says.

"Maybe he's moved to another neighborhood."

"He'll be back." Kurt opens his hand. The firefly is crushed in his palm, its light fading from yellow to green before going dark. He flicks it to the ground. "He'll be back and we'll catch him."

Back home, Sandra arranges laundry on her clothesline, trying to recapture the feeling of the pictures she shot before, but she can't get it right. It's too calm, and the shirts simply hang. After Jim's late-night call, she goes back outside and sits on the wet grass, hoping the wind will pick up. Fireflies light around her, an electric snowstorm with her at its center.

She looks up to the Texaco sign, staring at it absently until it seems to float by itself in the sky, until its red and white lights overlap. She rubs her eyes because she no longer sees a star, only shards of broken glass shattered by a blood-red T.

A soft thump interrupts the silence, and she turns to see the long-haired boy squatting among Kurt's trash cans. Sandra shrinks behind a hanging pillowcase, the material cool against her cheek. Her heart drums wildly. The boy rises and creeps across the lawn. His blonde hair is pulled into a ponytail, and Sandra can see his delicate features, the unshaven fuzz on his chin. He comes closer, unaware of her, his sneakers in a quiet trot over a lawn Sandra just now thinks should be cut. When he is less than ten feet away, she steps out from behind the clothesline. The boy stops, and they consider each other, the fireflies blinking between them, their bandaged hands mirroring each other's.

"What you're doing isn't right," Sandra whispers. "They'll catch you if you don't stop."

Her hand trembling, she tries to reach out and brush his cheek, his neck, her fingertips almost meshing with the soft strands of his ponytail.

The boy bolts across the lawn, and Sandra lights out behind him, chasing him into the deserted street. Her camera drops, the glass of her lens shattering. There's no way she can keep up with him, his form dwindling as he passes beneath the block's streetlight cones, yet she tries, willing every bit of strength into her pumping knees, running until he's swallowed by the dark.

HUNGER,
AN INTRODUCTION

I have a sturdy first sentence all prepared, and as soon as I settle down and get used to the reversal of our usual roles I'll give you the pleasure. Okay. Here goes. *Considering that everyone dies sooner or later, people know surprisingly little about ghosts.* Is my point clear? Every person on earth, whether saint or turd, is going to wind up as a ghost, but not one of them, I mean, of *you*, people, knows the first thing about them. Almost everything written, spoken or imagined about the subject is, I'm sorry, absolute junk. It's disgusting. I'm speaking from the heart here, I'm laying it on the line— disgusting. All it would take to get this business right is some common, everyday, sensible thinking, but sensible thinking is easier to ask for than to get, believe you me.

I see that I have already jumped my own gun, because the second sentence I intended to deliver was: *In fact, when it comes to the subject of ghosts, human beings are completely clueless.* And the third sentence, after which I am going to scrap my prepared text and speak from the heart, is: *A lot of us are kind of steamed about that.*

For! The most common notion about ghosts, the granddaddy, the one that parades as grown-up reason, shakes its head, grins, fixes you with a steely glint that asks if you're kidding, says—Ghosts don't exist.

Wrong.

Sorry, wrong.

Sorry, I know, you'd feel better if you could persuade yourself that accounts of encounters with beings previously but not presently alive are fictional. Doesn't matter how many people say they have seen a woman in black moving back and forth behind the window from which in 1892 the chambermaid Ethel Carroway defenestrated a newborn infant fathered by a seagoing rogue named Captain Starbuck, thousands of fools might swear to having seen Ethel's shade drag itself past that window, it don't, sorry, it doesn't matter, they're all deluded. They saw a breeze twitch the curtain and imagined the rest. *They want you to think they're interesting.* You're too clever for that one. You know what happens to people after they chuck it, and one thing that's sure is, they don't turn into ghosts. At the moment of death, people either (1) depart this and all other possible spheres, leaving their bodies to fade out in a messier, more time-consuming fashion; or (2) leave behind the poor old skinbag as their immortal part soars heavenward, rejoicing, or plummets wailing to eternal torment; or (3) shuffle out of one skinbag, take a few turns around the celestial block and reincarnate in a different, fresher skinbag, thereupon starting all over again. Isn't that more or less the menu? Extinction, moral payback or rebirth. During my own life, for example, I favored (1), a good clean departure.

Now we come to one of my personal bugaboos or I could say anathemas, in memory of someone I have to bring in sooner or later anyhow, my former employer, Mr. Harold McNair, a gentleman with an autodidact's fondness for big words. Mr. McNair once said to me, *Dishonesty is my particular anathema.* One other time, he used the word *peculation.* Peculation was his anathema, too. Mr. Harold McNair was confident of his personal relationship to his savior, and as a result he was also pretty confident that what lay ahead of him, after a dignified leave-taking in the big bed on the third floor, was a one-way excursion to paradise. As I say, he was pretty sure about that. Maybe now and then the thought came to him that a depraved, greedy, mean-spirited weasel like himself might have some trouble squeaking through the pearly gates, no matter how many Sundays he strutted over to the church on Abercrombie Road to lip-synch to the hymns and nod over the sermon—yes, maybe Harold McNair had more doubts than he let on. When it came down to what you have to call the crunch, he did not go peacefully. How he went was screeching and sweating and cursing, trying to shield his head from the hammer and struggling to get back on his feet, for all the world as though he feared spending eternity as a rasher of bacon. And if asked his opinion on the existence of ghosts, this big-shot retail magnate would probably have nodded slowly, sucked his lower lip, pondered mightily and opined—

All right, I never actually heard the position of my former employer in re ghostly beings despite our many, ofttimes tediously lengthy colloquies. Harold McNair spoke to me of many things, of the anathemas dishonesty and peculation, of yet more anathemas including the fair sex, any human being under the age of twenty, folk of the Hebraic, Afric or Papist persuasions, customers who demand twenty minutes of a salesman's attention and then sashay out without making a purchase, customers—*female* customers—who return undergarments soiled by use, residents of California or New York, all Europeans, especially bogtrotters and greaseballs, eggheads, per-fessers, pinkos, idiots who held hands in public, all music but the operettas of Gilbert & Sullivan, all literature not of the "improving" variety, tight shoes, small print, lumpy potatoes, dogs of any descrip-tion and much else. He delivered himself so thoroughly on the top-ics which excited his indignation that he never got around to describ-ing his vision of the afterlife, even while sputtering and screeching as the hammer sought out the tender spots on his tough little noggin. Yet I know what Mr. McNair would have said.

Though ghosts may fail to be nonexistent, they are at least com-fortingly small in number.

Wrong. This way of thinking disregards the difference between Ghosts Visible, like poor Ethel Carroway, who dropped that baby from the fourth-floor window of the Oliphant Hotel, and Invisible, which is exactly like pretending there is no difference between Living Visibles, like Mr. Harold McNair, and Living Invisibles—in spite of everything the way I was back then—not to mention most everyone else, when you get down to it. Most people are about as visible to others as the headlines on a week-old newspaper.

I desire with my entire heart to tell you what I am looking at, I yearn to describe the visible world as seen from my vantage point beside the great azalea bush on my old enemy's front lawn on Tulip Lane, the spot I head for every day at this time. That would clear up this whole *numbers* confusion right away. But before I can get into describing what I can see, I must at last get around to introducing myself, since that's the point of my being here today.

Francis T. Wardwell is my handle, Frank Wardwell as I was known, and old Frank can already feel himself getting heated up over third numbskull idea the run of people have about ghosts, so he better take care of that one before going any further. The third idea is: Ghosts are ghosts because they are unhappy. Far too many of you out there believe that every wandering spirit is atoning for some old heart-stuffed misery, which is why they suppose Ethel drifts past that window now and again.

Ask yourself, now. Is anything that simple, even in what *you* call experience? Are all the criminals in jail? Are all the innocent free? And if the price of misery is misery, what is the price of joy? In what coin do you pay for that, laddy: shekels, sweat or sleepless nights?

Though in every moment of my youthful existence I was sustained by a most glorious secret that was mine alone, I too was acquainted with shekels, sweat and what the poets call white nights. No child of luxury, I. Francis Wardwell, Frank to his chums, born to parents on the

ragged-most fringe of the lower middle class, was catapulted into cor-
poreality a great distance from the nearest silver spoon. We were
urban poor (lower middle-class poor, that is), not rural poor, and I feel
deeply within myself that a country landscape such as that of which I
was deprived would have yielded to my infant self a fund of riches
sorely needed. (Mark the first sounding of the hunger theme, to
which we will return betimes.) Is not Nature a friend and tutor to the
observant child? Does it not offer a steady flow of stuff like psychic
nutrient to the developing boy? Experts say it does, or so I hear, and
also that much do I recall from my reading, which was always far, far
in advance of my grade level. (I was reading on the *college level* before
I was out of short pants.) Old-time poets all said Nature is a better
teacher than any other. In my case, blocked off by city walls from the
wise friend Nature, I was forced to feed my infant mind on the
harsher realities of brick, barbed wire and peacock-feather oil slicks.
That I went as far as I did is testimony to my resilient soul-strength.
Forbidden was I to wander 'mongst the heather and cowslips, the fox-
gloves, purple vetch, tiger lilies, loosestrife and hawkweed on country
lanes; no larks or thrushes had I for company, and we never even
heard of nightingales where I came from. I wandered, when I had that
luxury—that is when I wasn't running my guts out to get away from a
long-nosed, red-eyed, smirking Boy Teuteburg—through unclean city
streets past taverns and boarding houses, and for streaky gold-red sunsets I had neon signs. The air was not, to put it good and plain, fresh.
The animals, when not domestic, were rodentine. And from the seventh grade on, at a time when I suffered under the tyranny of a ter-
maganty black-haired witch-thing named Missus Barksdale who
hated me because I knew more than she did, I was forced to endure
the further injustice of after-school employment. Daily had I to
trudge from the humiliations delivered upon my head by the witch-
thing, Missus Barfsbottom—humiliations earned only through an
inability to conceal entirely the mirth her errors caused in me—from

sadistic, unwarranted humiliations delivered upon the head of one of the topmost scholars ever seen at that crummy school, then to trudge through sordiosities to the place of my employment, Dockweder's Hardware, where I took up my broom and swept, swept, swept.

For shekels! In the sense of measly, greasy coins of low denomination in little number! Earned by my childish sweat, the honest sorrowful perspiration, each salty drop non-accidentally just exactly like a tear (and that, Miss Doggybreath, is what you call a metaphor, not a methapor, as your warty mustachy cake-hole misinformed the massed seventh grade of the Daniel Webster State Graded School in the winter of 1928), of a promising, I mean really and truly *promising* lad, an intelligent lad, a lad deserving of the finest this world had to offer in the way of breaks and opportunities, what you might want to call and I looking back am virtually forced to call a Shining Boy!

Who day and night had to check over his shoulder for the approach of, who had to strain his innocent ears in case he could hear the footfalls of, who was made to quench his glorious shining spirit because he had to live in total awful fear of the subhuman, soulless, snakelike figure of, Boy Teuteburg. Who would crouch behind garbage cans and conceal himself in doorways, was a lurker in alleys, would drag at his narrow cigarette with his narrow shoulders against the bricks and squint out from under the narrow brim of the cap on his narrow head, was a low being of no conscience or intelligence or any other merits altogether. A Boy Teuteburg is a not a fellow for your flowery fields and rending sunsets. And such as this, a lowly brutal creature with no promise to him at all save the promise to wind up in jail, became yet another, perhaps the most severe, bane of the Shining Boy's existence.

Between Daniel Webster State Graded School and Dockweder's Hardware Emporium would this young terrorist lurk of an afternoon, stealing some worthless tit-bit there, hawking on the sidewalk there, blowing his nose by pressing two fingers against one nostril, leaning over and firing, then repeating the gesture on the opposite side, all the while skulking along, flicking his puny red eyes over the passing throng (as *Dickens* had it) in search of children younger than he, any children in actual fact, but in most especial one certain child. This, you may have divined, was yours truly. I knew myself the object of Boy Teuteburg's special hatred because of what befell the child-me on those occasions when I managed to set sail from one place to another in convoy with other kidlings of my generation — other sparrows of the street (as *Blake* might put it) — to subsume myself within the shelter of a nattering throng of classmates. We all feared Boy, having suffered under his psychotic despotism through year after year of grade school. Our collective relief at his eventual graduation (he was sixteen!) chilled to dread when we discovered that his release from the eighth grade meant only that Boy had been freed to prowl eternally about Daniel Webster, a shark awaiting shoals of smaller fishes. (A *simile*, Missus Doggybark, a *simile*.) There he was, smirking as he tightened his skinny lips to draw on his skinny cigarette — circling. Let us say our convoy of joking lads rounds the corner of Erie Street by the Oliphant Hotel and spreads across the sidewalk as we carry on toward third street, home for some, Dockweder's and the broom for me. Then a stoaty shadow separates from the entrance of Candies & Newsagent, a thrill of fear passes through us, red eyes ignite and blaze, some dreary brat begins to weep, and the rest of us scatter as boy charges, already raising his sharp and pointy fists. And of all these larking children, which particular boy was his intended target? That child least like himself — the one he hated most — myself — and I knew why. Scatter though I would 'mongst my peers, rushing first to this one then to that, my friends, their morality stunted by the same brutal landscape which had shaped our tormentor, would'st thrust me away, abandon me, sacrifice me for their own ends. It was me, I mean I, he searched out, and we all knew it. Soon the others refused to leave the school in my presence, and I walked alone once more.

Oft were the days when the body that wielded the broom ached with bruises, when the eyes within the body were dimmed with tears of pain and sorrow, and the nose of the body contained screws of tissue paper within each nostril, purpose of, to staunch the flow of blood.

Oft, too, were the nights when from a multiplicity of causes young Frank Wardwell lay sleepless a-bed. His concave boyish tummy begged for sustenance, for the evening repast may have been but bread and sop, and the day's beating meant that certain much-favored positions were out of the question. Yet hunger and pain were as nothing when compared to the primary reason sleep refused to grant its healing balm. This was terror. Day came when night bowed out, and day brought Boy Teuteburg. So fearsome was my tormentor that I lay paralyzed 'neath my blankets, hoping without hope that I might the next day evade my nemesis. Desperate hours I spent mapping devious alternate routes from school to store while still knowing well that however mazy the streets I took, they would in the end but deliver me unto Boy. And many times I sensed that he had glided into our yard and stood smoking beneath our tree, staring red-eyed at my unlighted window. Other times, I heard him open our back door and float through the kitchen to hover motionless outside my door. What good now was my intellectual and spiritual superiority to Boy Teuteburg? Of what use my yearnings? Ice-cold fear was all I knew. Mornings, I dragged myself from bed, quaking opened my door to find Boy of course nowhere in sight, fed my ice-cold stomach a slice of bread and a glass of water, and dragged myself to school, hopeless as the junkman's nag.

Had I but known of the thousand eyes upon me . . .

Why does Ethel Carroway report to her window on the fourth floor of the Oliphant Hotel at the full of the moon? Guilt? Grief? Remorse?

In life, this was a thoughtless girl, vibrant but shallow, the epitome of a Visible, who felt no more of guilt than does a cast-iron pump. For a month, Ethel had gone about her duties in loose overblouses to conceal her condition, of which even her slatternly friends were ignorant. The infant signified no more than a threat to her employment. She never gave it a name or fantasized about it or thought of it with ought but distaste. Captain Starbuck had departed the day following conception, in any case a hasty, rather *scuffling* matter, no doubt to sow his seed in foreign ports. Delivery took place behind the locked door of Ethel's basement room and lasted approximately twelve hours, during which she had twice to shout from her bed that she was violently ill and could not work. During the process, she consumed much of a bottle of bourbon whisky given her by another priapic guest of the Oliphant. When at last the child bullied its way out between her legs, Ethel bit the umbilicus in two and observed that she had delivered a boy. Its swollen purple genitals were a vivid reminder of Captain Starbuck. Then she passed out. An hour later, consciousness returned on a tide of pain. Despite all, Ethel felt a curious new pride in herself—in what she had done. Her baby lay on her chest, uttering little kittenish mewls. It resembled a monkey, or a bald old man. She found herself regretting that she had to dispose of this creature who had brought her so much pain. They had shared an experience that now seemed almost hallucinatory in its intensity. She wished the baby were the kitten it sounded like, that she might keep it. She and the baby were companions of a sort. And she realized that it was hers—she had made this little being.

Yet her unanticipated affection for the infant did not alter the facts. Ethel needed her job, and that was that. The baby had to die. She moved her legs to the side of the bed, and a fresh wave of pain made her gasp. Her legs, her middle, the bed, all were soaked in blood. The baby mewed again, and more to comfort herself than it, she slid the squeaking child upward toward her right breast and bumped the nipple against his lips until he opened his mouth and tried to suck. Like Ethel, the baby was covered with blood, as well as with something that resembled grease. At that moment she wanted more than anything else to wash herself off. She wanted to wash the baby, too. At least he could die clean. She transferred him to her other breast, which gave no more milk than the first. When she stroked his body, some of the blood and grease came off on her hand, and she wiped his back with a clean part of the sheet.

Some time later, Ethel swung her feet off the bed, ignored the bolts of pain and stood up with the baby clamped to her bosom. Grimacing, she limped to the sink and filled it with tepid water. Then she lowered the baby into the sink. As soon as his skin met the water, his eyes flew open and appeared to search her face. For the first time, she noticed that their color was a violent purple-blue, like no other eyes she had ever seen. The infant was frowning magisterially. His legs contracted under him like a frog's. His violent eyes glowered up at her, as if he knew what she was ultimately going to do, did not at all like what she was going to do, but accepted it. As she swabbed him with the washcloth, he kept frowning up at her, scanning her face with his astonishing eyes.

Ethel considered drowning him, but if she did so, she would have to carry his body out of the hotel, and she didn't even have a suitcase. Besides, she did not enjoy the idea of holding him under the water while he looked up at her with that funny old-king frown. She let the water drain from the sink, wrapped the baby in a towel and gave herself a rudimentary sponge-bath. When she picked the baby off the floor, his eyes flew open again, then closed as his mouth gaped in an enormous yawn. She limped back to bed, tore the sheets off one-handed, cast a blanket over the mattress and fell asleep with the baby limp on her chest.

It was still dark when Ethel awakened, but the quality of the darkness told her that it would soon be morning. The baby stirred. Its arms, which had worked free of the towel, jerked upward, paused in the air and drifted down again. This was the hour when the hotel was still, but for the furnace-man. The hallways were empty; a single sleepy clerk manned the desk. In another hour, the bootboys would be setting out the night's polished shoes, and a few early-bird guests would be calling down their room-service orders. In two hours, a uniformed Ethel Carroway was supposed to report for duty. She intended to do this. When it became noticed that she was in pain, she would be allowed another day's sick leave, but report she must. She had approximately forty-five minutes in which to determine what to do with the baby and then to do it.

A flawless plan came to her. If she carried the baby to the service stairs, she would avoid the furnace-man's realm, and once on the service stairs, she could go anywhere without being seen. The hallways would remain empty. She could reach one of the upper floors, open a window and—let the baby fall. Her part in his death would be over in an instant, and the death itself would be a matter of a second, less than a second, a moment too brief for pain. Afterward, no one would be able to connect Ethel Carroway with the little corpse on the Erie Street pavement. It would seem as though a guest had dropped the baby, or as though an outsider had entered the hotel to rid herself of an unwanted child. It would be a mystery: a baby from nowhere, fallen from the Oliphant Hotel. Police Are Baffled.

She pulled on a night dress and wrapped herself in an old hotel bathrobe. Then she swaddled her child in the towel and silently left her room. On the other side of the basement, the furnace-man snored on his pallet. Gritting her teeth, Ethel limped to the stairs.

The second floor was too low, and the third seemed uncertain. To be safe, she would have to get to the fourth floor. Her legs trembled, and spears of pain shot through the center of her body. She was weeping and groaning when she reached the third floor, but for the sake of the baby forced herself to keep mounting the stairs. At the fourth floor, she opened the door to the empty, gas-lit hallway and leaned panting against the frame. Sweat stung in her eyes. Ethel staggered into the corridor and moved past numbered doors until she reached the elevator alcove. Opposite the closed bronze doors, two large casement windows looked out onto Erie Street. She hugged the baby to her chest, struggled with a catch and pushed the window open.

Cold air streamed in, and the baby tugged his brows together and scowled. Impulsively, Ethel kissed the top of his lolling head, then settled her waist against the ridge at the bottom of the casement. She gripped the baby beneath his armpits, and the towel dropped onto her feet. The baby drew up his legs and kicked, as if rejecting the cold. A bright, mottled pink covered his face like a rash. His mouth was a tiny red beak. One of his eyes squeezed shut. The other slid sideways in a gaze of unfocussed reproach.

Gripping his sides, Ethel extended her arms and moved his kicking body through the casement. She could feel the thin, sturdy ribs beneath his skin. The bottom of the frame dug into her belly. Ethel took a sharp inhalation and prepared to let go by loosening her grip. Instantly, unexpectedly, he slipped through her hands and dropped into the darkness. For a moment briefer than a second, she leaned forward, open-mouthed.

What happened to her in the moment she watched her baby fall away toward the Erie Street sidewalk is the reason Ethel Carroway returns to the window on the fourth floor of the Oliphant Hotel.

A doorman found the dead infant half an hour later. By the start of the morning shift, the entire staff knew that someone had thrown a baby from an upper window. Policemen went from room to room and in a maid's basement chamber came upon an exhausted young woman stuffing bloody sheets into a pillowcase. Despite her denials of having recently given birth, she was arrested and given a medical examination. At her trial, she was condemned to death, and in April,

1893, Ethel Carroway departed from her earthly state at the end of a hangman's rope.

During the next two decades, several fourth-floor guests at the Oliphant remarked a peculiar atmosphere in the area of the elevators: some found it unpleasantly chilly even in the dog days, others said it was overheated in winter, and Nelly Tetrazelli, "The Golden Thrush," an Italian mezzo-soprano touring the northern States with a program of songs related to faery legend, complained that a "nasty, nasty porridge" in the elevator alcove had constricted her voice. In 1916, the Oliphant went out of business. For three years, the hotel steadily deteriorated until new owners took it over and ran it until 1930, when they went broke and sold the building for use as a boarding school for young women. The first sightings of a ghostly figure on the fourth floor were made by students of the Erie Academy For Girls; by 1948, when the Academy closed its doors, local lore had supplied the name of the spectral figure, and a year later, when the Oliphant opened yet again, Ethel Carroway began putting in regular appearances, not unlike Nelly Tetrazelli, "The Golden Thrush." Over the decades, she acquired a modest notoriety. The Oliphant devotes a long paragraph of its brochure to the legend, an undoubtedly idealized portrait of the revenant hangs above the lobby fireplace, and a bronze plaque memorializes the site of the crime. Guests with amateur or professional interests in the paranormal have often spent weeks in residence, hoping for a glimpse, a blurry photograph, a sonic, tape-recorded rustle. (None have ever been granted their wish.)

Ethel Carroway does not reappear before her window to increase her fame. She does it for another reason altogether. She's hungry.

I have told you of bad Boy and the thousand eyes fixed upon the Shining Boy, and alluded to a secret. In the same forthright manner with which I introduced myself, I shall now introduce the matter of the wondrous secret, by laying it out upon the methaporical table.

All throughout my life I possessed a crystalline but painful awareness of my superiority to the common man. To put it squarely: I understood that I was better than the others. Just about *all* the others.

A fool may say this and be ridiculed. A madman may say it and be Bedlamized. What befalls the ordinary-seeming mortal whose great gifts, not displayed by any outward show, he dares proclaim? He risks the disbelief and growing ire of his peers, in humbler words, spitballs, furtive kicks and knocks, whispered obscenities and shoves into muddy ditches, that's what. Yet —and this must be allowed—*that the mortal in question is superior has already aroused ire and even hatred amongst those who have so perceived him.* Why was I the focus of Boy Teuteburg's psychopathic rage? And why did my fellow-kidlings not defend me from our common enemy? *What inflamed our enemy, Boy, chilled them.* It would have been the same had I never generously taken pains to illuminate their little errors, had I never pressed home the point by adding, *and I know this because I'm a lot smarter than you are.* They already knew the deal. They had observed my struggle to suppress my smiles as I instructed our teachers in their numerous errors, and surely they had likewise noted the inner soul-light within the precocious classmate.

Now I know better than to speak of these matters (save in privileged conditions such as these). In my midtwenties I gave all of that up, recognizing that my life had become a catastrophe, and that the gifts which so elevated me above the run of mankind (as the protagonists of the great *Poe* know themselves raised up) had not as it were elevated my outward circumstances accordingly. The inward soul-light had dimmed and guttered, would no longer draw the attacks of the envious. Life had circled 'round and stolen what was most essentially mine.

Not all ghosts are dead, but only the dread can be counted on for twenty-twenty vision. You only get to see what's in front of your nose when it's too late to do you any good.

At that point, enter hunger.

. . .

My life had already lost its luster before I understood that the process of diminishment had begun. Grade school went by in the manner described. My high school career, which should have been a four-year span of ever-increasing glories culminating in a 4.0 average and a full scholarship to a Harvard or even a College of William and Mary, ground into a weary pattern of Cs and Ds hurled at me by fools incapable of distinguishing the creative spirit from the glib, mendacious copycat. In his freshman year, young Frank Wardwell submitted to the school literary magazine under the pen name "Orion" three meritorious poems, all of which were summarily rejected on the grounds that several of their nobler phrases had been copied down from poets of the Romantic movement. Did the poets own these phrases, then? And would then a young chap like Frank Wardwell be forbidden to so much as *utter* these phrases in the course of literary conversations such as he never had, due to the absence of like-minded souls? Yes, one gathers, to the editors of a high-school literary magazine.

I turned to the creation of a private journal in which to inscribe my exalted thoughts and far-flung imaginings. But the poison had already begun its deadly work. Brutal surroundings and moral isolation had robbed my pen of freshness, and much of what I committed to the page was mere lamentation for my misunderstood and friendless state. In coming from the depths to reach expression, the gleaming heroes with cascading blond hair of my high-arching thoughts met the stultifying ignorance about me and promptly shriveled into gap-toothed dwarves. The tales with which I had vowed to storm this world's castles and four-star hotels refused to take wing. I blush to remember how, when stalled in the midst of what was to be a furious vision of awe and terror, my talent turned not to Great imagination for its forms but to popular serials broadcast at the time over the radio waves. "The Green Hornet" and "Jack Armstrong, the All-American

213

Boy," my personal favorites among these, supplied many of my plots
and even, I grant, some of my less pungent dialogue.

A young person suffering the gradual erosion of his spirit cannot
fully be aware of the ongoing damage to his being. Some vestige of
the inborn wonder will beat its wings and hope for flight, and I saw
with weary regularity the evidence that I was as far superior to my fellow students at Edna Ferber High as I had been at Daniel Webster
State Graded School. As before, my well-intentioned and instructive
exposures of intellectual errors earned me no gratitude. (Did you
really imagine, Tubby Shanks, you of the quill-like red hair and car-
buncled neck who sat before me in Sophomore English, that Joyce
Kilmer, immortal author of "Trees," was necessarily of the female
gender for the sole reason that your mother and sister shared his
Christian name? My rapier-like witticism that Irish scribe James
Joyce must then be a sideshow morphadite did not deserve the blow
you addressed to my sternum, nor the wad of phlegm deposited atop
my desk at close of day.) True, I had no more to fear the raids of Boy
Teuteburg, who had metamorphosed into a sleek ratty fellow in a
tight black overcoat and pearl grey snapbrim hat and who, by reason
of constant appointments in pool halls, the back rooms of taverns
and the basements of garages, had no time for childish pursuits. Dare
I say I almost missed the attentions of Boy Teuteburg? Almost longed
for the old terror he had aroused in me? That his indifference, what
might even have been his lack of recognition, awakened nameless
but unhappy emotions on the few occasions when we ancient enemies caught sight of one another, me, sorry, I mean I dragging
through our native by-ways at the end of another hopeless day at
Edna Ferber, he emerging from an Erie Street establishment known
as Jerry's *Hotcha!* Lounge, then his narrow still-red eye falling on
mine but failing to blaze (though the old terror did leap within me,
that time), then my immemorial foe sliding past without a word or
gesture to mark the momentous event? At such times even the dull

being I had become felt the passing of a never-to-be-recovered soul-state. Then, I had known of my preeminence and nurtured myself upon it; now, knowing of it still, I knew it did not make an ounce of difference. Boy Teuteburg had become a more consequential person than Francis T. Wardwell. I had seen the shades of the prison-house lowered 'til nearly all the light was blocked.

Soon after the unmarked momentousness, two other such yanked them all the way down.

After an unfortunate incident at school, admittedly not the first of its kind, involving the loss of a petty sum on the order of six or seven dollars from a handbag left hanging on a lunchroom chair, the meaningless coincidence of my having been seated adjacent to the chair from which hung the forgotten reticule somehow led to the accusation that I was the culprit. It was supposed, quite falsely and with no verification whatsoever, that I had also been responsible for the earlier incidents. I defended myself as any innocent party does, by declining to respond to the offensive accusations. I did possess a small, secret store of money, and when ordered to repay the careless slattern who had been the real source of the crime, I withdrew the wretched seven dollars from this source.

Humiliated, I chose to avoid the hostile stares and cruel taunts surely to greet me in our school's halls, so for some days I wandered the streets, squandering far too many quarters from my precious cache in diners and movie theaters when supposed to be in class, then reporting as ever to Dockweder's Hardware, where having passed down my broom to a shifty urchin of unclean habits, I was entrusted with the stocking of shelves, the fetching of merchandise to the counter, and during the generally inactive hour between 4:30 P.M. and 5:30 P.M., the manipulation of the cash register. After the fifth day of my self-imposed suspension from academe, Mr. Dockweder kept me after work as he ostentatiously balanced the day's receipts, the first time I had ever seen him do so, found the *awesome,* the *majestic* sum of $1.65 missing from the cash tray and immediately charged me with the theft. Not the boyish mistake of returning a surplus of change to an impatient customer or hitting a wrong button when ringing up a sale, but the theft. I protested, I denied, alas in vain. Then look to the boy, I advised, I believe he steals from the stock room, too, fire him and the pilfering will cease. As if he had forgotten my seven years of unstinting service, Mr. Dockweder informed me that sums of varying amounts had been missing from the register many nights during the period when I had been entrusted with its manipulation between the hours of 4:30 P.M. and 5:30 P.M. He demanded I turn out my pockets. When I did so, he smoothed out one of the three bills in my possession and indicated on its face the check mark he had placed upon each bill in the register before entrusting it to my charge.

In all honesty, check marks are entered upon dollar bills hundreds of times a day, and for hundreds of reasons. I have seen every possible sort of symbol used to deface our nation's currency. Mr. Dockweder, however, would accept none of my sensible explanations. He insisted to bring me home, and gripped my shoulder in an iron clamp as we took to the streets. Within our shabby dwelling, he denounced me. My denials went unheard. In fact, I was trembling and sweating and undergoing a thousand torments, for once or twice I had dipped into the register and extracted a quarter, a dime, a penny or two, coins I assumed would never be missed and with which I could sustain myself through the long day. I even *confessed* these paltry lapses, thinking to improve the situation with a show of honest remorse, but this fearless candor did nothing of the kind. After remunerating Dockweder from his own skimpy reserve of cash, my father announced that I personally would make good the (inflated) sum and must henceforth clear my head of nonsense and learn the ways of the real world. He was sick of my airs and highfalutin' manners, sick of my books, sick of the way I talked—sick of me. From that day forth I should work. As a dumb beast works (my father, an alcoholic welder, being a prime example of the species), without hope, without education, without letup, without meaning and with no reward save an inadequate weekly pay-packet.

Reeling from the depth and swiftness of my fall, that evening after the welder and his weeping spouse had retired I let myself out of our hovel and staggered through the darkness. What I had been, I scarcely knew; what I now was, I could not bear to contemplate; what I was to become, I could not imagine. On all sides life's prison-house rose up about me. In that prison-house lay a grave, and within that grave lay I. The streets took me, where I knew or cared not. At intervals I looked up to behold a dirty wall, a urine stain belt-high beneath a broken warehouse window, a mound of tires in a vacant lot. These things were *emblems*. Once I glimpsed a leering moon; once I heard the shuffle of feet close by and stopped in terror, sensing mortal danger, and looked all round at empty Erie Street.

Bitterly, childhood's stillborn fantasies returned to me, their former glow now corpse-gray. Never would I kneel in meadows and woods 'midst bird's-foot trefoil, daisy fleabane, devil's pulpit, Johnny-jump-up, jewelweed, the foxglove and the small sundrop. Never would I bend an enchanted ear to the lowing of the kine, the tolling of bells in a country rectory, the distant call of the shepherd, the chant of the lark. Mountain lakes and mountain streams would never enfold me in their chill, breath-giving embrace. The things I was to know were but *emblems* of the death-in-life ranged 'round me now.

I lifted my all-but-unseeing eyes to the facade, six stories high, of the Oliphant Hotel, dark dark dark. Above the lobby dimly visible through the great glass doors, the ranks of windows hung dark and empty in the darker brick. Behind those windows slept men and women endowed with college degrees and commercial or artistic skills, owners of property, sojourners in foreign lands, men and women on the inside of life. They would never know my name nor

would I ever be one of their Visible number. Radiantly Visible themselves, they would no more take note of me by daylight than at present—and if they happened to look my way, would see nothing!

A figure moved past an upper window, moved back and then reap-
peared behind the window. Dark dark dark. A guest, I imagined,
wandering sleepless in the halls, and thought to turn away for my
long journey home. Some small awareness held me, looking up.
High above behind a casement window hovered a figure in black
garb, that figure, I now observed, unmistakably a woman's. What was
she doing, why was she there? Some trouble had sent one of the
gilded travelers roaming the Oliphant, and on that trouble she
brooded now, pausing at the window. Recognizing a fellow-being in
misery akin to my own, I brazenly stepped forward and stared up,
silently demanding this woman to acknowledge that, despite all that
separated and divided us, we were essentially the same. White hands
twisted within her black garment. We were the same, our world the
same, being dark dark dark. Perhaps the woman would beckon to
me, that we each could soothe the shame of the other. For streaming
from her vague figure was shame—so I thought. An oval face
emerged from shadow or from beneath a hood and neared the glass.

You shall see me, you shall, I vowed, and stepped forward once
again. The alabaster face gazed at a point some five feet nearer the
hotel than myself. I moved to meet her gaze, and just before doing
so experienced a hopeless terror far worse than anything Boy
Teuteburg had ever raised in me. Yet my body had begun to move
and would not stop when the mind could not command it. Two
mental events had birthed this sick dread: I had seen enough of the
alabaster face to know that what I had sensed streaming out was
something far, far worse than shame; and I had suddenly remembered what the first sight of this figure at this window of this hotel
would have recalled had I been in my normal mind—the legend of
the ghost in the Oliphant. Ethel Carroway's eyes locked on mine and

scorched my innards. I could not cry out, I could not weep, with throat constricted and eyes singed. For a tremendous moment I could not move at all, but stood where her infant had fallen to the pavement and met her ravishing, her *self-ravishing* gaze. When it was over—when she released me—I turned and ran like a dog whom wanton boys had set on fire.

The following day my father commanded me to go to McNair's Fine Clothing and Draperies and enquire after a full-time position. He had recently done some work for Mr. Harold McNair, who had spoken of an opening available to an eager lad. Now that my circumstances had changed, I must try to claim this position and be grateful for the opportunity, if offered. I obeyed the paternal orders. Mr. Harold McNair had indeed a position avaliable, the position that of assistant stock-boy, hours 7:30 A.M.–6:00 P.M., Monday–Saturday, wages @ $0.45/hr., meals not supplied. He had thought the welder's boy might be responsive to his magnanimity, and the welder's boy, all that remained of me, was responsive, yes sir, Mr. McNair, sir. And so my endless drudgery began.

At first I worked to purchase, at the employee rate, the shirts and trousers with which an assistant stock-boy must be outfitted; and for the next twenty-nine years I spun long hours into dress shirts and cravats and worsted suits, as Rumpelstiltskin spun straw into gold, for a McNair's representative must advertise by wearing the very same articles of clothing offered its beloved customers. I had no friends. The only company I knew was that of my fellow employees, a half-brained lot devoted to sexual innuendo, sporting events and the moving pictures featuring Miss Jean Harlow. Later on, Wallace Beery and James Cagney were a big hit. Even later, one heard entirely too much of John Wayne. This, not forgetting the pages of our Sunday newspaper wasted upon the "funnies," was their culture, and it formed the whole of their conversation. Of course I held myself apart. It was the old story repeated once again, as all stories are repeated again and again, eternally, just look around you. You are myself, and I myself am you. What we did last week, last year, what we did in our infancy, shall we do again tomorrow. I could take no delight in the gulf dividing my intellect from theirs, nor could my fellow workers. Doubtless all of them, male and female alike, secretly shared the opinion expressed during our Christmas party in 1955 by Austin Hartlepoole, an Accounting junior who had imbibed too freely of the fish-house punch: "Mr. Wardwell, have you always been a stuck-up jerk?"

"No," I might have said, "once I was a Shining Boy." (What I did say is of no consequence.)

By then I was Mr. Wardwell, note. The superior qualities which condemned me to social and intellectual isolation had seen me through a series of promotions from assistant stock-boy to stock-boy, then head stock-boy, thence laterally to the shipping department, then upward again to counter staff, Shirts and Neckwear, followed by a promotion literally upstairs to second floor, counter staff, Better Shirts and Neckwear, then Assistant Manager, Menswear, in time Manager, Menswear, and ultimately, in 1955, the year soon-to-be-sacked Hartlepoole called me a stuck-up jerk, Vice-President and Buyer, Clothing Divisions. The welder's boy had come through. Just outside of town, I maintained a large residence, never seen by my coworkers, for myself and a companion who shall remain nameless. I dressed in excellent clothing, as was to be expected. A gray Bentley, which I pretended to have obtained at a "price," represented my single visible indulgence. Accompanied by Nameless Companion, I regularly visited the Caribbean on my annual two-week vacation to occupy comfortable quarters in the same luxurious "resort" hotel. By the middle of the nineteen-fifties, my salary had risen to thirty thousand dollars a year, and in my regular banking and savings accounts I had accumulated the respectable sum of forty-two thousand dollars.

In another, secret account, I had amassed the even more respectable sum of three hundred and sixty-eight thousand dollars, every cent of it winkled away a little at a time from one of the worst people, in fact by a considerable margin actually the worst person it has ever been my misfortune to know, my employer, Mr. Harold McNair.

All was well until my transfer to Better Shirts and Neckwear, my "Ascension," we called it, into the vaulted splendors of the second floor, where affluent customers were spared contamination by the commoners examining cheaper goods below, and where Mr. McNair, my jailer-benefactor of years ago, was wont to appear from the depths of his walnut-paneled office, wandering between the counters, adjusting the displays, remarking upon the quality of a freshly-purchased tweed jacket or fox stole (Ladies' was sited across the floor), taking in the state of his minions' figernails and shoes. Mr. McNair, a smallish, weaselish, darkish, baldish figure in a navy suit, his solid red tie anchored to his white shirt with a visible metal bar, demanded courteous smiles, upright postures, hygenic habits. Scuffed shoes earned an errant clerk a sharply worded rebuke, unclean nails an immediate trip to the employee washroom. The dead thing I was did not object to these simple, well-intentioned codes. Neither did I object to my employer—he was but a fixed point in the universe, like his own God enthroned in His heavens. I did not take him *personally*. Not until my ascension, when we each fell under the other's gaze.

Living Visibles like Harold McNair do not expect merely to be seen. Though they be discreetly attired, quietly-spoken and well-mannered, within they starve, they slaver for attention and exact it however they must. In Mr. McNair's case, this took the form of divisiveness, capriciousness, sanctimoniousness and for lack of a better word, tyranny. He would favor one counter clerk, then another, thereby creating enmity and rivalry and an ardent wish in two hearts to comprehend his own heart. He would select an obscure minion for weeks of special treatment, jokes, confidences, consultations, then without explanation drop the chosen one back into obscurity, to be pecked to death by his peers. He drew certain employees aside and whispered subtle criticisms of their dearest friends. Throughout, he searched for his true, secret favorites, those whose contempt for themselves, masked behind a smooth retailer's manner, matched his own for them, masked behind the same. In time I began to think of Harold McNair as a vast architectural structure something like his great store, a building charmingly appointed with fine though not ostentatious things, where a smiling but observant guide leads you ever deeper in, deciding room by room if you have earned the right to behold the next, by stages conducting you into chambers growing successively smaller, uglier, eventually even odorous, then through foul, reeking sties, and at last opens the final door to the central, the inmost room, the room at the heart of the structure, the most terrible of all, and admits you to—the real Mr. Harold McNair.

He knew I was his the first time he saw me behind the Better Shirts counter on the second floor. He may have known it on the day he hired me, long years before. In fact, he might even have regarded the alcoholic welder laboring in his basement and seen that this man's son, if he had one, would be his as if by Natural Law. His in the sense of easily flattered, thus easily dominated. Ready to be picked up by a kind word and downcast by a harsh one. Capable of attentive silences during the Great Man's monologues. Liable to be supine before power, abject before insult. A thorough and spineless subordinate. A kind of slave. Or, a slave. Long before my final promotion, I had been shown into the final room and met the true Harold McNair. I knew what he was and what I was. In many ways, I had fallen under the sway of a smoother, more corrupt Boy Teuteburg, a Boy who thought himself a noble being and wore the mask of a dignified, successful man of business.

I accepted this. But I had determined to be paid well for the role.

My thefts began with an impulsive act of revenge. I had just departed Mr. McNair's office after a session in which the whip lashed out more forcefully than was customary from within the velvet bag, both before and after my employer had expressed his apocalyptic disgust for womankind, those sly-scented obscenities, those temples of lust, etc., etc. Making my way granite-faced through Better Gowns, I observed an elderly temple of lust depositing her alligator bag upon the counter as she turned to scrutinize a bottle-green Better Gown with Regency sleeves. A wallet protruded slightly from the unclasped bag. Customer and Saleslady conferred in re the wisdom of Regency sleeves. My legs took me past the counter, my hand closed on the wallet, the wallet flew into my pocket, and I was gone.

Heart a-thud, I betook myself to a stall in the male employees' washroom, opened the wallet and discovered there sixty-eight dollars, now mine. I had been rash, I knew, but what an electric, unharnessed surge of life force! All I regretted was that the money had been the temple's, not Mr. McNair's. I left the stall and by reflex stepped up to the sinks and mirrors. Washing my spotless hands, I caught my face in the mirror and froze—a vibrant roguish Visible a decade younger than I looked back with blazing eyes, my own.

Anyone in a business that receives and disburses large amounts of cash will eventually devise a method for deflecting a portion of the moolah from its normal course. Some few will test their method, and most of those will be found out. A primitive snatch and grab like mine, unobserved, is as good as any. During my tenure in the store, many employees located the imperfections in their schemes only as the handcuffs closed around their wrists. (Mr. McNair never showed mercy or granted a second chance, ever.) From the moment I met my living eyes in the washroom mirror, I was withdrawing from the cash available an amount appropriate to my degredation, or *stealing my real salary*. All that remained was to work out a method that would pass undetected.

Many such methods exist, and I will not burden you with the details of mine, save to reveal that it involved a secret set of books. It proved successful for better than two decades and yielded a sum nearly compensatory to my endless humiliation. Mr. McNair knew that significant quantities of money were escaping his miserly grasp but despite feverish plotting and the construction of elaborate rat-traps could not discover how or where. The traps snapped down upon the necks of minor-league peculators, till-tappers, short-change artists, bill-padders, invoice-forgers, but never upon his greatest enemy's.

On the night I placed my hundred thousandth unofficial dollar in my secret account, I celebrated with a lobster dinner and a superior bottle of champagne in our finest seafood restaurant (alone, this being prior to the Nameless Friend era) and, when filled with alcohol and rich food, remembered that the moon was full, remembered also my night of misery so long ago and resolved to return to the Oliphant Hotel. Then, I had been a corpse within a grave within a prison; now, I was achieved, a walking secret on the inside of life, an invisible Visible. I would stand before Ethel Carroway and be witnessed—what had been written on her face now lay within me.

I walked (in those pre-Bentley days) to Erie Street and posted myself against a wall to await the appearance of the shade. By showing herself again to me, she would acknowledge that the intensity of my needs had raised me, as she was raised, above the common run. Mine was the confidence of a lover who, knowing this the night his beloved shall yield, savors each blissful, anticipated pleasure. Each moment she did not appear was made delicious by its being the moment before the moment when she would. When my neck began to ache, I lowered my chin to regard through enormous glass portals the Oliphant's lobby, once a place of unattainable luxury. Now I could take a fourth-floor suite, if I liked, and present myself to Ethel Carroway on home ground. Yet it was right to stand where I had before, the better to mark the distance I had come. An hour I waited, then another, growing cold and thirsty. My head throbbed with the champagne I had taken, and my feet complained. My faith wavered—another trial in a test more demanding with every passing minute. Determined not to fail, I turned up the collar of my coat, thrust my hands in my pockets and kept my eyes upon the dark window.

At times I heard movement around me but saw nothing when I looked toward the sound. Mysterious footfalls came teasingly out of the darkness of Erie Street, as if Ethel Carroway had descended to present herself before me, but these footfalls were many and varied, and no pale figure in black appeared to meet my consummating gaze.

I had not understood—I knew nothing of Visibles and those not, and what I took for confidence was but its misshapen nephew, arrogance. The cynosure and focus of myriad pairs of unseen eyes, I surrendered at last after 3:00 A.M. and wandered sore-footed home through an invisible crowd that understood exactly what had happened there and why. In the morn, I rose from the rumpled bed to steal again.

Understanding, ephemeral as a transcendent insight granted in a dream, ephemeral as *dew*, came only with exposure, which is to say with loss of fortune and handsome residence, loss of Nameless Companion, of super-duper Bentley, of elegant sobersides garb, of gay Caribbean holidays on the American Plan, loss of reputation, occupation (both occupations, retailer and thief), privacy, freedom, many Constitutionally guaranteed civil rights and, ultimately, of life. As with all of you, I would have chosen these forfeited possessions, persons, states and conditions over any mere act of understanding, yet I cannot deny the sudden startling consciousness of a certain piquant, indeterminate pleasure-state, unforeseen in the grunting violence of my last act as a free man, which surfaced hand in hand with my brief illumination. This sense of a deep but mysterious pleasure linked to my odd flash of comprehension often occupied my thoughts during the long months of trial and incarceration.

I had long since ceased to fear exposure, and the incarnadine (see *Shakespeare*) excess of exposure's aftermath would have seemed a nightmarish impossibility to the managerial Mr. Wardwell, stoutly serious and seriously stout, of 1960. Weekly, a gratifying sum wafted from Mr. McNair's gnarled, liver-spotted grip into my welcoming hands, and upon retirement some ten stony years hence I expected at last to float free in possession of approximately one and a quarter million dollars, maybe a million and a half. My employer's rat-traps continued to snap down on employees of the anathema stripe, of late less frequently due to widespread awareness of the Byzantinely complex modes of surveillance which universally "kicked in" at the stage beneath the introduction of my invented figures, on account of their having been set in place by the very anathema they were designed to entrap. Had not the odious McNair decided upon a store-wide renovation to mark the new decade, I should after twenty, with luck twenty-five, years of pampered existence in some tropic clime and sustained experience of every luxury from the highestly refined to basestly, piggishestly sensual, have attained upon death from corrupt old age an entire understanding of my frustrated vigil before the Oliphant, of the walkers and shufflers I had heard but were not there, also of Ethel Carroway and her refusal to recognize one who wrongly supposed himself her spiritual equal. But McNair proceeded upon his dubious inspiration, and I induced a premature understanding by smashing the fellow's brains into porridge—"nasty, nasty porridge"—with a workman's conveniently disposed ballpeen hammer.

The actual circumstances of my undoing were banal. Perhaps they always are. A groom neglects to shoe a horse, and a king is killed. A stranger hears a whisper in an ale-house, and—a king is killed. That sort of thing. In my case, coincidence of an otherwise harmless sort played a crucial role. The dread renovation had reached the rear of the second floor, lapping day by day nearer the Accounts Room, the Art Department and the offices, one mine, one Mr. McNair's. The tide of workers, ladders, drop cloths, yardsticks, plumb lines, saw-horses and so forth inevitably reached our doors and then swept in. As my employer lived above the store in a velvet lair only he and his courtiers had seen, he had directed that the repaneling and recarpet-ing, the virtual *regilding*, of his office be done during normal working hours, he then enduring only the minor inconvenience of descend-ing one flight to be about his normal business of oozing from cus-tomer to customer, sniffing, adjusting, prying, flattering. As I owned no such convenient bower and could not be permitted access to his, not even to one corner for business purposes, my own office received its less dramatic facelift during the hour between the closing of the store, 6:00 P.M., and the beginning of overtime, 7:00 P.M. A task that should have taken two days thus filled ten, at the close of every which, concurrent with my official duties, I must manage the unofficial duties centered on the fictive set of books and the disposition of the day's harvest of cash. All this under the indifferent eyes of laborers set-ting up their instruments of torture.

Callous, adamantine men shifted my desk from port to starboard, from bow to stern, and on the night of my downfall informed me I had to jump ship post haste that they might finish, our boss having lost patience with this stage of affairs. I jumped ship and bade farewells to departing employees from a position near the front doors. At 6:55 P.M. I made my way through the familiar aisles to my office door, through which I observed Harold McNair, on a busy-body's journey from the sultan's quarters above, standing alone before my exposed desk and contemplating the evidence of my vari-ous anathematic peculations.

The artisans should have been packing up but had finished early and departed unseen by the rear doors; McNair should have been consulting his genius for depravity in the velvet lair but had slithered down to ensure their obedience. We were alone in the building. As Mr. McNair whirled to confront me, a combination of joy and rage distorted his unpleasant features into a demonic mask. I could not save myself—he knew exactly what he had seen. He advanced toward me, spitting incoherent obscenities.

Mr. McNair arrived at a point a foot from my person and continued to berate me, jabbing a knobby forefinger at my chest as he did so. Unevenly, his face turned a dangerous shade of pink, hot pink I believe it is called. The forefinger hooked my lapel, and he tugged me deskward. His color heightened as he ranted on. Finally he hurled at my bowed head a series of questions, perhaps one question repeated many times, I don't know, I could not distinguish the words. My being quailed before the onslaught; I was transported back to Dockweder's. Here again were a marked bill, an irate merchant, a shamed Frank Wardwell—the wretched boy blazed forth within the ample, settled, secretive man.

And it came to the wretched boy that the ranter before him resembled two old tormentors, Missus Barksdale and Boy Teuteburg, especially the latter, not the sleek rodent in a pearl-gray hat but the red-eyed bane of childhood who came hurtling out of doorways to pummel head and body with sharp, accurate, knife-like fists. I experienced a moment of pure psychic sensation so foreign I could not at first affix a name to it. I knew only that an explosion had taken place. Then I recognized that what I felt was pain—everlasting, eternal pain long self-concealed. It was as though I had stepped outside my body. Or *into* it.

Before me on my oaken chair lay a ballpeen hammer forgotten by its owner. The instant I beheld this utilitarian object, I knew what I would do. My hand found the hammer, the hammer found Mr. McNair's head. Startled, amazed even, but not yet terrified, Mr. McNair jumped back, clamoring. I moved in. He reached for the weapon, and I captured his wizened arm in my hand. The head of the hammer tapped his tough little skull, twice. A wondrous, bright red feeling bloomed in me, and the name of that wondrous feeling was Great Anger. Mr. McNair wobbled to his knees. I rapped his forehead and set him on his back. He squirmed and shouted, and I tattooed his bonce another half-dozen times. Blood began to drizzle from his ears, also from the abrasions to his knotty head. I struck him well and truly above the right eye. At that, his frame twitched and jittered, and I leaned into my work and now delivered blow after blow while the head became a shapeless bloody brain-spattered . . . *mess*. As the blows landed, it seemed that each released a new explosion of blessed pain and anger within Frank Wardwell; it seemed too that these blessings took place in a realm, once known but long-forgotten, in which emotion stood forth as a separate entity, neither without nor within, observable, breathtaking, utterly alive, like Frank Wardwell, this entranced former servant swinging a dripping hammer at the corpse of his detested and worshiped enemy. And there arose in an unsuspected chamber of my mind the remembered face of Ethel Carroway gazing down at but in fact not seeing the disgraced boy-me on Erie Street, and, like a reward, there arrived my brief, exalted moment of comprehension, with it that uprising of inexplicable, almost intellectual pleasure on which I chewed so often in the months ahead. Ethel Carroway, I thought, had known this—this shock—this *gasp*—

Into the office in search of a forgotten hammer came a burly tough in a donkey jacket and a flat cap, accompanied by an even burlier same, and whatever I had comprehended blew away in the brief cyclone that followed. Fourteen months later, approximately dogging Ethel Carroway's footsteps, I moved like a wondering cloud out of a sizzling, still-jerking body strapped into our state's electric chair.

The first thing I noticed, apart from a sudden cessation of pain and a generalized sensation of *lightness* that seemed more the product of a new relationship to gravity than actual weight loss, was the

presence in the viewing room of many more people than I remembered in attendance at the great event. Surely there had been no
more than a dozen witnesses, surely all of them male and journalists
by profession, save two? During the interesting period between the
assumption of the greasy hood and the emergence of the wondering
cloud, thirty or forty onlookers, many of them female, had somehow
crowded into the sober little room. Despite the miraculous nature of
my exit from my corporal self, these new arrivals paid me no mind at
all. Unlike the original twelve, they did not face the large, oblong
window looking in upon the even smaller, infinitely grimmer chamber where all the action was going on.

I mean, although the obvious focus of the original twelve—one
nervously caressing a shabby Bible, one locking his hands over a ponderous gaberdine-swathed gut, the rest scratching "observations" into
their notebooks with chewed-looking pencils—was the hooded,
enthroned corpse of the fiend Francis T. Wardwell, from which rose
numerous curls and twists of white smoke as well as the mingled
odors of urine and burned meat, these new people were staring at
them—the Bible-stroker and the warden and the scribbling
reporters—really *staring* at them, I mean, *lapping up* these unremarkable people with their eyes, *devouring* them.

The second thing I noticed was that except for the thirty or forty
male and female shades who, it had just come to me, shared my new
state, everything in the two sober chambers, including the green
paint unevenly applied to the walls, including the calibrated dials
and the giant switch, including the blackened leather straps and the
vanishing twists of smoke, including even the bitten pencils of the
scribes, but most of all including those twelve mortal beings who had
gathered to witness the execution of the fiend Francis T. Wardwell,
mortal beings of deep, that is to say, radiant ordinariness, expansive
overflowing heartbreaking throat-catching light-shedding meaning-
steeped—

The second thing I noticed was that everything—

At that moment, hunger slammed into me, stronger, more force-ful and far more enduring than the river of volts which had separated me from my former self. As avid as the others, as raptly appreciative of all you still living could not see, I moved to the glass and fastened my ravenous gaze upon the nearest mortal man.

Posted beside the blazing azalea bush on Boy Teuteburg's front lawn, I observe, mild word, what is disposed so generously to be observed. After all that has been said, there is no need to describe, as I had intended at the beginning of our journey, all I see before me. Tulip Lane is thronged with my fellow Invisibles, wandering this way and that on their self-appointed rounds; some six or seven fellow Invisibles are at this moment stretched out upon Boy Teuteburg's high-grade lawn of imported Kentucky bluegrass, enjoying the par-ticularly lambent skies we have at this time of year while awaiting the all-important, significance-drenched arrival of a sweet human being, Tulip Lane resident or service personage. These waiting ones, myself included, resemble those eager ticket-buyers who, returning to a favorite play for the umpty-umpth time, clutch their handbags or opera glasses in the dark and lean forward as the curtain rises, breath suspended, eyes wide, hearts already trilling, as the actors begin to assemble in their accustomed places, their dear, familiar words to be spoken, the old dilemmas faced once again, and the plot to spin, this time perhaps toward a conclusion equal to the intensity of our atten-tion. Will they get it right, this time? Will they *see*? No, of course not, *they* will never see, but we lean forward in passionate concentration as their aching voices lift again and enthrall us with everything they do not know.

Boy is an old Boy now, in his eighties I believe, though it may be his nineties—distinctions of this sort no longer compel—and, won-derfully, an honored personage. He ascended, needless to say without

PETER STRAUB

my vote, into public life around the time of my own "Ascension" to
the second floor, and continued to rise until a convenient majority
elected him mayor shortly before my demise, and upon that plateau
he resided through four terms, or sixteen years, after which ill health
(emphysema) restrained him from further elevation. His mansion on
Tulip Lane contains, I am told, many rooms—seventeen, not count-
ing two kitchens and six bathrooms. I do not bring myself here to
admire the mansion of my old adversary, now confined, I gather, to
an upper floor and dependent on a wheelchair and an uninterrupted
flow of oxygen. I certainly do not report to Tulip Lane at this time of
the day to gloat. (Even Boy Teuteburg is a splendid presence now, a
figure who plants his feet on the stage and raises his brave and frail
voice.) I come here to witness a certain moment.

A little girl opens the door of the room beyond the window next
the azalea. She is Boy Teuteburg's youngest grandchild, the only offspring of the failed second marriage of his youngest child, Sherrie-
Lynn, daughter of his own failed second and final marriage. Her
name is Amber, Jasmine, Opal, something like that—Tiffany! Her
name is Tiffany! Tiffany is five or six, a solemn, dark-haired little person generally attired in a practical one-piece denim garment with bib
and shoulder straps, like a farmer's overall, but white, and printed
with a tiny, repeated pattern—flower, puppy, or kitten. Food stains,
small explosions of catsup and the like, provide a secondary layer of
decoration. Beneath this winning garment Tiffany most often wears
a long-sleeved cotton turtleneck, blue or white, or a white cotton T-
shirt, as appropriate to the season; on her feet are clumsy but infor-
mal shoes of a sort that first appeared about a decade or two ago,
somewhat resembling space boots, somewhat resembling basketball
sneakers; in Tiffany's case, the sides of these swollen-looking objects
sport pink check marks. Tiffany is a sallow, almost olive-skinned
child in whom almost none of her grandfather's genetic inheritance
is visible. Whitish-gray streaks of dust (housekeeping has slacked off

considerably since Mayor Teuteburg's retirement to the upper floor) can often be observed on her round, inward-looking little face, as well as upon the wrinkled sleeves of her turtleneck and the ironic pastoral of the white overall.

Smudgy of eye; streaky with white-gray dust; sallow of skin; dark hair depending in wisps and floaters from where it had been carelessly gathered at the back, and her wispy bangs unevenly cut; each pudgy hand dirt-crusted in a different fashion, one likely to be trailing a single foot-long blond hair, formerly her mother's; introspective without notable intelligence, this liable to fits of selfishness and brooding; round of face, arm, wrist, hand and belly, thus liable for obesity in adulthood; yet withal surpassingly charming; yet gloriously, wholly beautiful.

This little miracle enters the room at the usual hour, marches directly to the television set located beneath our window, tucks her lower lip beneath her teeth—pearly white, straight as a Roman road—and snaps the set on. It is time for the adventures of Tom and Jerry. By now, most of those Invisibles who had been sprawled on the Kentucky blue have joined me at the window, and as matters proceed, some of those who have found themselves on Tulip Lane will wander up, too. Tiffany backpedals to a point on the floor well in advance of the nearest chair. The chairs have been positioned for adults, who do not understand television as Tiffany does and in any case do not ever watch in wondering awe the multiform adventures of Tom and Jerry. She slumps over her crossed ankles, back bent, clumsy shoes with pink check marks nearly in her lap, hands at her sides, round face beneath uneven bangs dowsing the screen. Tiffany does not laugh and only rarely smiles. She is engaged in serious business.

Generally, her none-too-clean hands flop all anyhow on her flowered denim knees, on her pink-checked feet, or in the little well between the feet and the rest of her body. At other times, Tiffany's hands go exploring unregarded on the floor about her. These forays deposit another fine, mouse-gray layer of dust or grime on whatever sectors of the probing hands come in contact with the hardwood floor.

During the forays, the small person's face maintains a soft immobility, the soft unconscious composure of a deep-diving rapture; and the conjunction of softness and immobility renders each inner delight, each moment of identification or elation, each collusion between drama and witness, in short, you people, each emotion that would cause another child to roll giggling on the floor or draw her smeary fists up to her face, each emotion is rendered *instantly visible* —written in subtle but powerful runes on the blank page that is Tiffany's face. As the eerie tube-light washes over this enchanted child's features, her lips tighten or loosen; an adult frown redraws her forehead; mysterious pouches 'neath her eyes swell with horror or with tears; a hidden smile tucks the corners of her mouth; joy leaps candlelike into her eyes; the whole face irradiates with soul-pleasure. I have not even mentioned the dreamy play brought over the wide cheeks and the area beneath the eyes by thousands of tiny muscle-movements, each invoking the separate character, character as in fictional character, of a piquant, momentary shadow.

And from time to time, a probing hand returns to base and alights on a knee, a space-shoe, wanders for a second through the dangling wisps, hesitates, and then, with excruciating patience, approaches the opening mouth and, finger by finger, enters to be sucked, tongued, warmed, above all cleaned of its layers of debris. Tiffany is eating. She will eat anything she finds, anything she picks up. It all goes into her mouth and is absorbed into Tiffany. Cookie crumbs, maybe; mostly dust; loose threads from who knows what fabric; now and then a button or a coin. When she is through with her fingers, she might graze over the palm. More often, she will extend a newly washed forefinger and push it into a nostril, there to tease and rummage until a glistening morsel is extracted, this morsel unhesitatingly to be brought to the portals of the mouth and slipped within, then munched until it too has been absorbed into the Tiffany from whence it came.

We watch so intently, we crowd so close, thrusting into the azalea, breasting the window, that sometimes, having heard a dim version of what I twice heard on Erie Street, she yanks her eyes from the screen and glances upward. She sees but a window, a bush. Instantly, she returns to the screen and her ceaseless meal. I have given you Ethel Carroway letting fall her child, and I have given you myself, Frank Wardwell, battering in a tyrant's brains; but no riper spectacle have I summoned to the boards than Tiffany. She embraces and encompasses living Ethel and living Frank, and exactly so, my dear ones, does Tiffany embrace and encompass you.

THE INDIAN

The town, in New England, of Tarbox, restrained from embracing the sea by a margin of tawny salt marshes, locates its downtown four miles inland up the Musquenomenee River, which ceases to be tidal at the waterfall of the old hosiery mill, now given over to the manufacture of plastic toys. It was to the mouth of this river, in May of 1634, that the small party of seventeen men, led by the younger son of the governor of the Massachusetts Bay Colony—Jeremiah Tarbox being only his second in command—came in three rough skiffs with the purpose of establishing amid such an unpossessed abundance of salt hay a pastoral plantation. This, with God's forbearance, they did. They furled their sails and slowly rowed, each boat being equipped with four oarlocks, in search of firm land, through marshes that must appear, now that their grass is no longer harvested by men driving horses shod in great wooden discs, much the same today as they did then—though undoubtedly the natural abundance of ducks, cranes, otter, and deer has been somewhat diminished. Tarbox himself, in his invaluable diary, notes that the squealing of the livestock in the third skiff attracted a great cloud of "protestating sea-fowl." The first houses (not one of which still stands, the oldest in town dating, in at least its central timbers and fireplace, from 1642) were strung along the base of the rise of firm land called Near Hill, which, with its companion

Far Hill, a mile away, in effect bounds the densely populated section of the present township. In winter the population of Tarbox numbers something less than seven thousand; in summer the figure may be closer to nine thousand. The width of the river mouth and its sheltered advantage within Tarbox Bay seemed to promise the makings of a port to rival Boston; but in spite of repeated dredging operations the river has proved incorrigibly silty, and its shallow winding channels, rendered especially fickle where the fresh water of the river most powerfully clashes with the restless saline influx of the tide, frustrate all but pleasure craft. These Chris-Craft and Kit-Kats, skimming seaward through the exhilarating avenues of wild hay, in the early morning may pass, as the fluttering rust-colored horizon abruptly yields to the steely blue monotone of the open water, a few dour clammers in hip boots patiently harrowing the tidewater floor. The intent posture of their silhouettes distinguishes them from the few bathers who have drifted down from the dying campfires by whose side they have dozed and sung and drunk away a night on the beach—one of the finest and least spoiled, it should be said, on the North Atlantic coast. Picturesque as Millet's gleaners, their torsos doubled like playing cards in the rosy mirror of the dawn-stilled sea, these sparse representatives of the clamming industry, founded in the eighteen-eighties by an immigration of Greeks and continually harassed by the industrial pollution upriver, exploit the sole vein of profit left in the name of old Musquenomenee. This shadowy chief broke the bread of peace with the son of the governor, and within a year both were dead. The body of the one was returned to Boston to lie in the King's Chapel graveyard; the body of the other is supposedly buried, presumably upright, somewhere in the woods on the side of Far Hill where even now no houses have intruded, though the tract is rumored to have been sold to a divider. Until the postwar arrival of Boston commuters, still much of a minority, Tarbox lived (discounting the summer people, who came and went in the marshes each year like the migrations of mallards) as a town apart. A kind of curse has kept its peace. The handmade-lace industry, which reached its peak just before the American Revolution, was destroyed by the industrial revolution; the textile mills, never numerous, were finally emptied by the industrialization of the South. They have been succeeded by a scattering of small enterprises, electronic in the main, which have staved off decisive depression.

Viewed from the spur of Near Hill where the fifth edifice, now called Congregationalist, of the religious society incorporated in 1635 on this identical spot thrusts its spire into the sky, and into a hundred colored postcards purchasable at all four local drugstores—viewed from this eminence, the business district makes a neat and prosperous impression. This is especially true at Christmastime, when colored lights are strung from pole to pole, and at the height of summer, when girls in shorts and bathing suits decorate the pavements. A one-hour parking limit is enforced during business hours, but the traffic is congested only during the evening homeward exodus. A stoplight has never been thought quite necessary. A new Woolworth's with a noble façade of corrugated laminated Fiberglas has been erected on the site of a burned-out tenement. If the building which it vacated across the street went begging nearly a year for a tenant, and if some other properties along the street nervously change hands and wares now and then, nevertheless there is not that staring stretch of blank shopwindows which desolates the larger mill towns to the north and west. Two hardware stores confront each other without apparent rancor; three banks vie in promoting solvency; several luncheonettes withstand waves of factory workers and high-school students; and a small proud army of *petit-bourgeois* knights—realtors and lawyers and jewelers— parades up and down in clothes that would not look quaint on Madison Avenue. The explosive thrust of superhighways through the land has sprinkled on the town a cosmopolitan garnish; one resourceful divorcée has made a good thing of selling unabashedly smart women's clothes and Scandinavian kitchen accessories, and, next door, a foolish young matron nostalgic for Vassar has opened a combination paperback bookstore and art gallery, so that now the Tarbox town derelict, in sneaking with his cherry-red face and tot of rye from the liquor store to his home above the shoe-repair nook, must walk a garish gantlet of abstract paintings by a minister's wife from Gloucester. Indeed, the whole street is laid open to an accusatory chorus of brightly packaged titles by Freud, Camus, and those others through whose masterworks our civilization moves toward its dark climax. Strange to say, so virulent is the spread of modern culture, some of these same titles can be had, seventy-five cents cheaper, in the homely old magazine-and-newspaper store in the middle of the block. Here, sitting stoically on the spines of the radiator behind the large left-hand window, the Indian can often be seen.

He sits in this window for hours at a time, politely waving to any passerby who happens to glance his way. It is hard always to avoid his eye, his form is so unexpected, perched on the radiator above cards of pipes and pyramids of Prince Albert tins and fanned copies of *True* and *Male* and *Sport*. He looks, behind glass, somewhat shadowy and thin, but outdoors he is solid enough. During other hours he takes up a station by Leonard's Pharmaceutical on the corner. There is a splintered telephone pole here that he leans against when he wearies of leaning against the brick wall. Occasionally he even sits upon the fire hydrant as if upon a campstool, arms folded, legs crossed, gazing across at the renovations on the face of Poirier's Liquor Mart. In cold or wet weather he may sit inside the drugstore, expertly prolonging a coffee at the counter, running his tobacco-dyed fingertip around and around the rim of the cup as he watches the steam fade. There are other spots—untenanted doorways, the benches halfway up the hill, idle chairs in the barbershops—where he loiters, and indeed there cannot be a square foot of the downtown pavement where he has not at some time or other paused; but these two spots, the window of the news store and the wall of the drugstore, are his essential habitat.

It is difficult to discover anything about him. He wears a plaid lumberjack shirt with a gray turtleneck sweater underneath, and chino pants olive rather than khaki in color, and remarkably white tennis sneakers. He smokes and drinks coffee, so he must have some income, but he does not, apparently, work. Inquiry reveals that now and then he is employed—during the last Christmas rush he was seen carrying baskets of Hong Kong shirts and Italian crèche elements through the aisles of the five-and-ten—but he soon is fired or quits, and the word "lazy," given somehow more than its usual force of disapproval, sticks in the mind, as if this is the clue. Disconcertingly, he knows your name. Even though you are a young mutual-fund analyst newly bought into a neo-saltbox on the beach road and downtown on a Saturday morning to rent a wallpaper steamer, he smiles if he catches your eye, lifts his hand lightly, and says, "Good morning, Mr. ——," supplying your name. Yet his own name is impossible to learn. The simplest fact about a person, identity's very seed, is in his case utterly hidden. It can be determined, by matching consistencies of hearsay, that he lives in that tall, speckle-shingled, disreputable hotel overlooking the atrophied railroad tracks, just down from the Amvets, where shuffling Polish widowers and one-night-in-town salesmen hang out, and in whose bar, evidently, money can be wagered and women may be approached. But his name, whether it is given to you as Tugwell or Frisbee or Wigglesworth, even if it were always the same name would be in its almost parodic Yankeeness incredible. "But he's an Indian!"

The face of your informant—say, the chunky Irish dictator of the School Building Needs Committee, a dentist—undergoes a faint rapt transformation. His voice assumes its habitual whisper of extravagant discretion. "Don't go around saying that. He doesn't like it. He prides himself on being a typical run-down Yankee."

But he *is* an Indian. This is, alone, certain. Who but a savage would have such an immense capacity for repose? His cheekbones, his never-faded skin, the delicate little jut of his scowl, the drooping triangularity of his eye sockets, the way his vertically lined face takes the light, the lusterless black of his hair are all so profoundly Indian that the imagination, surprised by his silhouette as he sits on the hydrant gazing across at the changing face of the liquor store, effort- lessly plants a feather at the back of his head. His air of waiting, of gaz- ing; the softness of his motions; the odd sense of proprietorship and ease that envelops him; the good humor that makes his vigil gently dreadful—all these are totally foreign to the shambling shy-eyes and moist lower lip of the failed Yankee. His age and status are too pecu- liar. He is surely older than forty and younger than sixty—but *is* this sure? And, though he greets everyone by name with a light wave of his hand, the conversation never passes beyond a greeting, and even in the news store, when the political contention and convivial obscen- ity literally drive housewives away from the door, he does not seem to participate. He witnesses, and now and then offers in a gravelly voice a debated piece of town history, but he does not participate.

It is caring that makes mysteries. As you grow indifferent, they lift. You live longer in the town, season follows season, the half-naked urban people arrive on the beach, multiply, and like leaves fall away again, and you have ceased to identify with them. The marshes turn green and withdraw through gold into brown, and their indolent, untouched, enduring existence penetrates your fiber. You find you must drive down toward the beach once a week or it is like a week without love. The ice cakes pile up along the banks of the tidal inlets like the rubble of ruined temples. You begin to meet, without seek- ing them out, the vestigial people: the unmarried daughters of van- ished mill owners, the retired high-school teachers, the senile dea- cons in their unheated seventeenth-century houses with attics full of old church records in spidery brown ink. You enter, by way of an elderly baby-sitter, a world where at least they speak of him as "the Indian." An appalling snicker materializes in the darkness on the front seat beside you as you drive dear Mrs. Knowlton home to her shuttered house on a back road. "If you knew what they say, Mister, if you knew what they say." And at last, as when in a woods you break through miles of underbrush into a clearing, you stand up surprised, taking a deep breath of the obvious, agreeing with the trees that of course this is the case. Anybody who is anybody knew all along. The mystery lifts, with some impatience, here, in Miss Horne's low-ceilinged front parlor, which smells of warm fireplace ashes and of peppermint balls kept ready in red-tinted knobbed glass goblets for whatever openmouthed children might dare to come visit such a very old lady, all bent double like a little gripping rose clump, Miss Horne, a fable in her lifetime. Her father had been the sixth minister before the present one (whom she does *not* care for) at the First Church, and *his* father the next but one before him. There had been a Horne among those first seventeen men. Well—where was she?— yes, the Indian. The Indian had been loitering—waiting, if you prefer—in the center of town when she was a tiny girl in gingham. And he is no older now than he was then.

THE JIMI HENDRIX
EXPERIENCE

I t's the summer of 1970 and I've got one lovely ambition. I want to have been born in Seattle, to be black, to be Jimi Hendrix. I want a burst of afro ablaze in a bank of stage lights, to own a corona of genius. I ache in bed listening to "Purple Haze" over and over again on my record player; the next night it's "All Along the Watchtower." I'm fourteen and I want to be one of the chosen, one of the possessed. To soak a guitar in lighter fluid, burn baby burn, to smash it to bits to the howl of thousands. I want to be a crazy man like Jimi Hendrix.

What I didn't know then is that before my man Jimi flamed his guitar at Monterey he warned the cameraman to be sure to load plenty of film. This I learn much later, after he's dead.

It's not a good time for me; my father moves us to a new city when school finishes in Winnipeg; all I have is Jimi Hendrix, Conrad and Finty. I don't know what I am doing with these last two, except that with school out for the summer I lack opportunities to widen my circle of acquaintances. Beggars can't be choosers.

Finty I meet outside a convenience store. He introduces me to Conrad. There's not much wrong with Finty; born into a normal family he'd have had a chance. But Conrad is a different story. Finty proudly informs me that Conrad's been known to set fire to garbage

cans and heave them up on garage roofs, to prowl a car lot with a
rusty nail and do ten thousand dollars' worth of damage in the wink
of an eye. He's a sniffer of model-airplane glue, gasoline. That stuff I
don't touch. It's impossible to imagine the great Jimi Hendrix with
his head in a plastic bag. Occasionally, I'll pinch a little grass from
my big sister Corinne's stash in her panty drawer, have my own private Woodstock while Jimi looks down on me approvingly from the
poster on my bedroom wall. I tell myself this is who I am. Finty and
Conrad are just temporary way stations on the big journey.

Conrad scares me. His long hair isn't a statement, just a poverty
shag. His broken knuckles weep from hitting walls; he's an accident
willing itself to happen. The only person who comes close to scaring
me as much is my father, a night janitor who works the graveyard
shift in a deadly office complex downtown, midnight to eight in the
morning. A vampire who sleeps while the sun is up, sinks his teeth
into my neck at the supper table, goes off to work with a satisfied,
bloody, gray smile on his lips. So far as he's concerned there's only
one lesson I need to learn—don't be dumb when it comes to life. I
hear it every night, complete with illustrations.

I'm not dumb. It's my brilliant idea to entertain ourselves annoying
people because that's less dangerous than anything Conrad is likely to
suggest. The same principle as substituting methadone for heroin.

The three of us go around knocking on people's doors. I tell whoever answers we've come about the Jimi Hendrix album.

"What?"

"The Jimi Hendrix album you advertised for sale in the classifieds
in the newspaper."

I didn't advertise nothing of any description in any newspaper."

"Isn't this 1102 Maitland Crescent?"

"What does it look like? What does the number say?"

"Well, we must have the right house then. Maybe it was your wife.
Did your wife advertise a Jimi Hendrix album?"

"Nobody advertised nothing. There is no wife anymore. I live alone."

After my warm-up act, Finty jumps in all pathetic with misery and disappointment like I've coached him. "This isn't too funny you ask me. Changing your mind at the last minute. I promised my sister I'd buy your album for her birthday. A buck is all I got to buy her a lousy second-hand birthday present and then you go and do this. We had to transfer twice on the bus just to get here."

"His sister's got polio, mister." I tilt my head like I can't believe what he's doing to the poor girl.

Conrad says to Finty, "I got fifty cents. It's yours. Offer him a buck and a half. He'll take a buck and a half."

"I ain't going to take anything because I don't have no Jimmy Henson record. I don't even own a record player."

"I've got thirty-five cents," I tell the man. "That makes a buck eighty-five. He *needs* the album for his sister. Music is all she has in life."

"She can't go out on dates or nothing," Finty says, voice cracking. "It's the wheelchair."

"Look, I'm sorry about your sister, kid. But I'm swearing to you—on a stack of Bibles I'm swearing to you—I don't have this record."

"Maybe you've forgotten you have it," I say. "Does this ring a bell? Sound familiar?" And I start cranking air guitar, doing "Purple Haze," no way the poor wiener can stop me until I'm done screaming hard enough to make his ears bleed.

One afternoon we're cruising the suburbs, courtesy of three bikes we helped ourselves to from a rack outside a city swimming pool. Conrad's been sniffing. You can feel the heat coming off the asphalt into your face when you lean over the handlebars to pump the pedals. This is steaming the glue and producing dangerous vapors in Conrad's skull. Already he's yelled some nasty, rude remarks at a woman pushing a baby carriage; now he's lighting matches and flicking them at a yappy Pekinese on somebody's lawn, driving the dog out of its tiny mind. The lady of the house is watching him out her front window and I know that when she lets the drapes fall closed it'll be to call the cops.

Conrad is badly in need of structure, a sense of purpose at this particular moment, so I point to a bungalow across the street, a bungalow where every shrub in the yard has been trimmed to look like something else. For instance, a rooster. I definitely recall a rooster. It's easy to guess what sort of person will live in a house of that description. Prime territory for the Jimi Hendrix

Finty and Conrad are off their bikes in a flash; no explanation needed.

There's a sign on the front door, red crayon on cardboard, ENTRANCE ALARMED. PLEASE ENTER AT REAR. The old man who comes to the door is dressed like a bank manager on his day off. White shirt, striped tie, bright yellow alpaca cardigan. He's a very tall, spruce old guy with a glamour tan, and he's just wet-combed his white hair. You can see the teethmarks of the comb in it.

"We came to inquire about the album," I say.

"Yes, yes. Come in. Come in. I've been expecting you," he says, eyes fixed on something above my head. But when I turn to see what's caught his interest, there's nothing there.

"This way, this way," he urges us, eyes blinking up into a cloudless sky. For a second I wonder if he might be blind, but then he begins herding us through the porch, through the kitchen, into the living room, pushing air away from his knees palms-out like he's shooing chickens. Finty and Conrad are giggling and snorting. "Too rich," I hear Conrad say.

The old man points and mutters, "Have a seat. Have a seat," before he evaporates off into the back of the bungalow. Conrad and Finty start horsing around, scuffling over ownership of a recliner, but it's already a done deal who's going to end up with it. Like the big dog with the puppy, Conrad lets Finty nip a bit before he shoots him the stare, red little eyes like glazed maraschino cherries left in the jar too long, and Finty settles for the chesterfield. Big dog flops in the recliner, pops the footrest, grins at me over the toes of his sneakers. "Right on," he says.

I don't like it when Conrad says things like "right on." He's not entitled. He and Finty aren't on the same wavelength as people like me and Jimi Hendrix. Conrad would just as soon be asking people for Elvis Presley albums if I hadn't explained that the types whose doorbells we ring are likely to own them.

Finty is into a bowl of peanuts on the end table. He starts flicking them at Conrad. Conrad snaps at them like a dog trying to catch flies, snaps so hard you can hear his teeth click. The ones he misses rattle off the wall, skitter and spin on the hardwood floor.

I'm wondering where the old guy's gone. My ear is cocked in case he might be on the phone to the police. I don't appreciate the unexpected turn this has taken, the welcome mat he spread for us. I'm trying to figure out what's going on here, but there's this strange odor in the house which is worming into my nostrils and interfering with my thoughts. When I caught the first whiff of it, I thought it was the glue on Conrad's breath, but now I'm not so sure. A weird, gloomy smell. Like somebody's popped the door on a long-abandoned, derelict fridge, and dead oxygen and stale chemical coolant are fogging my brain.

I'm thinking all this weird stuff when Finty suddenly freezes on the chesterfield with a peanut between his thumb and middle finger, cocked to fire. His lips give a nervous, rabbity nibble to the air. I scoot a look over my shoulder and there's the old man blocking the entrance to the living room. With a rifle clutched across his chest.

Conrad's heels do a little dance of joy on the footrest.

The old gentleman pops the rifle over his head like he's fording a

249

stream, takes a couple of long, plunging strides into the room, and crisply snaps the gun back down on a diagonal across his shirt front, announcing, "My son carried a Lee-Enfield like this clear across Holland in the last war. He's no longer with us. I thought you boys would like to see a piece of history." He smiles and the Lee-Enfield starts moving like it has a mind of its own, the muzzle sliding slowly over to Finty on the chesterfield. One of the old guy's eyes is puckered shut; the other stares down the barrel straight into Finty's chest. "JFK," he says. Then the barrel makes a lazy sweep over to Conrad in the recliner. "Bobby. Bobby Kennedy."

Some nights I turn on the TV at four in the morning when all the stations have signed off the air. I like how the television fizzles in my ears, how my brain drifts over with electric blue and gray snow, how the phantom sparkles of light are blips on a radar screen tracking spaceships from distant planets. Similar things are happening in my head right now, but they feel bad instead of good.

"Get that out of my face," Conrad orders him.

The old man doesn't move. "I could feel John and Bobby giving off copper right through the television screen. Lee Harvey could feel it and Sirhan Sirhan could feel it. I think, as far as North America goes, we were the only three."

Conrad squints suspiciously. "What kind of bullshit are you talking?"

"And you," says the old man, voice rising, "you give off copper and so does your friend by the peanut bowl. Chemistry is destiny. Too much copper in the human system attracts the lightning bolt. Don't blame me. I'm not responsible."

There's a long silence. Conrad's heels jitter angrily up and down on the footrest.

"Do you understand?" the old man demands. "Am I making myself clear?"

The question is for Conrad but I'm the one who answers. I feel the old man requires something quick. "Sure. Right. We get it."

He sends me a thoughtful nod as he lays the gun down at his feet. A second later he's rummaging in his pockets, tearing out handfuls of change, spilling it down on the coffee table like metal hail, talking fast. "Of course, there are always exceptions to the rule. Me for one. I'm immune to the thunderbolt. I could walk clear through a mob of assassins with a pound of copper in my belly and no harm, no harm. Untouchable." His fingers jerk through the coins, shoving the pennies to one side. Suddenly his neck goes rigid, his tongue slowly pokes between his lips. A narrow, gray, furry trough. He picks up a penny and shows it to each of us in turn. Presses the penny carefully down on the tongue like he's sticking a stamp on an envelope. Squeezes his eyes tightly shut. Draws the penny slowly back into his mouth and swallows. We watch him standing there, swaying back and forth, a pulse beating in his eyelids.

Conrad's had enough of this. "Hey, you!" he shouts. "Hey, you, I'm talking to you!"

The old man's eyes flutter open. It's like watching a baby wake up.

"We don't give a shit how many pennies you can swallow," Conrad says. "We're here about the album. The famous album."

"Right, the album. Of course," says the old man, springing to the footstool, flipping up the lid.

"And another thing," Conrad warns him, winking at me. "Don't try and pass any golden oldies off on us. Troy here is a hippy. He's got standards. You know what a hippy is?"

"Yeah," says Finty, taking heart from Conrad. "You know what a hippy is?"

The old man drags a bulging photograph album out of the footstool, drops it on the coffee table, sinks to his knees on the hardwood beside it. You'd think it was story time at Pooh Corner in the children's room at the library the way he turns the pages for us.

The pictures are black and white, each one a snapshot of a road under construction. All of them taken just as the sun was rising or setting, the camera aimed straight down the highway to where it disappears into a haze of pale light riding the horizon. There are no people in any of the pictures, only occasional pieces of old-fashioned earth-moving equipment parked in the ditch, looking like they were abandoned when everybody fled from the aliens, from the plague, or whatever.

Conrad grunts, "What the hell is this?"

"An example of the law of diminishing returns," the old man answers, dreamily turning the pages. "In a former life I was a highway contractor. Unrecognized for my excellence."

"How come there's nobody in these pictures?" Conrad wants to know. Pictures without people in them don't make any sense to him.

"Oh but there is," the old man corrects him. "Identify the person. I think it's evident who he is, although there has been argument. If you would confirm his identity it would be very much appreciated."

Conrad and Finty peer down hard at the snapshots. As if there really might be a human being lurking in them. After a minute, Conrad irritably declares, "There's nobody in any picture here."

"He fades in and fades out; sometimes he's there and sometimes he's not. But he's very definitely there now. You'll recognize him," the old man assures us.

By now Conrad suspects the old man is pulling something, a senior citizen variation on the Jimi Hendrix experience. "Oh yeah, I see him now. Jimi Hendrix peeking around that big machine in the ditch. That's him isn't it, Finty? The nigger in the woodpile." He jabs Finty in the ribs with his elbow, hard enough to make him squeak.

"Wrong. The person in question is definitely in the middle of the road. Walking towards us. Look again."

This only pisses Conrad off. "Right. I ain't stupid. Don't try and pull this crap on me."

"Please describe him," the old man says calmly.

"Here's a description for you. An empty road. Get a pair of fucking glasses, you old prick."

"So that's your line." The old man's voice has started to tremble; it sounds like Finty's when he talks about his sister in the wheelchair, only genuine. "Just a road. Just an empty road." He stabs his forefinger down on the photograph so hard it crinkles. "You, Sir. Describe him," he says, turning to Finty.

"Huh?" Finty looks over at Conrad for help. Conrad's eyes are slits, glassy with the glue oozing out of his brain.

"Knock, knock. Who's there?" The old man's finger taps the photograph urgently, bouncing like a telegraph key. "Who's there? Who's there? Knock, knock."

Conrad juts his jaw at Finty, a warning. "Don't you say nothing."

The old man slaps his knee. "There, you've given it away!" he shouts. "Not thinking, were you? Telling him not to give it away — but that's an admission by the back door, isn't it?"

He snatches the album, shoves it into my hands. Tiny points of chilly sweat break out on his forehead. They make me think of liquefying Freon, or whatever gas they pump into refrigerators to keep them cold. The chemical smell is industrial strength. It's coming from him.

"The truth now," he whispers to me. "Tell me what you see."

I feel Conrad staring at me. I hear him say, "Nothing there, Troy. Nothing."

I gaze down at an empty road, scraped raw by grader blades, patches of greasy earth shining like freshly picked scabs. A burr of foggy light bristles on the horizon.

"Just a road," I say.

"But roads don't just happen," says the old man gently.

"No."

"So tell me, who else is in the photograph?"

It's no different from staring into a blank television screen. The snow shifting, forming the faces of famous people locked in the circuitry from old programs. The hiss of static turning into favorite songs, guitar chords whining and dying.

"He's playing head games with us, Troy," Conrad warns. "Fuck him. Fucking lunatic."

The old man leans in very close to me; I feel his alpaca sweater brushing the hairs on my bare arm. "Tell the truth," he murmurs. "Who do you see?"

I hold my breath, and then I say it. "You."

"Yes," says the old man. When he does, I sense Conrad rising to his feet, sense his shadow lurching down on the two of us.

"And my head. What do you see above my head?" the old man coaxes.

"Enough of this shit, Troy," Conrad says.

I look at the picture, the old man's finger guiding me to the pale gray froth on the horizon. He rests it there, the phantom light crowning his nail.

"Light."

"The aura."

"The aura," I repeat numbly after him.

All at once, Conrad boots the album out of my hand, sends it flying across the room, pages flapping. The old man and I dare not lift our heads; we just sit there looking at the floor, listening to the ragged whistle of Conrad's breathing. It goes on for a long time before he says, "You think I don't know what you're up to, Troy? But you don't fuck with me, man. Just don't try and fuck with me. Just don't."

The old man and I sit with bowed heads, listening to Conrad and Finty pass through the house, their voices getting louder the closer they get to the door. Then it slams, and the old man's head jerks up as if it were attached to it by a wire. Conrad and Finty hoot outside. I listen to their voices fade away, and then I realize the old man is talking to me.

"I knew you were the one to tell the truth. I knew it at the back door when I saw all the generous light . . ." He pauses, touches my head. "Here."

And I'm up and running through the house, colliding with a lamp, moving so fast the sound of breaking glass seems to have nothing to do with me. Out the screen door, hurdling my stolen bike, clearing the broken spokes, the twisted wheel rims that Finty and Conrad have stomped. I'm running, my scalp prickling with tiny flames, I feel them, the flames creeping down the nape of my neck, licking at my collar, breathing hotly in my ears.

And, Jimi, two months from being dead, is out there in front of me, stage-lights snared in his hair, a burning bush. And a young road builder is standing alone on a blank, unfinished road, his head blooming with a pale gray fire.

And here I am, running through the late afternoon stillness of an empty suburban street, sucked down it faster than my legs can carry me, this hollow, throaty roar of fire in my head, that tiny point on the horizon drawing me to where the sun is either coming up or going down.

Which?

AURA, CRY, FALL, AND FIT

I hold my twin brother's head in my skirt on the cool oak floor—the cut was slight; the seizure was not—until he recovers enough for me to leave then return to bathe his wound.

We come from a proud and ancient line of winemakers who spent centuries collecting antique mansions—not so haunted that just anyone wandering in could put their hand on what kept them on edge or slightly aroused. We grew up above it all on a third floor, but it was I, rifling a steamer trunk of diaries, who found that the concealed occupation of this place was to kill a relative on Christmas, Easter or a name day.

Before the grand mal but after listening to Uncle Constantine's history of our family, Karl looked right through me—I remember looking around for a mirror—forcing me, just nineteen, to thoroughly blush, as if crossing an ocean and the apron of the stage of our childhood at Uncle's invitation had divorced us from our sibling selves and turned us—black-haired, green-eyed and virgins—into lovers. Over Russian salad and Armagnac, Constantine was about to, as he put it, "finish my education," when Karl abruptly left the table.

"In 1823, one of your ancestors—who built this house out of cathedral windows and beams arching like the limbs of a praying mantis—seduced his daughter, who gave birth to a son, who suffocated his father, also his grandfather, in front of his mother, also his sister. These apparitions turn paintings upside-down in the corridors."

"Nonsense," said Aunt Zenia, his third wife, who, at table the next morning, announced that Constantine had died in his sleep.

Karl, looking at himself in his boots' high polish, said, "They came for him on his name day; they will come for me, and they will find you, Cassandra, on your toes trimming the Christmas tree, unless we gather our forces and speak to them in a way they'll never forget."

Hand-in-hand with an uncorked Montrachet, a gouda and apples, we climbed through a crush of family portraits, their faded, cracked indifferent eyes pushing us up then down on a quilt Karl spread over our uncle's oriental. We shaped a man with apples for eyes, a round of cheese for a belly, lit candles and lay next to him and drank. Ashes in the grate were stirring in a draft; the thin light of dusk poured cobalt through the leaded glass. He threw my dress over the head of our soft sculpture, entered me, and we fell, like a fairy tale, into a trance, all I remember . . . then a young man dressed in full fig, a wig, lace at the wrist and a short beard appeared from behind a tapestry. The eyes of the cheeseman rolled under the bed as we dived for the quilt to take cover. He lifted his coattails over his thighs, sat down and drank right from the bottle.

"You have been," he said, wiping wine off his lips with a finger, "misinformed about this house. I wish to clarify a few details."

Could I pass my hand through the bulge of his Adam's apple, I wondered; did he want me to?

"Years ago," he went on, looking into the fear and desire in the transfixed quartet of eyes steaming under the quilt, "our mutual relation was out for his morning ride through the trees. His horse reared, and to the peasant who found him he seemed no longer among the living. A brood of doctors pronounced him 'in a trance,' though, knowing little about it and caring less, they left him to the devices of Sister Madeleine, who washed, sang and talked to him late into the night.

"One evening, after several years, reading aloud from Revelations, she looked up to find him staring. A moment passed, and then he fell on her. She ran for Sister Evangeline, who looked gingerly through a crack, mesmerized by the man on his back asleep. She advised Madeleine to confess her dream.

"Instead, Madeleine ran, poor and without prospects, past the age of marriage, past the village of her childhood, past her parents, old and on their knees in a pew—running like a poet's ghost trying to free itself of voices, until, destitute and nearly broken, she returned as a nurse, no longer God's bride, to bathe the endless film of sleep and trim the beard that spread like frost grapes out of the sea of his steady breathing.

"She looked up again—a few years had passed—on his name day. He looked back. She said that she had loved him half-alive, that she was no longer a nun, if only he could stay awake. This time when she went for Evangeline the Sister stormed the room, a flurry of anger, derision, and it wasn't until months later—when she could put a glass and her ear to Madeleine's belly and hear the persistent, tidal rhythms of a child's heart—that she apologized, so mortified she made a pilgrimage to Bethlehem and never returned.

"Madeleine gave suck and the rudiments of an education to Christina in his hospital room, which they rarely left, caring for him for nearly thirteen years. One evening, Madeleine was about to read. He stirred, she ran, and he chased her down the hill to a fountain, where she threw herself into the turbulence flowing out of the marble-green mouths of tigers. He rescued her and they talked:

"'I've been sleeping for days.'

"'You've been sleeping for years and we have a child named Christina because you fell on me.'

"'If I've lost years, I'll take the child for what I've wasted, but you must leave.'

"He groomed Christina like an idiot-wife or an idolized mistress.

She had your eyes and artistic fingers and the dark spot you both share below your knee. She saw no one else, no room but this, and when their desires became urgent, he had his way with her.

"He summoned the old nurse back because of his wife-daughter's inability to raise a son, who, reaching his eighteenth year, his father about to die, was to become lord of the house and a wealthy man. The nurse laid the truth before the boy. That night, after dispatching three generations with two serene strokes of a razor, he threw himself from a parapet into the warm air.

"At the wake, the nurse looked beyond the two bodies lying in state to the still figure of her grandson and begged the priest, 'Don't bury this boy. Like his father in a trance for nearly twenty years, he's still alive.'"

A small meteor crashed into the churchyard. The town, forced to make repairs, found Uncle Constantine clutching himself, surrounded by fantastic carvings lining the coffin. Aunt Zenia, who went quietly in an asylum outside of Prague, willed the house and everything in it to me and Karl, who, like a superstitious child, had it shipped in pieces and reassembled near Salt Lake City, where we entertain an occasional stranger.

HYANNIS BOAT

U ncle Daniel became rich after the war, but not in spirit. And when I say rich, I mean in the inflated, midcentury way that only in this one particular time, in this one particular culture could ever have been thought of as normal. The split-level with four bedrooms and a pool, the beach house even larger, the new cars with their ceaseless carbonizations, the new appliances and complicated toys. And when I say poor in spirit, I refer to the meager rewards these things brought him — how his last years were spoiled by the kind of remorse a pirate king might feel on the day the booty turns to ashes in his hands.

Of the war itself, I only heard him tell one story, this in the softened, apologetic voice that was all his disappointment left him. He had graduated a year ahead of his class at Boston Latin and spent the bulk of 1945 waiting for the fighting to end or his eighteenth birthday, whichever should come first. In the meantime, with the shortage of men, he found a job as deckhand on the old *Sconset* ferrying passengers and foodstuffs between Nantucket and Cape Cod. It was back-breaking work, with endless hours loading bulky containers of freight, but at least it helped exhaust the patriotic energy that — between newsreels and bond drives and victory gardens — coursed through his veins in unadulterated adrenaline.

At times it was better than that. At times they would leave the island late and be caught midpassage by darkness so there was no separation between the sea below and the sky above, and their wake would sparkle with phosphorescence like a furrow plowed through stars. Watching it, Daniel would imagine he was on a troopship bound for Guadalcanal, an LST bound for Normandy, the *Queen Elizabeth* bound for home—feel danger and safety surge in alternate thrills of pleasure down his spine. Two miles out from Nantucket, Captain Bowen would douse all the lights, heightening the effect even more. U-boats were about, at least off Chatham, and though they had never actually seen one, there were gasoline cans piled on the stern to be floated toward anything suspicious and set ablaze with a deer rifle Newcomb, the mate, had commandeered from a sporting goods store back in Bourne.

Real or not, the threat helped them through the tedium of the night. Before long, what few passengers they had would be wrapped in their overcoats asleep, and Daniel would be left alone with his imaginings, staring out across the rail toward the uneven darkening that was America fifteen miles off the bow. Chalke, the engineer, would bring him coffee at midnight. The hot taste of it against his shivering gave Daniel a happiness that went beyond anything he had ever known.

This was May, the last few moments of the European war. Each of the crew felt the excitement of this, and all their actions had been subconsciously quickened. With no returning passengers to worry about, the cargo was loaded at Nantucket that evening in record time. Bowen—prudent, unhurried Bowen—steamed them backward from the pier before the cargo doors were even secured, narrowly avoiding collision with a barge. The hurry was wasted though. They caught the first wisps of fog off Brant Point, and by the time they left the breakwater, long marbled strands of it had become caught up in the radio mast like streamers of taffy.

Bowen pitched around in it for an hour, then—with darkness—
shut down the engines and glided the *Sconset* to a stop. Certain fogs
on that sound seemed to sharpen and particularize, coating everything
with wetness like a moist lens, but this was the darker, more dangerous
fog that swelled and distorted, until even a bobbing seagull, ten yards
off the stern, loomed as large and threatening as a tanker.

Daniel was sent aft to keep watch. The sea was weed-slicked and
still—still enough that he took a seat on the biggest, most precari-
ously balanced of the gasoline cans, straddling it like a pony. For
three hours he sat there, blowing on his hands to warm them, stomp-
ing his feet up and down, working his gum around to sweeten the
coppery taste of the fog.

By the fourth hour he was cold—cold and mutinous. It was ridiculous posting him there. No trawler in its right mind would blunder
about in a pea soup like that. Even if one approached, there was nothing he could do to stop them short of launching Newcomb's gasoline
bombs. He teetered there in indecision for another half hour, then
with a righteous disregard of all consequence, swung himself down
and began groping his way along the oily deck toward the bridge.

Daniel, in telling this, would clear his throat here, attempting to
find the proper register to convey what happened next. He had
walked all the way to the bow, cut through the deserted passenger
lounge, and was just beginning to climb the iron stairway to the
upper deck, when from the oval swelling in the side where the
Number Two lifeboat hung there came a voice. A voice, or rather a
voicelike sound, so deep and so troubled his first impression was that
the fog, pressed so thickly, had chosen that moment to groan.

"Away!"

It was startling enough, coming out of the dark like that, but at the
same time there was something so impossible about the deepness that
Daniel hurried past the word's echo with the same kind of heedless,
swiping gesture he would have used to brush away spray. He ran up

the stairs to the next deck, felt his way around some hawsers, then continued on toward the wedge of orange that leaked from the blacked-out bridge.

The *Sconset's* bridge was as round and rusty as the turret off an old Civil War ironclad, and it took a determined shove to open the door. Inside, the only light came from the crimson of the binnacle, but compared to the fog it was like daybreak. Daniel blinked his eyes to adjust. Bowen's pipe, the baked smell of the heater—he was aware of these first. Softly, braced for a scolding, he felt his way to the corner by the chart table where he would be out of the way.

No one bothered noticing him. Bowen sat on a stool to the side of the wheel, his mouth arranged in the thin smile that was his habitual expression, his pipe underlining it, his lips working meditatively on the stem. To his left stood Medeiros, his hands on the wheel even though the ship was motionless, his chin jutting out between spokes like a grizzled figurehead's. Chalke stood toward the front by the window, dressed in overalls. Beside him, balancing nervously on the balls of his feet, Newcomb rubbed sloppy circles across the glass.

"It was right there, I tell you," he said, to no one in particular. "Right smack there off the starboard bow."

"You're dreaming," Bowen said pleasantly. "Bullshit I'm dreaming. Pat saw it too, didn't you, Pat?" "Sure I saw it," Chalke said, without conviction. He wiped a mustache of grease across his lip. "It was . . . uh. It was yellow and red." He glanced over his shoulder for support. "Right, Joe?" Medeiros—who was oldest—snapped his head forward in a spitting motion. "Fucking Krauts," he mumbled. The three of them stared toward the window and the holes Newcomb was making in the steam. Only Bowen seemed disinterested. He swiveled around to refill his pipe, caught sight of Daniel, and winked.

"Pretty chilly there on the stern, eh, Mr. Mathews? Deserting your post is a capital offense. Pull up a stool and make yourself at home."

That was Bowen's way—not to miss anything, but to scold only gently—and Daniel idolized him as a result. He was the senior captain on the sound, retired when war broke out, then pressed back into service with a schedule that could kill a younger man. He was showing the strain of it now; despite the smile, there was a stiff, formal weariness about him, as if he were waiting for history to snap his picture so he could relax.

"The mate here's been seeing Martians," he said, without malice. "You might slide yourself forward and take a look. Fog like this needs young eyes to penetrate. You see anything with a green complexion, you let Mr. Newcomb know."

Newcomb spun around in Bowen's direction, saw Daniel, and vented his fury on him instead.

"Your post is at the stern, Mathews! Who the hell gave you permission to come forward?"

Newcomb was only two years older than Daniel and hard toward him for that reason. He was a big man, quick and alert—handsome if you didn't count the withered arm that made him 4F. His personality was a mix of boyish exuberance and low cunning, and he was spoken of among the ferry men as an up and coming young man.

"You get on back there now," he said. "You leave again, I'll—"

He was cut off by Chalke's yell. "There it is! There it is! Three points off the starboard bow!"

His voice was so certain that the five of them, even Bowen, rushed to the window this time. Daniel used his sleeve to clear off a space. At first, all he could see was the same impenetrable fog they had been wrapped in since stopping, but toward the top the droplets were less opaque, more scrimlike, and above that was a slight blackening that might possibly with some imagination be taken as sky.

"There's nothing," Bowen said.

Newcomb tapped the glass with his fist. "There to the right. Up high off the horizon. It must be every thirty seconds. . . . Twenty-seven . . . twenty-eight . . . twenty-nine. . . ."

Daniel, staring toward the blackness, saw it quiver—saw it spiral upward in a shaft of something red, then stop, widen, and drop.

"Over to port." Chalke yelled. "Orange this time. No, cherry. Cherry-colored and higher."

"There's a silver one back the other way!" Newcomb said. "Silver and red and blue!"

Bowen, who had taken the binoculars out, focused them in the direction Newcomb pointed. "Flares," he said, after a time.

Medeiros nodded. "Ship in distress. U-boats. . . . Fucking Krauts."

"Flares my ass!" Newcomb shouted. He bobbed his head up and down and made little boxing motions with his fists. "Flares over dry land? Flares my ass! Flares don't blossom out like that. Flares aren't in colors. Those are fireworks!"

"In the middle of May?" Chalke said.

"Middle of May my ass! They're celebrating. The Cape is celebrating. You know what they're celebrating? You know what they're hot goddam fucking celebrating? The war is over! The war is fucking over!"

The moment he said it the fog, with its own sense of drama, parted enough to admit a narrow opening off the bow. Through it, a packet of light climbed into the sky and burst apart in a red, white, and blue cloud. A moment later the fog closed back again, but not until—very faint, more as a tapping sensation on the chest than anything aural—came the faintest, vaguest of booms.

"Sweet God in heaven," Bowen said. He put the binoculars down and wiped his eyes, suddenly very old. "You're right, Mr. Newcomb, and I apologize. Those are fireworks and there can be only one reason for them. The war is over."

With that they grew very solemn. Newcomb went around pumping all their hands, then Bowen did the same more formally, then Chalke with an embarrassed swiping, then Medeiros with cranky jerks. They went back to the window after that. Chalke fiddled with the radio but nothing came in.

"Well, what are we waiting for?" Newcomb said, when the silence grew noticeable.

"Waiting?" Bowen said.

"The war is over. The Cape is celebrating. Let's go."

"In this fog? We'd run straight up on a rock—a rock or a trawler."

Newcomb threw his arms apart and appealed in agony to the ceiling. "Then we'll miss it!"

"Now calm down, Mr. Newcomb. Let's not get hasty."

"Hasty!"

"What we need are those stronger glasses. Daniel? You know that locker back in the stern under the collapsibles? Go back and fetch it. . . . And Daniel?"

"Yes, sir?"

"Mind your footing. The last thing we need is an unconscious deckhand."

Daniel nodded, pressed his shoulder against the door to open it, then pressed it shut again on the angry, muffled sound of Newcomb's voice.

It didn't take long to retrace his steps. Despite Bowen's caution, he ran as fast as he could, hurdling the hawsers, swinging around a stanchion, all but flying down the stairway in sheer exhilaration. The war was over! The war was over and it was the happiest moment in his life and the happiest moment in America's life and the happiest moment in history and it was so happy that happiness swarmed in front of him like the fog and he couldn't think.

He was down to the main deck, ducking to get beneath the lifeboat davits, when out of the corner of his eye he noticed a blurred, back and forth motion slightly higher than the rail. At the same time, or even a split second sooner, he remembered the strange sound he had heard there on his way to the bridge. Between them, the blur and the remembering seemed to squeeze out a word the same way the fog had earlier, only this time in a whisper that was so throaty and urgent it stopped him dead in his tracks.

"Away!"

Daniel looked toward the lifeboat, saw nothing, and was just about to continue on when another, more distinct motion made him cross to the railing where he could stare up toward the L-shaped mount. There perched on the metal lip of it, his hands braced against the lifeboat's side, was a man dressed in a white linen suit.

Daniel's reaction came in three parts, the second and third following so hard upon the first it was impossible to separate them. It was a ghost he was looking at, a ghost materializing out of the mist, but not a ghost, a German saboteur bent on revenge, only not a saboteur but a stowaway—a stowaway who was athletic and nimble and deranged.

Was he dreaming? He craned back his head. There was a man there, only now he had left the relative security of the mount and was kneeling on the taut canvas of the lifeboat's cover, pulling frantically at the snaps. He seemed infuriated at their stubbornness; he ripped off his jacket, flung it sideways like a matador, then turned and went back at the snaps with redoubled fury.

"Away!" he said. "Away! Away!"

Daniel watched him with his mouth open, his fright changing very rapidly into guilt. Passengers were his responsibility, from the moment they boarded to the moment they disembarked, and to admit one had slipped aboard without paying would mean a tongue-lashing from Newcomb, possibly even firing. So there was no use being polite about it. He cleared his throat self-importantly, reached up, and rapped his fist against the lifeboat's keel.

"Hey you! Get down off there!"

"Away!"

"You heard me. Down from there!"

"Away!"

"Get down!"

Slowly, reluctantly, the man balanced his way along the boat's side and let himself down onto the locker where the lifejackets were stored. It still wasn't all the way to the deck, but it was flatter there and he was less likely to fall overboard.

"That's better," Daniel said. "Lifeboats are off-limits to passengers except during drills. Now where's your ticket? You're supposed to hand it in when you board. Come down here where I can make you out."

The man took a cautious step forward, but seemed unwilling to move beyond reaching distance of the boat. The white of its lap-strake, backing him, caught what soft light his face managed to cast, catching him up in his own milky radiance. He was thirty at most—blond and oval-faced, handsome in a leathery way, but with cheeks that seemed deflated and eye sockets that looked gouged. The rest of him looked drawn as well. His neck where his tie was loosened, his arms where his sleeves were rolled back. As strong as they were, they were lined with veins and prominent tendons, making it seem as if his body had been twisted together from cords.

"Here, all the way," Daniel said, softening his tone. He pointed toward the bridge. "It's not too late. I can sell you a one-way and nobody has to be the wiser."

The man was kneeling on the rail—he had started to lower a cautious leg to the deck— when behind him in the distance a new salvo of fireworks went shooting skyward, coloring the top of the fog in a hazy filigree of red and yellow.

The man's expression, wound so tight already, now seemed to snap past bearing. He leapt to his feet and hurled himself toward the lifeboat, beating the davits with the rolled mallets of his fists.

"Away!" he shouted. "Away, away, away!"

Each new blaze of light terrified him more than the last—he jerked crazily about, as if the explosions weren't on the horizon but in his heart. Daniel, for his part, had a new rush of panic, but only because he suddenly realized who the man must be.

The military squareness of his shoulders, his tanned face that displayed so much suffering, the horror the flaring caused. He was obviously a discharged soldier suffering shell shock—someone whose nerves had been shattered by artillery fire in Italy or France. A soldier, not a sailor. A sailor would have known where the winch was that lowered the lifeboat. He was still fumbling with the davits, all but biting them in frustration, sobbing out the same word again and again.

"Away! Away! Away!"

I must humor him, Daniel decided. I must speak plainly and simply like a friend.

"Don't be frightened. It's all right now. Those are fireworks, that's all. The Cape's celebrating. The war is over—at least we think so. Word must have come in tonight on the news."

"Away!"

"Away where? We're not in a battle or anything. Uh, were you in tanks? The Captain's son is in tanks. I think tanks must be . . . well, demanding. Pretty goddam demanding. It worries him but he never lets on."

"Away!"

"You must be happy it's over."

"Away!"

Daniel started to say something, then shrugged. Short of wrestling with him, there was nothing he could do alone. He waited to make sure the man had his balance, then turned and hurried toward the bridge for help.

They had taken down the blackout curtains since he left; the chart light and overhead were both fully on. Bowen and Medeiros stood near the wheel, saying nothing. Newcomb and Chalke stood to starboard as far from them as possible. From the way they glared at each other, it was obvious the silence had lasted a long time.

They waited while Daniel brushed the damp off his jacket. He had finished—he was trying to find the right words to explain—when

Newcomb made a snorting sound and stepped forward.

"Okay, there it is. Two for, two against. Mathews, your vote decides. . . . Joe and the Captain say we molder in the fog where we are. Pat and I say we stop pussyfooting around and get under way and be part of the greatest celebration the Cape's ever known. . . . Which one for you?"

The four men looked at him—it was as if each had reached over and grabbed a separate limb. Go, with caution, Daniel decided to say, but before he could, Bowen leaned over and rapped his pipe against the wheel.

"You've been watching too many newsreels, Mr. Newcomb," he said quietly. "This isn't a democracy, not while I'm in charge. The kid doesn't vote. We wait out this fog if it takes a week."

Newcomb clutched his middle as if he'd been drilled. "Then we'll be late!"

"Late for what?" Bowen said.

"Late for everything! Late for the broads! Late for the booze! What's waiting there? I don't know. Let's get this tub moving and find out. All it's been for four lousy years is the war this and the war that and now it's the war nothing and every poor lonely slob in the world is celebrating except us."

Bowen shook his head. "There's still Japan."

"Japan," Medeiros mumbled. He ground his dentures together, rearranging them from right to left. "Fucking Nips."

"Fuck Japan!" Newcomb yelled. "That's the other half of the world for crissake! In my half, the war's over. . . . Look," he said, changing tacks, "it doesn't have to be all that dangerous. The fireworks are enough to give us a horizon. We'll keep her down to six knots, keep blasting the hooter, stop the moment we see anything. In an hour we'll be docked at Hyannis cranking up my Ford ready to trot. . . . Right, Pat?"

Chalke, who was twirling pliers around on his finger, caught them and shrugged. "It's wiped the slate clean. The war, I mean. It's wiped the slate clean for the start of a new dawn." He looked up and shrugged again. "I read it in the *Post*."

Ahead of him and quite plainly, a firework climbed above the fog. Its explosion, coming clearer now, rattled around the bridge like something trapped.

"You know what this night is going to be known as?" Newcomb said, staring straight at Bowen. "It's going to be known as Victory Night 1945—the night old Isaac Bowen lost his nerve."

Bowen, back on his stool now, didn't seem to hear. When he spoke it was very softly, to the glass.

"You don't push out here, understand? You poke and you probe and gain a few yards, but you never push, never force yourself. I can wait forever, that's my strength. That was the strength of the men that taught me, that was the strength of the men that taught them. That was all our strength."

"But not mine," Newcomb said. He crossed to the wheel. "I'll steer. Mathews, you go down to the bow and mount a lookout. The minute you see anything, scream."

"We're waiting it out," Bowen said, but the vigor was gone from his voice. "Ken, I'll tell you this man to man. It's going to sit bad with the authority your talking like this. It's going to mean a black mark when it comes to your future."

"My future?" Newcomb threw his arm toward the window. "There's my future! There with those lights. You think I'd stay in this lousy dead-end job one second after getting ashore? Fart around playing sailor for a lousy fifty a week? The minute my feet hit that dock I'm gone. . . . And why the hell are you standing there playing with yourself, Mathews? You heard me. Move!"

Daniel took a step toward the door, checked himself, and looked toward Bowen for confirmation. All during the argument he had found himself sharing Newcomb's impatience, but at the same time wanting the Captain to stand firm. Now, facing him, he saw something he had been too stupid to notice before—that Bowen himself shared their impatience; that his haste leaving Nantucket hadn't been a fluke; that his eyes, wherever else they went, kept swinging back to the distant glowing.

"You go down there like the mate says, Mr. Mathews," he said. "Mr. Chalke, you go down to the engine room and get up steam. If the fog breaks enough to see our bow lights, we'll get under way." He glanced over at Newcomb. "But only then, understand? Until it does, we're staying put."

Across the binnacle, Newcomb smiled. "Suit yourself, Captain," he said, stroking his arm. "Hey, I'm in no hurry. No hurry at all."

Chalke grabbed his pliers off the transom and shot out the door like an unwound spring. Daniel, though, still hesitated.

"Well, what is it, Mr. Mathews?" Bowen said. "Are you going or not?"

"There's a man."

"What man?" Newcomb demanded.

"A man . . . I have to see a man. There in Hyannis, I mean."

Bowen rolled his eyes toward the ceiling in a Mother of God expression. "Now don't you start in on me too, Daniel. Get on forward like the mate says."

"Yes, sir."

Again, for the second time that night, Daniel pushed his way back out into the dark. It was harder this time. It was as if the fireworks had tilted the ship toward land, so that he had to fight gravity to make any way. He felt burdened besides—burdened with the weight of a secret and a lie. Between his worry over this, the clatter of his shoes, and the muffle of the fog, he didn't hear anything until he actually reached Number Two, and even then the sound seemed weaker than before, more wistful and slurred.

"Away . . . away . . . away . . ."

The man was still there, only now he knelt partially obscured in the center of the lifeboat, where he had managed to find the winch. He ran his hands over its mechanism quickly and carefully, probing like a safecracker, but without success. As simple as the winch was, there was a sleeve across the safety catch that kept the lifeboat from dropping. It took a certain familiarity to work it, and there was no risk of him doing it alone.

Daniel coughed to announce his presence, then spoke very quietly, in the tone someone might use in coaxing a cat down out of a tree.

"I just talked to the Captain. He says you can ride free the rest of the crossing. In honor of the war being over, that is."

"Away."

"You could sit in the lounge if you wanted. It's a lot warmer in there. There's a cigarette machine. I could brew up some coffee."

"Away."

"There's a boat back to Nantucket at eight tomorrow morning. We could put you on that. That'll get you away, all right. I mean, you are from Nantucket. Your loved ones and so on?"

"Away!"

Each time he said it, a little more of his face edged past the planking, until all of it was exposed but the mouth. If anything, it showed even more desperation than before. Sweat made his forehead look feverish; grease underlined the skeletal ridges of his cheeks. When it became obvious the winch wouldn't release, he threw himself sideways across the middle seat, then sideways back the other way, trying to shake the boat loose by sheer force.

"Away!" he yelled, louder this time. "Away!"

Five minutes, ten minutes—Daniel wasn't sure how long the swaying lasted. As abruptly as he'd begun, the man left off and went back to running his hands along the winch.

"Wow," Daniel said, forcing a laugh. "You rock pretty good there.

I bet this would be a good time for a rest. Besides, I see your suit is torn and—"

"Away!"

"I mean . . .Well, put it this way. I've been trying to help you for quite a while now. I've risked my job, stood out here in the cold, even lied for you. Don't you think it's time you compromised a little?" He put his hand up. "No, that's okay. I know what you're going to say. But just trust me. Here, put your feet on the davit over here and I'll give you a boost down."

"Away!"

Daniel brought his hands back as if burned. "Okay! That's it! I give up. You want to stay up there, that's fine by me. Sorry. Stay up there all night for all I care. I'm going to leave you all by your lonesome. . . . I'm going now. I won't be able to help you down anymore. . . . I'm going to the bow. See? I'm going up to the bow where I was supposed to be all along. Here I go then. Here's my first step. . . ."

The man showed no sign of noticing. Daniel took a second step, scuffing his shoes, but the man still didn't notice and, by the time Daniel had backed all the way to the stairway, he was pawing as single-mindedly as ever at the winch.

"Have it your way then!" Daniel yelled.

He continued on toward the bow, his face burning the way it did under one of Newcomb's tongue-lashings. There was a tangle of cable there and he kicked it angrily apart, then—his fury slacken-ing—stepped up onto the anchor flukes so he could look out toward the fog. It was worse than before—thicker, blacker, with a faster roll off the water. Still, there was a top to it, and by craning back his head—craning it far back the way he did at the movies when he sat too close—he could make out the horizon above the Cape.

The celebration there was reaching its climax. There were fire-works far to the west over New Bedford, fireworks dead ahead over Hyannis, fireworks over Brewster and Falmouth and Orleans. They shot into the air in bundled columns of sparks, disappeared momentarily, then burst apart in out-spreading umbrellas that slowly merged, until the coast was covered with a dome of shimmering, parti-colored flakes. And what was odd, though the sound traveled across the water like the pops of opened champagne, the light, as it lingered, seemed to become more garish and confused, so that at the last moments—as the final jubilant barrages were flung into the sky all at once—the horizon took on the molten, churning ugliness of overheated metal the instant before it cools into slag.

Daniel watched it wash out into the fog, trying to make sense of it all. It wasn't simple—nowhere near as simple as he had thought. His guilt over leaving the man alone, his guilt over letting him slip aboard in the first place, the danger of his falling overboard and drowning. Daniel's responsibility was too great, and after another minute of helpless staring, he clapped his hands together in decision and started back toward the lifeboat.

"Away?" he said, out loud. "I'll show him away, all right."

He was halfway there, plotting out exactly where on the body he would tackle the man in order to haul him down, when there was a scraping noise up above him to port—a scraping, then a hissing. He looked and was just in time to see a flare shoot up from the bridge and burst apart in white sparklers, illuminating the entire ship. Immediately, there was a second, third, and fourth, the booms and the flashing coming so hard upon each other that he was deafened and blinded all at once. There were whistles, blasts of the foghorn, smoke pouring from the stacks. Beneath his feet, the deck plates, already shaking, sagged, stiffened, and throbbed.

What happened next came fast in a blur. The ship shot forward with a lurch hard enough to throw him against the rail. By the time he picked himself up again they were moving through the fog at what for the *Sconset* was breakneck speed. Up near the bridge, silhouetted in its light, Newcomb launched flare after flare toward the horizon, whooping and yelling at the top of his lungs. Below him, the smoke went from vertical to horizontal in one abrupt tilting, enveloping his legs. Closer, to starboard, the sea slid past like a slide down which they were racing; the fog, so flat until now, streamed backward with the smoke, stinging Daniel's eyes until they filled with tears.

The suddenness of it was enough to knock a steady man overboard, let alone a shaky one, and Daniel forced himself aft against the ship's momentum, expecting the worst. Back to him, he told himself, beating at the fog to clear his eyes. Back to him! Back to him! Back to him!

When he reached the lifeboat the man was where he had left him by the winch, only now he was holding it in close to his cheek, hanging from it, his shoulders slumped in exhaustion, the cords of his muscles extended and slack.

"Away," he mumbled, barely managing the sound.

He didn't see Daniel approach. It would have been no trick at all to grab him by his arms and cradle him like a baby to the deck. Daniel was bracing himself against the rail to do just that when the man's head lolled to the side and his eyes flickered open and he stared at Daniel as if seeing him for the first time.

"Away," he murmured. "Away."

Daniel was close enough now that he could see the reddish stubble of the man's beard, feel the soft touch of his breath against his cheek. "Away," he pleaded, but only in a whisper, and Daniel had to lean even closer and cup his hands over his ears to make the word out.

"Away?" Daniel said gently. "Away where?"

"Away," the man whispered.

"Far away?"

"Away!"

"Away?"

"Away!"

"Away where, goddammit!"

"Away!"

Above them the flares were exploding and the foghorn was booming and the whistle was screaming and their voices grew louder to sur-
mount all the din until they were both yelling the word as loud as they
could, their faces touching, their hands meeting on the winch. They
were yelling and the man was pounding his head on the winch in
agony and Daniel was sobbing and everything became mixed with the
night and the flashing and the rushing until it was too much for him
and Daniel slid the man's hand down the winch to the sleeve and
pushed with him until the safety snapped free.

With a tearing sound and a furious kicking, the winch started to
unwind.

It didn't take long. In a second the lifeboat had dropped below the
rail, and a second after that came a splintering sound as it careened
off the side and slapped against the water twenty feet below. Daniel,
certain the man had been spilled out, grabbed hold of the empty
davit and swung himself onto the locker so he could see down.
Though the concussion had knocked him back off the seat, the man
was still aboard—he was scrambling to right himself, grabbing furiously for the oars. There was a critical moment as the lines came
taught—the boat hydroplaned wildly, nearly capsizing—but the
man somehow managed to balance his way forward to unfasten the
last hook.

As the boat dropped loose, the billow of the side took it from view
and Daniel had to rush to the stern to pick it up again. By the time
he did, the lifeboat was already well back of them, pitching in the
heavy V of the wake. The man, shirtless now, had the oars out and
was rowing steadily toward the open sea, his back dipping and
straightening with each new stroke.

"Away!" he yelled, the distance emphasizing the force of his voice,
so that it rang across the water with the pealing, tolling defiance of a
bell. "Away! Away!"

He pulled the boat through the froth of black weed and creamy phosphorescence the propellers churned up, until the gap between them was twenty yards, then forty yards, and then the boat was into the fog, the bow disappearing first, then the man's shoulders, then the man's head, then the tapered pentagon of the lifeboat's stern, and then there was nothing left in the story but Daniel as a young man watching it and Daniel as an old man telling it and the senselessness of the word's repetition and the final diminishing echo drawing the circle fully shut.

"Away. Away, away, away, away . . . away, away . . . away . . . away."

Away.

THE WAY HE KNEW IT

I t's not apparent now, but I was a beautiful woman. I don't mean emaciated supermodel beauty, or that teased-hair designer-nail kind you see breeding in malls. I'm talking real beauty. Healthy. Natural. Down-to-the-bone.

So it was no wonder he wanted me. No wonder he trolled after me, six nights in a row, studying my habits. When I left for work or took out the trash. When I got my mail. Where I went shopping. Not to mention who came over. Did I have a boyfriend? Was I a dyke? Did my brother drop by to fix my plumbing?

He had a lot to figure out in six days. I give him credit. Am I flattered? There are over three hundred thousand single women in this city he could have raped and murdered, and he chose me.

What he did to me, it wasn't love. Not in the traditional sense. When you kill someone, you're making a statement. You're saying, our relationship has no future. That's not love. Not the way most of us know it. But it was love the way he knows it. In the crudest, most vulgar, pathetic sense, it was love. His hands on my skin, his eyes wide and reckless, the words he used (some I can't even repeat), the spittle that rained on my face when he spoke them—all were signs of his love, the only way he knows how to express it.

My friends would disagree. They would say that what he did to me was worse than simply raping my beautiful body, torturing it, strangling it to death. He objectified me as a woman. He didn't regard my intelligence. Didn't acknowledge my freedom, my liberation. He perpetrated an act of patriarchal misogyny by how he perceived me.

True, he brought my female identity back to the Middle Ages. But there are things I know that my friends never will. That's what happens when you die by someone's hand. You take on a complete, unabridged knowledge of his (or her) life's story. I don't know why this occurs any more than I know why I still have a consciousness able to perceive it, but it does.

For example, I know that his name is Michael Rivers. Nice name. I didn't know it before he killed me. He was born in St. Louis and moved to Denver when he was eighteen. He owns a catering business. Works on the crisis center hot line. Once a year, he throws a free picnic in Curtis Park for the underprivileged. He uses all his resources, waiters, cooks, burns two thousand of his own dollars buying food, all so that a few poor people can have a nice snack come the end of summer. How great is that?

He even has a girlfriend. Get this, she's a struggling actress, and he supports her so she can chase her dream. I don't know if she's any good. I know they don't always get along. He has his temperamental side. He gets moody—gregarious one day, suicidal the next. He disappears at night. Out driving around. Drinking beer. Suddenly he quits; he stays in bed, depressed. Slowly, he comes out of his blue period, until everything's back to normal. Once again he's the loving boyfriend, the prolific chef, the philanthropist. Then, after a couple of months, he gets the urge. Typical serial-killer-profile stuff. Bundy was the same way. They wear one mask for the outside world, the fake selves they've created out of the expectations they've perceived others to have of them. Then there's the monster in the box, their inner selves. The sadistic murderers. Pick up any book out of the True Crime section at Barnes & Noble. You'll get the same story.

And the abused childhood. Drunk father, whoring mother, sticks up the rectum, forced to sleep with his dead cat. The usual stuff that makes you feel sorry for them as kids, electrocute them as adults. Did lousy in school even though he was smart, always smelled like he'd urinated himself. A disgrace, one teacher called him. A filthy nuisance. An animal.

He created his own secret world by hiding under his porch. He invented friends like Sandy Suckacock and Barry Shitforbrains, taken from names he'd heard around the house. They gave him alternate identities to enable him to cope, I guess. I don't know all the psychology. I worked in retirement bonds.

But I can tell you that when a kid picked a fight with him on the way home from school and Michael started crying, Barry Shitforbrains jumped in and kicked the kid's ass. And if Michael got in trouble in class and a teacher had to grab his arm, take him out into the hall and set him straight, along came Sandy Suckacock to field the humiliation.

That's the baggage I carry—the miserable life of Michael Rivers, who took mine with his bare hands after kidnapping and having his way with me out in a field east of Denver. It's also why, when he had his hands around my throat, pressing on my windpipe so that my tongue felt like a steel rod protruding from my mouth, I know that what he felt just prior to ejaculation was the nearest thing to love of which he is capable.

I had something of a life. I was only twenty-six years old. I went to movies, skied Crested Butte, white-water rafted down the Royal Gorge. But what I really miss is buying a new pair of shoes. Shopping for cashmere sweaters at Lord & Taylor. Going out to lunch at some nice microbrewery. Korean takeout. Ethiopian steamed sourdough bread. I miss drinking espressos late at night, when I was right in the middle of a good book. I miss sleeping on my Sealy, goose down pillow under my head. Waking with the sun slicing through the curtain, the aroma of automatic drip coffee wafting in from the kitchen. I miss my morning pee.

My body is a crippled resurrection of my former self. I told you I was healthy, beautiful. Although I know that part of me still exists at least in bone structure, I no longer have either of those qualities. I am decaying. I smell like spoiled meat. My complexion, once enviably ruddy, is blotchy with liver spots. On top of that, I'm a vagrant. I push a shopping cart. I collect cans for the deposit and bum cigarette change. Food is no longer an issue, but I've learned to like smoking, something I never did when I was alive.

I'm greeted with looks of disgust, sighs, a reluctant gift of a quarter from some young man too naive to realize it's a fiscal taboo to give non-tax-deductible charity. I know. I used to think that way.

But there are advantages. I don't feel the cold. I don't eat, shit, piss, have headaches or cramps. I don't get my period.

I never feel great, either. I don't have much energy. It's some kind of postmortem chronic-fatigue syndrome. I'm content just to plant myself on a door stoop for the day and sleep.

Thursdays I take all my quarters and get to a pay phone. Michael's night on the crisis line.

"Crisis center, this is Sandy." They're required to use phony names.

"Michael."

"No, this is Sandy."

"Michael."

"There's no one here by that name. How can I help you?"

"This is your mother, Michael. I know what you've been doing."

Click.

I wait fifteen minutes.

"Crisis center, this is Sandy."

"I'm Lisa Rivers."

Click.

"I'm the ghost of Lisa Rivers."

Click.

"I'm your mother the whore."

Click.

"I'm onto you, Michael."

And it goes on like this every Thursday. I don't know why he keeps returning.

"Crisis center, Sandy speaking."

"Sandy Suckacock?"

Dead silence.

"This is Barry Shitforbrains."

Click.

I know all of Michael Rivers's dirty little secrets. Not just the terrible ones, like about women he's murdered. But those childhood things. The dried booger collection he kept underneath his desk. The scabs he ate. The fantasies he had about the girls who found him revolting. Fantasies of getting even, of forcing his love on them. And the compulsive masturbation, including his whole evolution of techniques, from the pulsating ball throttle to the double-twirl-around-head maneuver. I know about every time he ever touched himself somewhere and sniffed his fingers. Every gross thing he did, I know about.

I know his feelings, too. Constant humiliation. Fear. Anger. Of course, all fueled by his mother. Isn't that just always the case? She called him a dirty pig, nicknamed him Pigboy. Told him he was born out her asshole. No wonder he cut out her vocal cords and flushed them down the toilet. I won't say what he did with her severed head. There are some things I can't bring myself to talk about.

He was only thirteen. His dad had taken off a year before, gone on a drinking binge and never came back. They found the murder somewhat justifiable after testimonies from teachers and neighbors, from local law enforcement, painted the horrible portrait of Lisa Rivers. Whore. Drug addict. Abuser.

He spent five years in a juvenile corrections facility. When he got out he moved straight to Denver. There was a culinary school he wanted to attend. He'd done a lot of cooking in the facility, learned to like it.

He was a student at the culinary school when he killed again. Sharon Stanley of Littleton, a funny, cheery, overly optimistic girl. Not particularly attractive. Flat nose. Thick lips, only not in a sensual way.

He'd met her at a party, one of those friend-of-a-friend things where nobody knew him. They'd talked for a while, that was about it. Then she left. He caught up as she was unlocking her car. Asked her if going for a drive didn't sound like a great idea. He knew a spot with a view. They could bring some beer, smoke a joint. She went for it. With her looks, she probably didn't get many chances.

They found her body tossed off the edge of Lookout Mountain. People who'd seen them talking couldn't remember his name. No one was sure whose friend he'd been.

But he realized his luck. What if one person had known him? What if they'd been seen leaving in his car by someone, anyone, on the street? He got more careful after that.

He also became more selective. He discovered pretty women were just as vulnerable as plain ones, so why not at least choose someone attractive? He honed his skills, began trolling strangers, learning their habits, finding those perfect windows of opportunity. He nabbed one woman as she was closing the bookstore where she worked. Another coming out of the gym. After a PTA meeting. In the supermarket parking lot. At the Taco Bell drive-thru. With me, it happened in back of my apartment building while I was bringing out the trash. All it took was a whisper from his open car door, the steely flash of his gun.

· · ·

Michael and I first met at the Christmas party he catered for my office. He served spinach pies in the most delicious pastry shell, pesto bruschetta topped with roasted red peppers (for the holiday colors effect), a medley of grilled vegetables, ranging from butternut squash to Jerusalem artichokes. This was my fourth Christmas party with this commodities firm, and he was by far the most talented caterer we'd had. There were special touches—the swan ice sculpture on the dessert table, the fact that he used real crystal punch mugs and champagne flutes, provided cloth napkins instead of the standard paper hors d'oeuvres size with the cheap holly wreath prints. I was so impressed I went to where he was reconstituting the goat cheese fondue with heavy cream and told him so.

"Thanks," he said. "There's nothing I enjoy more."

Of course I didn't know the degree of peril this lie would impose on me in the long run.

"You're very welcome," I said. And I walked away never expecting to lay eyes on him again.

So you can imagine how surprised I was to see him parked near my Dumpster, door wide open, gun on his lap. The caterer, forcing me into his car at gun point. The caterer, of all people. I almost threw up a hand, turned and walked away, leaving my trash bags next to his car. What would he have done? Shot me in the back? Sensible Sandy Suckacock wouldn't have allowed it. There was only so much he was willing to tolerate.

Of course, I only know that now, when it's too late. One scream would have sent him packing. One shade in my expression that reflected anything but fear. Because once I got over the absurdity that the man who catered our office Christmas party, who'd made that fine dark chocolate mousse served in marzipan poinsettia cups, was sitting six feet away with a gun pointed directly at me, I succumbed to complete horror. It wasn't even the gun that frightened me. It was the look in his eyes.

. . .

My body gets worse every day. My limbs grow increasingly difficult to maneuver as I lose motor skills, as my muscles corrode. Until now I've enjoyed leaving notes on Michael's car. I acquired a pad of Post-its and a pen from a drugstore so that whenever I see him parked, I stick one on his windshield.

> *Michael,*
> *I had such a great time on our date.*
> *Wish you hadn't left me cold.*
> *Signed,*
> *Your last victim.*

> *Michael,*
> *Come out to the field, dig me up*
> *and fuck me, you stud.*
> *Sincerely,*
> *Your latest dead love.*

But my handwriting's gotten so bad that there's no point to it anymore. I see his car, watch him get out. I limp over and show him my hand.

He presses a five-dollar bill into my palm. "Bless your heart," he says. "Get yourself something hot to eat." He's dressed in a tie, suede jacket, his almond hair combed back. Overall, he's fairly handsome.

I try to say, "I bet you're a real lady-killer." But my speech has become too slurred. The joke is lost.

"Don't even mention it," he says, pretending to understand. And then he's gone, driving off in his midnight-blue Escort. I wonder if he's got an eye on somebody these days. A new flame.

I give the money to a drunk who sometimes shares a stoop with me. He uses it to buy a bottle of Night Train, offers me some. Even if I could drink it, I wouldn't.

One morning I step right out of my body. It's become so heavy and useless, I can't bend a single finger. Suddenly, I'm completely free. I leave it huddled in the corner of the stoop, lifeless at last.

I'm light, invisible. I've graduated from zombie to ghost, no longer encumbered by the weight and awkwardness of a physical body; I'm air. Maybe it's in my nature to first find the downside to everything, but what I realize is that I'll never again wear any nice clothes. No new shoes or silk blouses. I know, it's superficial. It's stereotypical, my friends would argue. I'm reinforcing the subversive feminine paradigm of vanity as self-worth. Guilty. But none of my friends has ever lost her body. They don't know what it's like.

I can't pick things up, but I travel with amazing speed. I feel no resistance from the wind and nothing obstructs me. People, light posts, traffic—I move right through them. The tiredness and lethargy have completely vanished.

And I know where Michael Rivers is. It's as though he's a beacon sending out a signal. I follow it, and *boom!* There I am. Watching as he carves a roast beef, bastes a tray of ducklings, filets a smoked salmon. Witnessing his careful attention to detail as he makes sure the help wipes each serving utensil with vinegar-water for a streak-free shine, steams each wine glass over a pot of hot water, then polishes it with a lint-free cloth. Scrutinizes every sauce, rearranges the decorative kale. When I see him work like this, I'm in awe.

I'm also amazed by the way he speaks. His voice sounds so different than it did in the field. Of course, it's the same one he used at the Christmas party. Gracious. Articulate. Not a trace of malice.

I spend days with him. I follow him home at night, watch him sleeping next to his actress girlfriend. They hardly ever have sex. He'd have to kill her to really get turned on. Sometimes he goes through the motions for the sake of appearances. But there's no passion in it. No love.

She doesn't complain. Maybe because her acting career hasn't really taken off, so she can't afford a breakup. Or maybe she's afraid of the temper that comes out at the strangest times. Everything will be going smoothly. Then one wrong word and he explodes. Something about him coming home late, or how he's not paying attention to their relationship, doesn't listen to what she has to say. Then she's a bitch. Then she's riding him. Then she doesn't know what the fuck she's talking about.

After it's over, he's sorry. He takes her out to dinner, buys her some little present. A turquoise bracelet. Jade earrings. A book on tapping your creative energy. He takes her home and fucks her lamely. Because it's the best he can do without strangling her to death.

And every day, I follow. Watching.

Of course it's just a matter of time before he finds someone new. She does the flowers at a wedding he's catering. Jennifer Roth. Younger than I was; my guess is twenty-two. Pretty, but not beautiful. Ponytail, faded jeans, old T-shirt. Camping-trip pretty. Nobody who'd impress you at a party, though.

It doesn't take much. He compliments her arrangements, the oriental lilies framed by white larkspur, champagne roses nested in Queen Anne's lace. The next step is natural, inevitable.

"I often make recommendations to people I cater for," he says. He doesn't even ask for her business card. She slips it right into his hand.

Then it's just a matter of using the phone book to find her home address, driving to her house and parking across the street. Nursing a six-pack, waiting. Finding out what time she gets back. When does her live-in boyfriend come home? How long is she alone?

I felt a special bond because Michael had chosen me. And now, I have to admit, I'm jealous. It cheapens my murder. I gave my life for this man, literally, so that he could experience, if not love itself, some twisted semblance of love. It was genuine. Passionate.

What was my passion? Retirement bonds. 401K plans. Evenings home with my cat, reading books without plots. Dates that went nowhere. Ski lifts and stationary bikes. Endlessly shopping for nothing in particular. My life was a collection of activities that filled space vacant of any real ardor.

I haven't even been with that many men. Twelve, count them, since my senior year of high school. Six in college alone. The rest along the roadside stands of my career. Not that I was looking for anyone in particular—most guys I went out with annoyed me. They got nervous, flubbed their words. It took them an entire date to build the confidence to touch me with one sweaty hand. They got eager, tried to cover it up with aloofness, then overcompensated by feigning genuine interest. Was it love? Was it sublimity? At best, if they succeeded, it was unremarkable conquest.

Michael Rivers showed me real passion. Let me tell you about his hands. Strong. Deliberate. Hungry. I'd never been touched by hands like his. Never knew they existed.

I could be accused of condoning his crime. Don't get me wrong—I experienced nothing less than sheer pain and terror. But the truth is, I've never felt as alive as I did in those moments just prior to death. His lust, relentless and vengeful, stirred something within me. Something primal. Perhaps I only truly appreciate it now, when death has lost its finality, but I've never felt so emotionally charged.

I don't like the thought of him with another woman. Of course, my notes and phone calls deterred him from going out for a while. But now that some time has passed, his courage is back. It was a fluke, as far as he is concerned. An uncanny coincidence.

My presence, as I've come to call it, whatever it is that I am, my awareness, my traveling perception, locates itself in the backseat of his car. I am neither comfortable nor uncomfortable, those sensations no longer available. I simply am here, perceiving the world from Michael Rivers's vehicle. We park down the street to avoid detection. Jennifer follows her walkway down to the mailbox. The sun has just set. The porch light is on. A small dog runs behind her, stops to piss on a shrub. Michael notes the time, starts the car.

"She's not that attractive," I say.

Michael swivels around, panicked. "Fucking Christ," he says. He shakes his head.

"Michael?"

He turns white in the face. "What the fuck?"

I've never actually spoken. I thought I'd left all my physical abilities behind with what remained of my body. So I'm just as surprised as Michael that he's hearing me. I don't say another word, to avoid alarming him. Maybe he chalks it up to paranoia and too much Budweiser. He shrugs it off, turns on the radio. Of all things, it's Elvis Costello singing "Allison."

I wonder if anyone else can hear me. I'm on Broadway, in front of an artsy movie theater I used to frequent. I shout at people waiting in line to see some sleeper from Cannes; I scream in their ears, curse them. Men in long wool coats, women wearing smart rayon-blend sweaters and insulated silk jackets. Bitch. Fuckhead. Hey, asshole. I'm gonna shoot a flame up your ass, motherfucker!

Nothing. I don't register on the scale of subatomic friction.

I find Michael home alone. The budding young actress whom he doesn't love is probably at a workshop or an audition. He opens another can of beer, sits on the couch and starts rubbing himself. Maybe imagines he's grasping the neck of Jennifer Roth, her chest heaving under him. Picturing Jennifer choking, just as he squeezes his erection, fingers the head. Michael, slumping into the couch, messing on his shirt.

But this is a lame substitute. It doesn't compare to the passion he experienced with me. He cleans off with a dish towel, wraps it back through the handle of the refrigerator. He zips himself up and lies on his bed.

I lower my presence onto him, feel his heart beating. I sense the swirl of desire and malice, as if I've discovered a deep cavern filled by a wind. As if I've reached the inner recesses of Michael's subconscious and found Barry Shitforbrains brooding. And I can inhabit this space, unnoticed, in the presence of his latent passion. I want desperately to ignite it, to feel it burn.

Michael has a big day. I catch up with him catering a luncheon at the Governor's Mansion. First, hors d'oeuvres, *clams en coquille* and mushrooms Copenhagen. State politicians nibble at them with a reserved sensibility, as if they can't allow themselves to fully experience the flavor. Then they sit for an impressive multicourse meal, starting with pumpkin soup garnished with puff pastry. For the main course, a choice of *coq au vin* or *truite en chemise*, the sauces brushed so delicately over the entrees one could imagine it done by da Vinci or Michelangelo. The red and green cabbage salad affords the dishes texture, tangibility. The chocolate soufflés, delicately powdered, perfectly dimensioned, might collapse from the weight of a touch.

And Michael, in his white chef's cap and smock, his black-and-white-checkered pants, is the creator. The same hands that strangled the life out of me also orchestrated this beauty. Couldn't both stand as works of art? In my case, a life-beyond-death affirmation that smacks of Italian renaissance painting?

I've fallen in love with Michael Rivers, the man who took my life. Maybe I've gained too much distance from my old physical self, my allegiance to commonly held social mores. What would my friends think? What if I tried to explain my feelings to a therapist? But does it even matter now that I'm dead?

After the luncheon Michael breaks down the stainless steel food trays, the tables, packs the leftovers in Rubbermaid containers, then loads them into a plastic storage bin. He extinguishes the Sterno candles. He polishes the metal hoods before wrapping them in their linen jackets.

I'm imagining all the things a man can do with his hands.

After sunset, Michael and I drive away from his house. He's been drinking. Watching as the actress paints her toenails, recites lines from some insipid amateur script. I couldn't bear sharing the same room with her, so I waited in the car.

"Michael."

He turns around. "Goddammit," he says, tearing up. After a moment, he takes a deep breath. His shoulders relax. His face goes flaccid. He turns into Sandy Suckacock.

"Pull over, Michael. Don't worry, you're not hearing things. Pull over and I'll explain."

"Jesus fucking Christ." He pulls in front of a Victorian-style mansion turned into a law office.

"There's no reason to be afraid," I tell him. "I'm not going to hurt you. Do you know who I am?"

He shakes his head, hands stuck to the steering wheel. "You don't sound like my mother."

"You're right, I'm not. Do you remember your last victim, Michael? The good-looking blonde you kidnapped by her Dumpster?"

"I didn't—"

"Don't fuck with me, Michael. I'm not playing games. I'm the woman you dragged to that field, raped and strangled and buried out there. Now do you remember me?"

"I do," he says. "I remember you."

"Tell me something, Michael. Did you find me attractive?"

He squeezes the steering wheel, turns around and looks back at nothing. "You're the blonde?"

"Yes."

"I found you very attractive. That's why I picked you up."

"I was beautiful, wasn't I, Michael?"

"I'd say so."

294

"Wouldn't you like to be with me again?"

"Again?"

"Michael, I want you to go ahead with your plan. Pick up Jennifer Roth. Force her into your car and take her out to the field."

"You want me to—"

"Now."

The assumption is that Jennifer gets her mail around the same time every day. We wait. We watch for an hour. She never shows. When the door finally opens the little dog comes out by himself, pisses on a dwarf pine, and is let back in the house.

"Maybe you should just go knock on the door."

"No."

"Look, Michael, it's obvious she either came out early and got her mail, or doesn't give a shit. Make up some excuse. Tell her you have a peony in your trunk you want her to take a look at."

"You think she's going to buy that?"

"You ended up with it and don't know what to do. You don't know anything about plants, tell her. It's a two-hundred-dollar bush and she can have it for nothing if she just takes it off your hands."

Michael narrows his gray eyes. "What the shit," he says.

How could he ever doubt me? Would I steer him wrong? He comes out with Jennifer Roth, brings her straight to the car, shows her the gun, and before you know it, we're driving east. She's crying, begging for her life. Pulling out all the predictable clichés like, "I have so much to live for," and "I'll give you anything you want." Michael's used to this talk. He's unaffected. I'm satisfied that at least when it was my turn, I retained my dignity. Of course, I didn't think he'd kill me. I really did believe I was going home alive.

We drive across the field, kill the engine. The moon is a thick crescent, a cloud touching off its tip. The wind makes a sound against the doors. Michael forces her into the backseat. I guess it's too cold out for any romance under the stars.

"Pretend she's me," I tell him. "Close your eyes. Can you see me? Remember my—"

"I know, the blonde."

"Huh?" Jennifer cries.

"Show me your love, Michael."

I bring my presence toward him. I can feel his anger, his violence. I am part of that, fused between him and Jennifer, caught in the erupting passion, neither receiving nor perpetrating, but connecting to it. I am submerged in his love, so intense, so concentrated, that it radiates through me until almost nothing else exists.

The sex I experienced with men in the past did provide me occasional satisfaction. Maybe you could call it passion, the tears of sweat they shed from their faces, the boyish whimpers of orgasm, followed by my own shallow tremors. But compared with Michael's consuming love, it amounts to a mere gust in the face of a hurricane.

Jennifer Roth was the first virginal touch, the opening dance. The blush of sex is still hot within my—being? Consciousness? Rather than satiating, the experience only piques my craving. Michael unlocked that secret door within me and released a single drop of water onto my soul. My parched landscape craves a river, Michael.

Unfortunately, he's in a slump. He carries the emotional baggage, suffers the repercussions. The real guilty party, i.e., Barry Shitforbrains, has gone into hibernation. Michael himself has retreated into his bedroom. The actress seems to know enough not to bother him during these melancholic periods.

"There's nothing to feel sorry for," I tell him.

"Somebody should kill me."

"You followed what was in your nature. I felt your love, and it was beautiful."

Michael wipes his eyes with the edge of the sheet. "You call that love?"

"Michael, it was your kind of love. You just don't do it like other people."

In life, I would have felt more guilty than he does. So why don't I? I have friends who would claim I'm facilitating. I'm exhibiting codependent tendencies. This is all I can offer in my defense: The view is different from the other side. From here, death doesn't appear so fatal. It is merely an extension of life, energy changing from one form to another. It's like a reversible garment. I don't know what happened to Jennifer Roth. I didn't see her soul leave her body. But she's somewhere, in a zombie-like state or a presence as I am. Maybe she got catapulted into the cosmos. But on she went.

Eventually Michael pulls out of his depression. He caters a born-again Christian dinner-dance, a reunion for the '98 class of recovering cocaine and barbiturate addicts, a merchandisers' luncheon. He's pounding veal steaks for marsala.

"I see that old aggression's back," I tell him.

"Shut up. I can't talk right now."

"Testy. What do you say we go out tonight? See what's around?"

He drives the mallet into the meat with exaggerated force. "I don't know."

"Come on, lover. I promise, it'll be fun."

"Ask me later."

"How about those born-again Christian women? Stir any puritanical fetish?"

"Leave me alone," he says.

I pick her out from the merchandisers' luncheon. Clothes have a lot to do with it, I'll admit. The Christians' were too lacy, the addicts' baggy, like their street-survivor looks. Hannah King (placards make it easy to see everyone's name) wears a simple but elegant Fatima Batista black halter dress, accessorized with earrings and matching necklace made of antique blue glass (Venetian?). And she has that beauty that can't be artificially rendered: high

Slavic cheekbones, icy-green eyes, short blond hair cut to the roundness of her face.

"Check out Hannah King," I tell Michael. "She's sitting on the end, near the back window."

He takes out a tray of crème brûlée. When he comes back he tells me, "I don't like her."

"She's perfect."

"No."

"She's the one."

"Then you take her."

That night the star of the stage is stretched out on the carpet. She's watching some mindless TV drama, presumably absorbing tips on method acting. Michael sits on the sofa, drinking a beer.

The afterglow of our lovemaking has worn off. I could fly away somewhere, go haunt an old house. Or a department store. I could be the ghoul of Neiman Marcus. But a fear has developed I've never before experienced. Loneliness. Not the temporary kind, like when it's been a while since the phone rang, or since you've been asked out on a date. That can always be diverted with some good chocolate and a movie.

This loneliness is terminal. Infinite. Because what if I end up spending eternity by myself, never having contact with anyone? What if I drift the streets, an invisible vapor, undetected, uncared for?

One person stands between me and the blackness of solitude: Michael Rivers.

"Let's get out of here," I tell him.

"No."

"What?" the actress asks. She doesn't turn her head from the screen.

"I didn't say anything," Michael tells her. I follow him into the kitchen.

"How about we just go on a drive?"

He swallows, glances around. The room is done in too much sunflower.

"Michael, I need to be with you."

"A drive, that's all." He opens the fridge and grabs the rest of the six-pack.

I plant myself in the passenger seat. Outside, it's snowing, the flakes falling like white ashes between the skeletons of trees. I'm right next to Michael, but we may as well be a thousand miles apart. "I can't feel anything you're feeling," I tell him. "I want to be close to you."

"Yeah?"

"You know how we can get close?"

We stop at a pay phone, look up Hannah's address, drive to her listing. Of course, it's an apartment in a security building.

I convince Michael to wait until someone goes in, then catch the door before it closes. He drinks another beer. He was reluctant at first, but I can tell he's getting anxious. Barry Shitforbrains is coming to. Finally we go outside and wait. When a couple slides their security card through the lock, Michael catches the door behind them. The man gives him a suspicious look, but Michael just smiles.

"Cold out," he says. He brushes the snow from his hair. Charmer.

Hannah King lives on the eighth floor. We take the elevator. It's one of those sixties-era postmodern structures, with cheap Renoir prints to give it that French-sidewalk-café flare that only points to the irony.

We find her door unlocked and go right in. There is a boyfriend, but guns are wonderful mechanisms in that they override anybody's maverick impulses. Michael ties his hands, shoves a dishrag in his mouth.

Ms. Hannah King, dressed informally in Capri slacks and an ivory silk blouse, is stricken with terror and disbelief. Of course, I know just how she feels. I really am sorry for her. He knocks her to the floor, grabs her expensive hairdo. Tells her that if she screams, he'll make it hurt. Bad. Barry Shitforbrains has taken over; I can feel his animosity swell.

I say, "Tell me you love me."

"Shut up, you cunt."

I am alive in the space of Michael's love, made of equal parts spite and desire. But to me, this is as rich as any mother's love for her child, because I was born out of this feeling, born into death. His love is the very substance of which I am made. And am made whole.

This is the river, outpouring.

When I look back at Hannah's body, limp and lifeless as a discarded vacuum-cleaner bag, her slacks bunched around her ankles, her blouse torn open, I feel a small kindred tug considering the road we've both had to travel.

While Michael caters, I'm trolling. I go to malls, fly through office buildings, comb supermarkets, bookstores, salons. I gather names and addresses, prioritizing by desirability. One interesting thing I notice — when I pass beyond a twenty-mile radius from Michael, I no longer sense his signal. I move within that radius, and I know exactly where he is.

At night, I recruit Michael and tell him where to drive. I'm able to go in ahead and scope things out. If our pick is on the phone, we wait until she gets off. If someone else is there, a boyfriend or grandmother, we figure out how to deal with it. We are a perfect team. A power duo. Unstoppable.

We catch Margaret Hayes while she's taking a bath. Surprise!

The next night it's Julie Foxx, doing aerobics.

Then Wendy Holcombe.

Cynthia Barrett.

Brenda Moss.

We're on a roll.

The argument could be made that I'm just as guilty as Michael. I'm responsible for spilling the innocent blood of these women, for enacting violence on their bodies and denying them their right to live safe, fulfilling lives. But at the same time I'm freeing them from slavery to jobs and bills, from lives lived out in cubicles and efficiency apartments, disappointing relationships and the futility of therapy, the addiction to consumer trends. Over and over, I am liberating women from the pathetic, moribund existence I myself once suffered. And the price they pay—the pain, the fear—is so ephemeral in comparison to the eternity before them.

It's also worth noting that the women I choose are single, no kids. I'm drafting only the most expendable. Those whose lives most resemble my former one.

To the degree I relish spending time with Michael, I can no longer stand the sight of that actress. I know she's cheating on him. I followed her one night on her way to rehearsal. She met some guy in a bar. Turtleneck, goatee—some fellow artist, I suppose. They had drinks, talked about movies, then went to his place and fucked on his cheap area rug. Turns out, she didn't even make the play.

One night after she leaves, I tell Michael he should get rid of her.

"I can't," he says.

"You don't love her."

"It's not about love."

It doesn't take a panel guest to figure it out. This is about Sandy Suckacock's need for stability. This is about Sandy Suckacock having the security of a warm body next to him at night. A need I can't fulfill.

"She knows something's up," I tell him.

Michael sips his beer, contemplates. "I know she does."

I wonder why he doesn't suspect anything about her. But I think the truth would do more harm than good at this point, coming from me.

"Do you ever feel my presence when we're making love?"

"It's not love," he says.

"Whatever you want to call it. Do you feel me?"

"I feel what I feel. What I've always felt. No different."

"For me, it's like I've entered your passion. It's the only way I have of being close to you."

"I don't want to hear this shit," Michael says. "I don't feel any love for you."

"Love to you is pain. It's charged emotions. You feel that."

"I feel that," he says.

"Let's go out, Michael. Be together."

"I don't want to."

"Please? I have someone picked. It'll be easy." If I could have rubbed his neck, touched the inside of his thigh to excite him. But I only had words. "Barry Shitforbrains, you in there? I got a sexy young woman, if you're interested."

Sometimes, words were all it took.

Michael is suppressed most of the time by either Sandy, who's always guarding against me, or Barry, the real center of passion. The suppression of Michael is destroying the catering business. He's the genius behind it. Sandy, it turns out, isn't a very good cook. He serves canned chili to the press club, macaroni and cheese to women against exploitation, corned beef hash to the Jewish community leaders. People cancel their catering reservations. The Rotary Club takes its monthly business elsewhere. Money stops coming in.

Michael's home is a disaster with food garbage, beer cans, dirty clothes strewn about. It's just the way Lisa Rivers used to keep house. And he's drinking almost nonstop, like his father did.

It's during turbulent times such as these people turn against each other. Barry Shitforbrains decides he doesn't like a mouthy ghost bitch telling him what to do. He won't go along with any more of my arrangements. And conservative Sandy Suckacock has always considered me a danger. Now he wants me gone.

"Listen," I tell them, "we've got to stick together. We get Michael working again, and we're all back on the same page."

"Not so long as you're around."

The actress, who hasn't lifted a finger to clean up around the house, who has rehearsals until three o'clock in the morning, then all night, and finally clear into the afternoon, comes home dragging her heels, hair matted, looking like she's been fucked around the block and back. Even Michael can see that now.

"You've been with somebody," he tells her.

"You're one to talk, gone half the night, come home smelling like sex and beer." She's wearing some god-awful outfit from the Kathy Lee Gifford collection, wrinkled front and back.

"It's not what you think," he says.

"Tell the bitch she's out of here, Michael," I tell him.

"Look, I'm just going through a difficult time right now," he says to her.

"Give her her walking papers. Good luck in Hollywood, babe."

"Shut up!" he screams. "You can't tell me what to do with my life. You get the hell out of here, you fucking cunt."

The actress walks straight into the bathroom, starts packing up her whole gaudy palette of Maybelline.

Michael chases after her. "I didn't mean you," he tells her.

"Who did you mean, Michael? Who did you imagine you were talking to? You don't think I hear you whispering to some invisible person, having conversations with yourself in the kitchen? And look at yourself, you haven't showered in a week. You haven't shaved. You look like a pig."

Michael's words come out slowly: "I . . . look . . . like . . . a . . . what?"

"I said you're a fucking pig."

He takes hold of her hair and whips her head against the counter, like he's cracking open a huge egg. She's dead before her ass hits the linoleum. Then he does the same things to her he did to his mother.

303

I don't even get close. This isn't any kind of love. I pull away, retreat into the living room, bolt outside. I wish I could feel the wind on my body; I see it, rocking the branches, pushing a plastic bag down the street. I wish I could smell the winter air.

What is our love? Some twisted hybrid of violence? I should be sick from what I've seen, the things I've done. Jennifer Roth, Hannah King, all the others. I should carry the pain of those women, suffer their agony. But when it's us together, when I'm part of it, it's beautiful. When it's just him, alone with his anger lashing out, it's hideous, terrible.

Inside the theater, I place myself right in the middle of the aisle. Nobody knows the difference. I can take the best seat in the house. But movies don't make sense to me anymore. They don't resemble anything coherent, any more than life itself. It used to be life was a series of events that related to each other. This idea of order seems irrelevant now. The actress could have been killed last year or next week, it's really all the same. Not that the pattern has vanished, but it's shifted. And the idea that anything, even a movie, could have a beginning and an end seems absurd.

Eventually I make my way back to the house. The actress was destined to die anyway, just as I was. The event itself holds no particular meaning. It's the spirit in which the act was committed. With the two of us, it was always about love. That's what made it right. I'm now forced to admit that this is the most unhealthy relationship I've ever been in. But the alternative is the abyss below, over which I dangle by the thread which is Michael. I can't help myself. I can't let go. Now I understand why women repeatedly seek out guys who treat them like shit, why battered wives return to their abusive husbands. It's the passion. Nothing else can come close.

Michael doesn't go out for days, doesn't answer the phone. A man comes and knocks on the door. He knocks and knocks and knocks.

He tries to look through the windows, but the curtains are drawn. I know who he's looking for.

A new catch might get us back on track. Rekindle the flame.

I find a great score. Find her, of all things, exiting a place that does spiritual readings. I'm taken by her coat, not only that it's a white fox fur, but that she has the fortitude to wear it.

I return to Michael. He hasn't budged from the couch. I'm lucky not to have my sense of smell. What I'm seeing is completely repugnant.

"I found someone, Michael. She's perfect."

"No."

"She's beautiful."

"No."

"Let's make love, Michael. It'll be good for us."

"There is no us."

"She's just your type."

"You always pick blondes. I'm sick of them."

"I thought they reminded you of me."

"I like brunettes."

The police come. Must be six or seven cars in front of the house. They take Michael out in handcuffs. There are photographers snapping pictures and a TV van, the News 4 crew sticking a microphone in his face.

"Did you kill all those women?" a pock-faced reporter asks. Michael keeps his head down.

"Hang in there, baby," I tell him. But he's too sick-hearted to even look up.

Inside, they gather the pieces of the actress. I can't help but think, She's finally gotten herself into some parts. I wonder if Michael would appreciate the joke.

He's examined by four different psychiatrists. They give him tests, where he rates statements from disagree to strongly agree. "I think I have made things happen by my mental powers." And, "Voices give me directions as to what I should do." Two determine that he suffers from an auditory psychosis, i.e., a voice that tells him to kill. The other two say he's full of shit. Either way, our world is sinking fast.

Michael is placed in a psychiatric hospital for more observation. They dress him in an unsightly hospital gown that snaps in the back. Really, if you treat someone like he's sick . . . but at this point, what does it matter? He lays in bed, one hand and the opposite foot each cuffed to the railing, the electronic mattress adjusted so that he's sitting up.

"You look awful," I tell him.

"Go to hell."

Should I try to be more supportive? I don't know what my friends would say. I don't care. "We'll find a way out of this, honey."

"I fucking hate you, okay?"

"Hate is an emotion inexorably bound in your love. That's part of the beauty of your passion, Michael."

What's clear is that Barry Shitforbrains may never show himself again, considering Michael will be institutionalized for the remainder of his life, if not on death row then in a place like this. It's pitiful, heartbreaking. His hands, once such powerful instruments, are now limp, one manacled, the other lifeless beside him. He reminds me of a broken Christ in an Italian fresco.

"I love you, Michael. And no matter what happens, I'm here for you."

He turns his head, as if to look at me. "I wish I'd never killed you," he says.

"You don't mean that."

I know all there is to know about Michael Rivers. Considering how he grew up, it's amazing he made it this far. He could have ended up in prison long ago, a common hood. A petty thief. But something in

Michael shined through all of the darkness. Something genuine. Beautiful. But I realize that I can't stay with him forever. Who knows, maybe when they execute him, our souls will reach out and bond. But that's years and years of appeals from now. I can't wait that long. A girlfriend once told me there had to be more than one person for everyone. Even if your lover is one in a million, there are six billion people inhabiting this planet. Don't get me wrong—I will always love Michael. He took me with his passionate hands, breached the threshold of my soul. He taught me the true difference between life and death. But there may be someone like him, still roaming free. Someone else who can hear my voice and is willing to listen. Someone who knows love, the way Michael did.

CONTRIBUTORS' NOTES

JENNIFER RACHEL BAUMER lives and writes in Reno, Nevada, where she makes her home with her husband Rick and seven oversized cats. A full-time freelancer since 1999, Jennifer writes nonfiction for a living while pursuing a career in fiction. A member of the Horror Writers' Association and Reno's Unnamed Writers' Group, Baumer has sold stories to *Talebones*, *Not One of Us*, *More Monsters from Memphis*, and the upcoming anthology *Extremes: Horror from the Ends of the Earth: Darkest Africa*.

T. CORAGHESSAN BOYLE is the author of the novels *Riven Rock*, *The Tortilla Curtain*, *The Road to Wellville*, *East is East*, *World's End* (winner of the PEN/Faulkner Award), *Budding Prospects*, and *Water Music*. *T. C. Boyle Stories*, his collected stories, was recently published. Boyle, the recipient of the 1999 PEN/Malamud Award for Excellence in Short Fiction, lives in Santa Barbara, California.

ROBERT COOVER is the author of fourteen books, including *Whatever Happened to Gloomy Gus of the Chicago Bears?*, *Spanking the Maid*, *Pinocchio in Venice*, *Pricksongs and Descants*, *A Night at the Movies*, *Briar Rose*, *The Universal Baseball Association, Inc.: J. Henry Waugh, Prop.*, and the collection of plays *A Theological Position*. He has received numerous awards, including the William Faulkner Award for best first novel for *Origin of the Brunists*, the Brandeis Citation for Fiction, three Obie awards, and the American Academy of Arts and Letters Award, and he has been nominated for a National Book Award for his novel *The Public Burning*. Coover has held teaching positions at Bard, the University of Iowa, Princeton, and Brown.

LAURENCE DAVIES, a native of Wales, lives in Vermont. He has coauthored a biography of Cunninghame Graham, Scottish writer, traveler, and political activist, and coedited the collected letters of Joseph Conrad for Cambridge University Press. His fiction has appeared in *New England Review* and *StoryQuarterly*, and *Elsaveta*, his collaboration with composer Steve Dembski, has had a workshop production with American Opera Projects, New York. "Run Ragged" comes from *Infinity Theatre*, a collection in progress; he is also working on *The Cup of the Dead*, a novel shaped around the old Welsh custom of sin-eating.

KATHRYN DAVIS's first novel, *Labrador*, won the Kafka Award. Her other novels include *The Girl Who Trod on a Loaf*, *Hell*, and *The Walking Tour*. A recipient of the Morton Dawen Zabel Prize from the American Academy of Arts and Letters, and a Year 2000 Guggenheim Fellow, Davis teaches creative writing at Skidmore College and lives in Vermont with her husband and daughter.

LOUISE ERDRICH—novelist, story writer, children's writer, memoirist, and poet—is the award-winning author of *The Birchbark House*, *The Antelope Wife*, *The Blue Jay's Dance*, *The Bingo Palace*, *Jacklight*, *Grandmother's Pigeon*, *Tracks*, *The Beet Queen*, and *Love Medicine*, and coauthor of *The Crown of Columbus*.

DOUGLAS GLOVER is the author of three story collections, three novels and, most recently, the book of essays *Notes Home from a Prodigal Son*. Glover's critically acclaimed novel *The Life and Times of Captain N.* was listed by *The Chicago Tribune* as one of the best books of 1993. His storybook *A Guide to Animal Behavior* was nominated for the 1990 Governor-General's Award, Canada's highest literary prize. His stories have been frequently anthologized, notably in *The Best American Short Stories, Best Canadian Stories,* and *The New Oxford Book of Canadian Stories.* His criticism has appeared in *The New York Times Book Review, The Washington Post Book World, The Boston Globe Books,* and *The Los Angeles Times.* He has edited the annual *Best Canadian Stories* since 1997.

NICOLA GRIFFITH is a native of Yorkshire, England, where she taught self-defense and was singer and songwriter for the band Janes Plane. She is the author of *Ammonite, Slow River, The Blue Place,* and *Red Raw,* and the editor of the *Bending the Landscape* original anthology series. Her honors and awards include the Nebula Award, World Fantasy Award, James Tiptree Jr. Memorial Award, and the Lambda Literary Award (five times), and her work has been translated into eight languages. She lives in Seattle with her partner, writer Kelley Eskridge.

SHELBY HEARON is the author of fifteen novels, including *Ella in Bloom, Life Estates,* and *Owning Jolene,* which won an American Academy of Arts and Letters Literature Award. She has received fellowships for fiction from the John Simon Guggenheim Foundation and the National Endowment for the Arts, Ingram Merrill and Writer's Voice grants, and has twice won the Texas Institute of Letters fiction award. Her short fiction has appeared in *Cosmopolitan, Redbook, Southern Review,* and other magazines and anthologies. She lives in Burlington, Vermont, with her husband, physiologist William Halpern.

DAVID HUDDLE, originally from Ivanhoe, Virginia, has lived in Vermont for thirty years. His first novel, *The Story of a Million Years,* appeared in 1999 and was chosen by *Esquire* and *The Los Angeles*

Times Book Review as a Best Book of the Year. His other books include *The Writing Habit, Paper Boy, Only The Little Bone, The Nature of Yearning, Intimates,* and *Stopping by Home.*

BRET LOTT is the author of a memoir, *Fathers, Sons, and Brothers;* three story collections, including *An Evening on the Cusp of the Apocalypse,* to be published by Invisible Cities Press; and five novels, including *The Man who Owned Vermont, The Hunt Club, Reed's Beach* and *Jewel,* which was selected by Oprah Winfrey for her book club. He received his MFA from the University of Massachusetts, Amherst, where he studied under the late James Baldwin, and currently teaches at the College of Charleston and in the MFA Program at Vermont College. He lives with his wife and children in Mount Pleasant, South Carolina.

PAMELA PAINTER is the author of the award-winning story collection *Getting to Know the Weather,* and coauthor of *What If? Writing Exercises for Fiction Writers.* Her stories have appeared *in The Atlantic, Harper's, Kenyon Review, Ploughshares,* and *Story,* and in numerous anthologies. She has received grants from The Massachusetts Artists Foundation and the National Endowment of the Arts, and has won a Pushcart Prize and Agony Review's The John Cheaper Award for Fiction. She is a founding editor of *StoryQuarterly* and teaches at Emerson College and in the MFA Program at Vermont College. Her newest collection of stories is *The Long and Short of It.* "Doors" first appeared in *StoryQuarterly.*

BEN PASTOR has been writing mystery and ghost stories ever since her interest in archaeology widened into curiosity for other things hidden and arcane. She has been featured in Alfred Hitchcock's *Mystery Magazine, Ellery Queen's, Yellow Silk,* and is a regular contributor to *The Strand.* Her critically acclaimed first literary mystery novel, *Lumen,* will be followed by a sequel later this year. A D.Litt. from the

University of Rome, she also holds an MFA in writing from Vermont College of Norwich University, where she is an associate professor of graduate studies.

TIMOTHY SCHMAND won the 1999 Calvino Prize for Short Fiction for his story *The Great Deadly Malpus*. He is a writer who lives in South Miami, Florida.

CURTIS SMITH has published short stories in over a dozen literary journals including *Antietam Review*, *Mid-American Review*, and *The William and Mary Review*. "Insomnia" first appeared in *The Pittsburgh Quarterly*. For the past seventeen years he has taught special learning students in Hummelstown, Pennsylvania.

PETER STRAUB is the author of *Ghost Story*, one of the most acclaimed horror novels of the last two decades. He is also the author of *Koko*, winner of the World Fantasy Best Novel award. He coauthored *The Talisman* with Stephen King. Recent novels include *Mr. X*, *The Throat*, and *The Hellfire Club*.

JOHN UPDIKE, award-winning author of over fifty books, including novels, collections of short stories and connected short stories, poetry, children's literature, plays, essays and literary criticism, art criticism, and autobiography, has written one ghost story.

GUY VANDERHAEGHE is the author of *The Englishman's Boy*, winner of The Governor General's Award for Fiction and the Saskatchewan Book Award for Best Novel. He is the author of three collections of short fiction, *Man Descending*, *The Trouble with Heroes*, and *Things As They Are*. His other novel, *Homesick*, was cowinner of The City of Toronto Book Award. His second play, *Dancock's Dance*, was produced in 1995. He lives in Saskatoon, Saskatchewan, where he is a visiting professor of English at S.T.M. College.

ROGER WEINGARTEN is the author of eight collections of poetry, including *Ghost Wrestling, Infant Bonds of Joy, Shadow Shadow, The Vermont Suicides,* and *Ethan Benjamin Boldt.* He has coedited four poetry anthologies, including *New American Poets of the '90s* and the forthcoming *Poets of the New Century.* He has been a fellow of the Ingram Merrill Foundation and the National Endowment for the Arts. He founded and teaches in the MFA Program at Vermont College.

W. D. WETHERELL has written novels, short story collections, and nonfiction books, including *One River More: A Celebration of Rivers and Flyfishing, The Wisest Man in America, Wherever that Great Heart Might Be, The Smithsonian Guide to the Natural Places of Northern New England, Vermont River, Upland Stream, Hyannis Boat and Other Stories,* and *The Man Who Loved Levittown.* He has won two National Endowment for the Arts Fellowships, the Drue Heinz Literature Prize, the National Magazine Award, and other honors. His novel *Chekhov's Sister* was selected as one of the Notable Books of 1990 by the *New York Times.*

RICK ZIND grew up in the Southwest. He is a graduate of the University of Colorado and the MFA program at Vermont College. He now lives in Vermont, where he teaches writing and literature. He is working on his first novel.

CREDITS